EXECUTING THE MENTALLY ILL

For Richard H. Burr

The [people] who made the world wiser,
better and holier were ever battling
with the law and customs and institutions
of the world

—Clarence Darrow

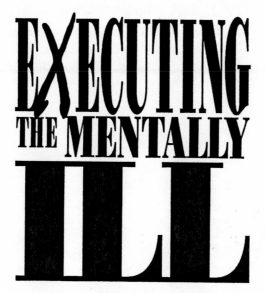

EXECUTING THE MENTALLY ILL

THE CRIMINAL JUSTICE SYSTEM AND THE CASE OF ALVIN FORD

KENT S. MILLER
MICHAEL L. RADELET

SAGE Publications
International Educational and Professional Publisher
Newbury Park   London   New Delhi

41,95

For information address:

SAGE Publications, Inc.
2455 Teller Road
Newbury Park, California 91320

SAGE Publications Ltd.
6 Bonhill Street
London EC2A 4PU
United Kingdom

SAGE Publications India Pvt. Ltd.
M-32 Market
Greater Kailash I
New Delhi 110 048 India

Printed in the United States of America

Library of Congress Cataloging-in-Publication Data

Miller, Kent S.
  Executing the mentally ill : the criminal justice system and the case of Alvin Ford / Kent S. Miller, Michael L. Radelet.
      p. cm.
  Includes bibliographical references and index.
    ISBN 0-8039-5149-3 (cl.). — ISBN 0-8039-5150-7 (pb)
    1. Ford, Alvin Bernard, d. 1991—Trials, litigation, etc.
  2. Trials (Murder)—Florida. 3. Capital punishment—United States.
  4. Insanity—Jurisprudence—United States. 5. Death row inmates—Mental health—United States. I. Radelet, Michael L. II. Title.
  KF224.F665M55   1993
  364.6'6'092—dc20
  [B]   93-999

93 94 95 96   10 9 8 7 6 5 4 3 2 1

Sage Production Editor: Judith L. Hunter

Contents

Acknowledgments

This book would not have been possible without the assistance of several people who played critical roles in Alvin Ford's life. In particular, we are indebted to his attorneys, Robert Adams, Richard H. Burr, Deborah Fins, and Laurin Wollan; to his mother, Connie Ford; to his sister, Gwendolyn; and to Gail Rowland, who worked on the case as a paralegal and became one of Mr. Ford's closest friends. Larry Spalding, director of Florida's Office of Capital Collateral Representative, gave us access to his files; and his staff, especially Faith Blake, Terry Farley, and Steve Walter, were very helpful. As with several other research projects in which we have been involved, we thank Watt Espy for his assistance and unparalleled knowledge of the history of the death penalty in the United States.

Valuable comments on previous drafts of this manuscript were made by Richard H. Burr, Susan Cary, Kellogg W. Hunt, Betty Davis Miller, Lisa Radelet, Windsor Schmidt, Jill Theg, Neil Walker, Laurin Wollan, and three anonymous reviewers retained by Sage Publications and later identified to us as Kirk Heilbrun, James W. Marquart, and Robert Bohm. We are especially indebted to Hugo Adam Bedau, Scharlette Holdman, and Constance E. Putnam for their extensive comments. We also thank our colleagues George Barnard and Kirk Heilbrun, whose work with us helped shape many of the observations made in the following pages.

Professor Radelet's work on this monograph was supported in part by a postdoctoral research fellowship under NIMH Grant T32 MH15161, administered through the Family Research Laboratory, University of New Hampshire. An earlier draft of portions of Chapter 9 first appeared in *Behavioral Sciences & the Law*, Summer 1992, and is reprinted by permission of John Wiley & Sons, Ltd.

KENT S. MILLER
MICHAEL L. RADELET
Tallahassee and Gainesville
March 15, 1993

Preface

Unlike every other western democracy in the world, the United States has made it clear that capital punishment will remain an active part of its criminal justice system. By the end of 1992, there were some 2,700 men and 43 women living under sentence of death in the United States.[1] These inmates, all of whom were convicted of murder, were living in 34 states, with Texas, Florida, and California each housing death rows of more than 300. The sheer numbers of condemned inmates, coupled with political pressure for executions and a judiciary that is growing increasingly tired of death penalty appeals, indicate that America may soon see executions at rates not seen before in this century.

Since 1900 there have been 7,000 executions in America, with just slightly more than 4,000 since 1930. All nonmandatory death penalty statutes in the United States were ruled unconstitutional by the U.S. Supreme Court in *Furman v. Georgia* in 1972.[2] Led by Florida, states began to rewrite their laws. In 1976 the Supreme Court, while invalidating statutes that provided for a mandatory death penalty for certain types of crimes,[3] approved other statutes that specified aggravating and mitigating circumstances designed to guide jurors and judges in deciding which convicted murderers to sentence to death.[4] After a 10-year moratorium, executions in the United States resumed in 1977. By the end of 1992, 188 inmates in 20 states had been put to death since *Furman*.

Several books now available review the arguments for and against capital punishment.[5] Those who support the death penalty use three primary arguments: retribution, incapacitation, and deterrence. By far the most often cited justification is retribution: Because of the enormous suffering caused by heinous murderers, they deserve maximum suffering in return.[6] The second justification, incapacitation, holds that the only way to guarantee that murderers will not kill again is to execute them. A third argument, though less pronounced than it was even a few years ago,[7] is general deterrence: Society needs to execute murderers to discourage its members who otherwise may be thinking of imitating the crime.[8]

Death penalty abolitionists are unconvinced by these justifications and argue that, absent solid reasons in favor of the death penalty, states should not be in the business of deciding which of their citizens should live and which should die. Abolitionists point out that who is selected for death is often unpredictable (reflecting arbitrariness), or influenced more by class and race than by legally relevant facts of the case.[9] In addition, innocent people have been and will continue to be executed.[10] They argue that the widespread opposition to capital punishment by organized religions reflects the death penalty's basic immorality, and that whatever benefits the death penalty may have are not worth the enormous fiscal costs (several times the cost of life imprisonment).[11]

This book focuses on the issues raised when the criminal justice system attempts to apply the death penalty to one type of defendant: prisoners who are, at least arguably, mentally impaired. That group is composed of two broad subsets. The first includes those whose mental status should have kept them off death row in the first place—a group of mentally ill and mentally retarded defendants who, for a variety of reasons, were unsuccessful in convincing their juries that mental abnormalities either caused the crime or contributed to it to an extent that should have mitigated the severity of punishment. To be sure, some of those whose mental illness led to criminal homicide are found incompetent to stand trial, or not guilty by reason of insanity, or are sentenced to terms of imprisonment rather than death. But because many mentally impaired defendants charged with murder do not have their illnesses recognized or acknowledged at trial (just as the illness was unrecognized or at least untreated in the years before the murder, when proper mental health care might have prevented the tragedy in the first place), the question of competence for execution can arise in cases of defendants whose history of mental illness predates their arrival on death row and who "slipped through the cracks." The second subset includes defendants who did not suffer from extreme mental abnormalities before their death sentences were first pronounced, but who became mentally ill while on death row awaiting their date with the executioner. Regardless of when the mental pathologies first developed, we are interested in the total class of mentally impaired death row inmates.

In the 1986 case of *Ford v. Wainwright*, the U.S. Supreme Court firmly stated that a narrowly defined class of mentally ill death row inmates could not be executed. The Court held that the determination of who belongs in this group could not be made solely by the state's executive branch as a clemency function, as it previously had been; a decision not to exempt a defendant from execution because of mental illness must also be subject to judicial review. The case involved Florida death row inmate Alvin Ford. Left unanswered by the Court's decision, however, are such questions as how mental illness should be defined for purposes of the exemption; how mental health professionals should evaluate competence for execution; what to do when the mental health professionals disagree among themselves about the defendant's mental status; how strong any doubts about mental status should be before the execution is stopped; and what to do with prisoners if they are found incompetent.

This book examines the *Ford* case as a vehicle for discussing these questions. In so doing, we will present materials in roughly concentric circles. At the center is information relating to Ford's unique history, crime, mental state, and how he was handled by the criminal justice system. The mental health issues raised in his case force us to deal with more general questions about the involvement of physicians and mental health professionals in various aspects of modern capital sentencing. The *Ford* case also raised some nonmental health issues (to be discussed in Chapter 7), such as the problems of racial bias in death sentencing and of securing competent attorneys for defendants charged with capital crimes. Hence, surrounding the unique aspects of *Ford* are a plethora of more general issues about the administration of the death penalty in America today. And, while the *Ford* case dealt with psychotic mental disorders (problems of thought and mood), in the final chapter we will examine how similar issues are involved in the execution of the mentally retarded (problems of intelligence). The book is intended as an introduction to this area of mental health law, and, for mental health professionals and students of mental health law, as an introduction to the death penalty.

A theme to be addressed throughout this book is that decisions of who should live and who should die require that hairs be split on several continua. Where do we draw the line to distinguish death-deserving criminal responsibility, premeditation, heinousness of offense, severity of prior record, and the like—and how should these lines be drawn? The case of Alvin Ford demonstrates that in drawing the line on at least one of these dimensions—mental status—we are making godlike decisions without godlike perfection.

Since no work in this area can be done without the moral and political positions of the authors quickly emerging, we state from the onset that after we began studying this issue and Alvin Ford in 1984, we gradually became more and more appalled at how hard the State of Florida worked to put Alvin Ford in his grave, and how easy it was for the state to involve mental health professionals in this effort. Over the years we have come to believe that Mr. Ford's case tells us much about the absurdities of capital punishment as practiced in America today, regardless of whether the penalty is imposed on healthy or mentally impaired defendants. Our 9 years of studying the case and the issues it raised have led us to the conclusion that governments do a very poor job of determining which of their citizens should live or die. We therefore cast our vote with those who stand opposed to capital punishment.

Notes

1. NAACP Legal Defense and Educational Fund, "Death Row, U.S.A." (Winter 1992). Because America's death rows house relatively few women, we use masculine pronouns in this book to refer to all inmates under a sentence of death.

2. *Furman v. Georgia*, 408 U.S. 238 (1972). For a history of events leading up to this decision, see Meltsner, 1973. For an overview of all literature published on capital punishment, 1972–1987, see Radelet and Vandiver, 1988.

3. *Woodson v. North Carolina*, 428 U.S. 280 (1976); *Roberts* (Stanislaus) *v. Louisiana*, 428 U.S. 325 (1976). The final type of mandatory death penalty statute, providing for a death sentence for prisoners who kill while serving a term of life imprisonment, was invalidated in 1987 (*Sumner v. Schuman*, 483 U.S. 66).

4. *Gregg v. Georgia*, 428 U.S. 153 (1976). "Aggravating" circumstances (e.g., the homicide was especially heinous or cruel) are those that increase the defendant's culpability for the death penalty; "mitigating" circumstances (e.g., the lack of a prior criminal record) lessen culpability. For extended discussion of discretionary and mandatory statutes, see Bedau, 1987.

5. See, for example, Bedau, 1982, 1987; Berns, 1979; Bohm, 1991; Paternoster, 1991; Zimring and Hawkins, 1986.

6. Carver, 1991; van den Haag, 1986.

7. Today there are virtually no criminologists who argue that the death penalty is or could be more of a deterrent to criminal homicides than alternative punishments of long imprisonment (Radelet & Vandiver, 1988). Among those Americans who support the death penalty, the proportion who base their support on a belief in a deterrent effect declined from 22% in 1985 to 13% in 1989 (Gallup & Newport, 1991, p. 42).

8. For a review of some of the deterrence research, see Hood, 1989 (prepared for the United Nations); Klein, Forst, and Filatov, 1978 (prepared for the National Academy of Sciences).

9. Baldus, Woodworth, and Pulaski, 1990; General Accounting Office, 1990; Gross and Mauro, 1989; Paternoster, 1991; Radelet and Pierce, 1991.

10. Bedau and Radelet, 1987; Radelet, Bedau, and Putnam, 1992.

11. Spangenberg and Walsh, 1989.

1

Drawing the Lines:
Who Lives and Who Dies?

The exclusion of the mentally incompetent from execution has a history in Anglo-American law dating back to the medieval period.[1] English common law prohibited the execution of such prisoners as a "savage and inhuman" practice; "a miserable spectacle . . . of extreme inhumanity and cruelty."[2] This attitude toward mentally disordered death row inmates carried over to nineteenth-century America, and legislators and courts to this day continue to voice prohibitions against executing the mentally incompetent. "Virtually every state that authorizes the death penalty has adopted by case law, statute, or implication, the common law rule prohibiting the use of that sanction against an insane prisoner."[3] Thus, at least according to *formal* rules, there is virtually unanimous agreement that mentally disordered inmates should not be executed, and that their sentences should be commuted to terms of long (or life) imprisonment. As we shall see, the extent to which this prohibition is actually observed is a separate question.

Before grappling with the question of what sorts of mentally ill or mentally retarded prisoners should be or are exempted from execution, a more fundamental question must first be asked: Why *not* execute the mentally ill? There are several reasons for the presence of this exemption in the statute books, but no single reason alone is sufficient to explain it. Confusion surrounding the reasons for this prohibition is in part attributable to a lack of agreement surrounding the purpose of capital punishment.[4] That is, the answer to the question of why some prisoners should not be executed is in part dependent upon the answer to the question of why others should be executed, and what procedures are necessary to ensure the legitimacy of the capital punishment process.

There are six primary (and somewhat overlapping) reasons why mentally ill inmates have been exempted from execution. First, resting on socially defined standards of decency, is the humanitarian argument. The mental illness itself is enough punishment. We do not execute the mentally ill because—criminal or not—they are a unique group in society, deserving of special concern, protection, and care. The exemption of the mentally incompetent from execution is a public and symbolic way of reaffirming consensual social commitments to make special efforts to understand and accept the mentally ill, even if the acceptance is conditional on a term of long imprisonment. Executing the mentally ill threatens societal values of humanitarianism. Mentally incompetent prisoners are exempted from execution not so much because of concern for them as individuals, but because of concern for the mentally ill as a group and concern for what executions say about standards of decency of the society as a whole.

Second, such exemptions further the image of "fair play." Mentally ill prisoners are not able to assist in crucial efforts by defense attorneys to challenge their convictions or sentences. Because this point focuses on public perceptions, fair play itself is less important than the *image* of fair play. The state would at least want to go through the ritual of evaluating mentally ill prisoners for competence so that an image of the prisoner's having a fair chance to contest the impending execution is presented. Public support for the death penalty might diminish if citizens believed the state's powers were being launched against a prisoner who could not assist in his own defense. The image of fair play will help reduce any guilt or ambivalence held in the society concerning the morality of capital punishment.

Third, the retributive goals of capital punishment are not achieved by executing the mentally ill. Because of the immense suffering caused by the prisoner's criminal actions, he is to suffer in anticipation of his death, and this goal cannot be achieved if he does not appreciate his impending fate because of mental illness. The mental impairment prevents the inmate from suffering a fear of death while on death row any more than he already suffers in living with the illness, thereby removing a major goal that the execution is purported to serve. According to this argument, society exempts the mentally ill from execution because of vindictiveness, not humanitarianism. Paradoxically, by so doing, the criminal justice system reaffirms the accountability of the sane.[5] However, if this were the sole reason for the exemption, it would be difficult to find physicians or mental health professionals who would evaluate death-sentenced inmates for competence, as ethical principles (to be reviewed in Chapter 6) would discourage the evaluation of prisoners to see whether they are, in effect, capable of more suffering.

Fourth, exempting the mentally ill from execution is necessary because they cannot spiritually prepare for death and an anticipated afterlife. This is a relatively minor explanation for why the mentally ill are not executed; as with the goal of exempting the mentally ill so they can help with their defense, in practice there are no states that actually apply the exemption in a way that would achieve such goals. If these goals were of paramount importance, the statutes would ask the evaluating mental health professionals to evaluate either the condemned man's ability to assist in his defense, or his realization of moral guilt and ability to ask forgiveness and competence to engage in religious pursuits.[6] Statutes ordering the exemption of the mentally ill from execution do not ask for such determinations; at best, statutes simply ask whether the prisoner understands the nature and effect of the death penalty and why it is to be imposed upon him. (Statutes in some states are even less specific, simply asking if the prisoner is "insane" or "unfit.")

Fifth, to the extent that the goal of the death penalty is to deter others from imitating the prisoner's criminality, the goal is not achieved by executing the mentally ill. Deterrence theory suggests that executions are most effective (if at all) in deterring future *premeditated* homicides; therefore, executing those who commit premeditated homicides—not those whose crimes were spontaneous or the result of a mental disorder—sends the clearest message. Further, the deterrence message is likely to be overshadowed by the message of how horrible it is for the state to fail to show mercy to the mentally ill.

Sixth, exempting the mentally incompetent from execution can also be a double check on the original trial. In some cases a mentally ill defendant, who should have been found incompetent to stand trial, insane at the time of the crime, or mentally unable to have the intent and/or premeditation sufficient for a capital crime, slips through the cracks and, for whatever shortcoming of the criminal justice system, is convicted and condemned to death. Recent studies point to an unknown but significant number of death row inmates who suffer from severe mental retardation or neurological impairments.[7]

There is a major fault with humanitarian explanations for the exemption of the mentally incompetent from execution. If a death row inmate is found to be insane[8] or, more specifically, *incompetent for execution* (and being psychotic or mentally ill or mentally retarded does not necessarily make one incompetent), in most jurisdictions the exemption from execution is temporary. To be sure, the defendant's mental status may give judges or governors sufficient reason to commute the death sentence to a term of imprisonment; but in most jurisdictions, incompetence for execution does not necessarily entitle the prisoner to permanent commutation. In England, since at least the 1840s, no prisoner has ever been executed after a previous finding of mental incompetency, but that is a tradition, not a rule.[9] As Weihofen put it, "The real issue is whether it is less humane to execute a guilty criminal while he is insane than it is to postpone the execution until we make sure that he understands what we mean to do to him—and then kill him."[10]

On the other hand, those who argue that the mentally ill should not be excluded from execution believe that virtually nothing should interfere with a death sentence once it is levied by the courts. Further, they contend that exempting the mentally incompetent would send an invitation to all death row inmates to feign symptoms of mental illness and try to fool the mental health experts.

The relevance of such arguments for the administration of capital punishment today is not in whether the mentally ill should be excluded from execution (since every state that still uses the death penalty has procedures for exempting at least some of the mentally ill from execution), but in how broadly the concept of incompetence for execution should be defined. Once defined, the methodological/diagnostic question of how to apply the criteria and separate the insane from the rest is reached. Even if opposing sides in a specific case argue that the defendant in question does or does not qualify for the exemption, all parties agree that at least a certain proportion of death row inmates *should* be exempted.

Whatever the rationale for exempting the mentally ill from execution, American history is replete with examples where the exemption has not been applied, and defendants with severe mental illnesses have been put to death. Consider, for example, the 1936 execution in New York of Albert Fish.

Fish was convicted of strangling 10-year-old Grace Budd to death on June 3, 1928.[11] He may have also killed as many as 14 additional victims.

The Budd family lived in New York City. Grace's brother had put an advertisement in a local newspaper, hoping to find work. The following Sunday afternoon, Fish appeared at the Budd's home, responding to the ad by saying that he owned a farm in New Jersey and was interested in hiring Grace's brother. After some friendly chatting, the job was offered and accepted. Just before leaving, Fish asked whether he could take Grace to a birthday party that his sister was giving for one of her children. The family never saw her again.

The disappearance remained a mystery until 6 years later, when Fish wrote to the Budds, admitting that he had choked Grace to death—and eaten her flesh. While the letter was unsigned, it did include a partial return address, so it was relatively easy for the authorities to trace. Fish was arrested on December 13, 1934.

At police headquarters Fish gave a detailed confession, admitting that he choked the child to death, cut her body into three sections, and ate part of each. He later took police to where the murder had occurred, where they discovered what remained of the child's bones. Fish's confession detailed 9 days of constant sexual excitement while he cooked Grace's body with carrots, onions, and strips of bacon, and then ate it.

Fish had several relatives who suffered from mental problems: a paternal uncle and a half brother (both of whom died in state hospitals), a paternal aunt, two brothers, a sister, and his mother. According to Dr. Fredric Wertham—one of the country's foremost forensic psychiatrists in this century—Fish's mother and six other relatives "suffered from psychosis or were severely psychopathic personalities."[12] Dr. Wertham, who examined Fish, described Fish's sexual life as one of "unparalleled perversity. . . . There was no known perversion that he did not practice and practice frequently."[13]

In addition to being a killer, a cannibal, and a sexual pervert, Fish was also a sadomasochist. He enjoyed taking bits of cotton, saturating them with alcohol, inserting them into his rectum, and setting them on fire. He also did that to some of the children he victimized. Dr. Wertham estimated that Fish had assaulted at least 100 children in 23 states (Fish preferred African-American children because the authorities did not pay much attention if they disappeared or were assaulted).

For years Fish enjoyed sticking needles into his body; he preferred the area between his scrotum and rectum (he also did this to some of his victims). Some of the needles were as big as sail needles, and, while Fish usually removed them, some were pushed in too far to be removed. At the time of his arrest, X-rays revealed that 29 needles remained inside his body. Fish was also coprophagic—he ate human feces.

Dr. Wertham testified at Fish's trial on behalf of the defense. In his words, "In response to a hypothetical question that was fifteen thousand words long, covered forty-five typewritten pages, and took an hour and a half to be read, I declared that in my opinion Fish was legally insane."[14] Nonetheless, four prosecution psychiatrists disagreed. Some of the statements of the physicians who testified for the state are revealing:

"Well, a man might for nine days eat that [human] flesh and still not have a psychosis. There is no accounting for taste."

"Coprophagia is a common sort of thing. We don't call people who do that mentally sick. A man who does that is socially perfectly all right."

"They [people with coprophagia] are very successful people, successful artists, successful teachers, successful financiers."

"I know of individuals prominent in society—one individual in particular that we all know. He ate human feces as a side dish with salad. . . . I had a patient who was a very prominent public official who did it."[15]

After the trial, according to Dr. Wertham, one of the jurors commented that most of the members of the jury agreed that Fish was indeed insane, but that he should be executed anyhow. Upon being found guilty, Fish's response was, "What a thrill that will be, if I have to die in the electric chair. It will be a supreme thrill—the only one I haven't tried."[16] Fish was executed in the electric chair at Sing Sing Prison on January 16, 1936. More than two dozen needles in his body apparently caused a minor short circuit in the execution apparatus; a second jolt of electricity was necessary to finish the job.[17]

While a half century has passed since Fish's execution, there is no scarcity of similar cases. Two 1992 executions are among them. The first occurred under the signature of then-Arkansas governor and presidential candidate Bill Clinton, who in January returned to Arkansas from the New Hampshire campaign trail to preside over the execution. The inmate was Ricky Ray Rector, who was convicted of murdering two people, including a police officer, in 1981. Rector had shot himself in the forehead at the time of his arrest, destroying a 3-inch section of his left frontal lobe. The ensuing surgery resulted in a frontal lobotomy, leaving him with little mental capacity, no understanding of the difference between life and death, no idea that he was going to be executed, the thinking capacity of a 10-year old, and, in the words of his attorney, a "zombie."[18] Court-ordered mental examinations led to the uncontested conclusion that Rector "would not be able to recognize or understand facts which might be related to his case which might make his punishment unjust or unlawful."[19] Nonetheless, the courts refused to intervene, and Governor Clinton denied pleas for clemency. Despite the governor's actions, an hour before the execution Rector told friends that he still planned to vote for Clinton for president. As he left his cell for the death chamber, Rector told his attorneys that he was saving a piece of pecan pie from his last meal to eat just before bedtime (a habit he had developed over the years). The untouched pie was found by guards after Rector's death.[20]

Another case comes from Texas, where on February 11, 1992, Johnny Frank Garrett was executed for the gruesome rape and murder of a 76-year-old nun in an Amarillo convent. While this is not the type of crime that normally invites sympathy (to say the least), investigation into Garrett's background revealed a childhood of severe physical torture, sexual abuse, and chronic psychosis. In addition, Garrett was only age 17 at the time of the crime—a factor that alone would make him ineligible for the death penalty in every country in the world except Iran, Iraq, Nigeria, Pakistan, Bangladesh, and the United States. None of these factors was considered by the jury that sentenced Garrett to death. As the case wound its way through the appellate courts, pleas for clemency came from the Bishop of Amarillo, 16 other Catholic bishops, the nun's community (Sisters of St. Francis), and even Pope John Paul II. These special circumstances led Texas Governor Ann Richards to issue a 30-day reprieve in January, just 2 hours before Garrett's first date with the executioner, and to refer the clemency appeal to the Texas Board of Pardons and Paroles (the agency in Texas that makes all clemency decisions). The prosecutors were livid, and doubled their efforts to carry out the execution. Three weeks later, when the Board voted on Garrett's motion for commutation, the vote against it was 17-0 (with one abstention). Outside the prison during the execution, a crowd of students from Sam Houston State University stood cheering and applauding, yelling "kill the freak" and singing "na-na-na-na, hey-hey-hey, good bye."[21]

The prosecutors and judges involved in the Fish, Rector, and Garrett cases are not alone in believing that mental illness should not be a reason to exclude criminal offenders from capital pun-ishment.[22] In fact, some research suggests that a "mental illness defense" in a capital trial, or in the sentencing proceeding that follows the determination of guilt,[23] can sometimes hurt the defendant more than it can help.[24] One of the first steps in selecting a jury in a capital case is to eliminate any potential juror who stands opposed to the death penalty. Any number of poten-tial jurors with such views can be excused by the prosecution for cause. Experiments with mock jurors show that those remaining tend to be comparatively unsympathetic to psychological expla-nations of criminal behavior.[25] Jurors have the tendency to be-lieve that mental illness is no excuse, that it is too easy for a defendant to fake symptoms of mental illness, and that even if mentally ill, he or she should have gotten help for it before the occurrence of criminal violence. In addition, raising mental health questions can mislead the jury into believing that the defendant, if not executed, will be dangerous and unpredictable while in prison or if ever let out.

This is only one of the reasons why every state allows governors and/or pardon boards to commute any death sentences that are perceived to be inappropriate or comparatively excessive. Few rules govern the exercise of clemency. Nonetheless, clemency hearings are often perfunctory or meaningless, as are the health or medical evaluations used in them. The rate of clemencies in capital cases in the United States since 1972 has been a small fraction of comparable rates in the pre-*Furman* years.[26]

Yet executive clemency is supposed to be the final safety net that is responsible for preventing American jurisdictions from executing severely impaired death row inmates. The attorneys in Alvin Ford's case claimed that the safety net of clemency was insufficient. Eventu-ally that claim made the U.S. Supreme Court acknowledge that the courts, too, must take some of that responsibility.

Notes

1. Broderick, 1979; Larkin, 1980; *Solesbee v. Balkcom*, 339 U.S. 9 (1950); Walker, 1968.
2. Brief for Petitioner, *Ford v. Wainwright*, p. 12.

3. Broderick, 1979, p. 533 (footnotes omitted).

4. Guttmacher and Weihofen, 1952; Hazard and Louisell, 1962; Schopp, 1991; Weihofen, 1951.

5. For further analysis, see Schopp, 1991.

6. Weihofen, 1951.

7. Blume and Bruck, 1988; Lewis, Pincus, Feldman, Jackson, and Bard, 1986; Lewis, Pincus, Bard, Richardson, Prichep, Feldman, and Yeager, 1988.

8. The term *insanity* usually applies only to the time the crime was committed. *Insanity* is legally defined; it is not a medical diagnosis. However, the statutes in some states, such as Florida, use the term *insanity* to refer to the person's mental status while on death row. For a recent discussion of the distinction between sanity and competence, see Rachlin and Weiner, 1992.

9. Walker, 1968.

10. Weihofen, 1951, p. 652.

11. This account is taken from Heimer (1971) and Wertham (1949, pp. 65-94).

12. Wertham, 1949, p. 70.

13. Wertham, 1949, p. 72.

14. Wertham, 1949, p. 84.

15. Wertham, 1949, p. 88.

16. Heimer, 1971, p. 129.

17. Heimer, 1971, p. 139.

18. Frady, 1993; *Newsday*, January 23, 1992, p. 112; *The New York Times*, January 25, 1992, p. 8.

19. *Rector v. Bryant*, 111 S.Ct. 2872 (1991), p. 2873.

20. *Newsday*, May 4, 1992, p. 19. The execution was also botched: It took the medical personnel almost an hour of probing before they found a suitable vein for the lethal injection. *The New York Times*, January 24, 1992, p. 8.

21. Fitzpatrick, 1992; *The New York Times*, February 12, 1992, p. 22.

22. For other examples of mentally ill prisoners who have been executed, see Ehrmann, 1962, pp. 19-21.

23. One of the reforms introduced after the *Furman* decision is that capital trials are now separated into two parts. The first part determines guilt or innocence. In the second part, held only if a capital guilty verdict is returned, the jury decides on sentence. In most states, a judge cannot sentence a defendant to death unless the jury agrees.

24. White, 1987a.

25. White, 1987b.

26. Bedau, 1990-1991.

2

An Introduction to Alvin Ford

Florida State Prison sits 40 miles south of the Georgia border, midway between Jacksonville and Gainesville, and 9 miles northwest of the appropriately named town of Starke. It is stark and bleak, not the section of the state that tourists visit on their Florida vacations. After a ride through seemingly endless stretches of swamps, pine woods, and then open fields, the prison finally comes into view on the horizon. Just in case the visitor failed to notice the change in scenery, until 1989 an arch with "Florida State Prison" written across it spanned the highway (the arch was then rebuilt across the prison's driveway). The prison is sizable, with 1,200 inmates. Approximately 325 of them are condemned to die and are housed in 6 × 9-foot cells in four wings that contain the prison's death row.

The prison was built in 1964. It is a light-green, three-story block building surrounded by a double row of chain-link fences, 12 feet high on the outside and 8 feet high on the inside. Both are topped with bales of barbed wire. The dogs that used to patrol the 8-foot area between the fences were replaced in 1980 with rolls of steel razor-ribbon, a technological innovation that resulted from America's involvement in the Vietnam war. A few palm trees in the parking lot are the only trees within a half mile. The shrubs surrounding the red-brick administration building, which is set just east of the prison's main entrance, are regularly trimmed to keep their height less than 24 inches. At night the building and grounds are flooded in light; no inmate has seen any stars since arriving. As visitors walk toward the front gate, they are increasingly aware of men shouting to one another from their cells and the blare of radios echoing on the other side of the perimeter fences.

To get to the area where interviews between inmates and their attorneys are conducted, visitors must first pass through the gates in the two perimeter fences that are operated from a nearby guard tower, and then through two more barred gates that are controlled from inside the prison. After all metal is removed, including shoes, belts, pens, jewelry, and coins, a walk through a sensitive metal detector is a further reminder of the maximum security environment. Visitors are then joined by an escort and pass through three more steel-barred gates before arriving at "The Colonel's Office." Here there are three small rooms available for legal visits. Inmates especially appreciate visits from members of their defense teams in the summer: This is the only section of the prison that is air-conditioned, and the summer temperature in the cells can, on occasion, surpass 100 degrees.

What turned out to be our final visit with Alvin Ford was on September 13, 1990. We were accompanied by Mr. Laurin (Larry) Wollan, an attorney from Tallahassee who had joined Ford's defense team in 1981.

Soon after we arrived, Alvin Ford was brought into the room, hands cuffed behind his back, by the correctional officer who had escorted him from his cell. The handcuffs were unlocked for a moment and then refastened after the prisoner had moved his hands to the front; he shook hands with us and we all sat down at a small plywood table.

An African-American, Ford stood 5 feet, 8 inches tall and weighed about 160 pounds. His outward appearance seemed to have changed little since 1987, when we last saw him. An earlier Afro haircut was gone; his head was now shaved. We also noted that he did not appear to be as neat and orderly as he had previously been. His fingernails were filthy; overall, he appeared disheveled and unkempt.

On the other hand, it was apparent that Ford's demeanor had improved since our 1987 visit—when it was obvious to us that if his health did not improve, his survival was highly questionable. As the handcuffs were moved from behind Ford's back to the front, he acknowledged our presence, although he avoided direct eye contact. That acknowledgement alone signaled some improvement over the previous 3 years. Wollan did most of the talking, greeting Ford, reminding him that we were writing a book about his case, and attempting to explain the status of his appeals. Ford responded with a brief question (the only one he was to ask that day), but he seemed to have little interest in or comprehension of the answer. Still, this was improvement.

He sat quietly, except for some involuntary shaking of his right arm and leg—signs of tardive dyskinesia, a neurological disorder caused by the antipsychotic medication he had been taking. He responded to questions with few words and with emotional flatness. He yawned frequently. Conversation was awkward and seemed pointless; he asked us only that one question and he offered no spontaneous comments. There was an aura of resignation, depression, and fatigue. He did not know the names of his neighbors in adjacent cells. He no longer took advantage of the twice-weekly, 2-hour recreation break in the prison yard, and he had quit exercising several years earlier.

Shortly before the 1990 visit, Ford had been moved from his cell to the prison's psychiatric unit. His explanation for the move was "My eye feels like it has a needle in it. A lady in 1974 said she stuck a needle in my eye while I was asleep. I feel that it is there now. It hurts." Notes in the medical records for 1990 described him as "filthy dirty," urinating on his clothes, and generally having horrible personal hygiene. Prison medical records reveal that he had been placed on suicide watch. (Paradoxically, even though the state wants to speed the inmate's death, the prison goes to considerable effort to prevent death row inmates from committing suicide.)

Ford's current appearance and manner were in marked contrast to his condition in early 1975, when he first arrived on death row after being convicted of killing a police officer in Ft. Lauderdale. Friends and fellow inmates described him at the time as bright, articulate, responsive, and fastidious in appearance. For the first 6 years on death row Ford was active and involved in day-to-day prison life. He read, took an interest in his appeals, lifted weights, and watched television. With meticulous handwriting, he carried on regular correspondence with family, friends, and his attorneys, showing concern for other inmates on death row—especially those who had no attorneys, family, or friends.

But living on death row was not easy. As Albert Camus wrote:

> The devastating, degrading fear that is imposed on the condemned for months or years is more terrible than death, and one that was not imposed on the victim. . . . As a general rule, a man is undone by waiting for capital punishment well before he dies. Two deaths are inflicted on him, the first being worse than the second, whereas he killed but once.[1]

Although the vast majority of condemned inmates are somehow able to withstand the physical and psychological pressures of death row without losing their mental faculties, Alvin Ford was not. His mental condition began to unravel dramatically when his first death warrant (an order signed by the governor that specifies an execution date, usually within the forthcoming month) was signed in late 1981. During and after litigation in state and federal courts that eventually blocked the execution (with only 14 hours to spare), Ford gradually began to exhibit all of the classic signs of thought disorder typical of schizophrenia, a condition that he moved into and out of for the next 9 years. Until just before our 1990 visit he rarely ventured out of his cell to meet with his attorneys and friends; his family had finally quit coming to visit with him after he consistently refused to leave his cell.

After 1981 there were long periods of time when Ford sat with his eyes closed or stared off into space while mumbling in a code-like fashion, all but totally unaware of what was going on around him. He was observed walking around his cell like a robot, occasionally making strange growling noises. He moved through stages of increasing paranoia and incoherence and into aggressive activity, throwing food, punching at imaginary opponents, rolling on the floor, and throwing unopened mail into the hall. He made marks on the wall and subsequently touched them with various body parts. One minute he thought the inmate in an adjacent cell was dangerous and threatening; the next minute he was asking the same man for a cigarette. By the time a second death warrant in the case was signed in 1984, Ford was at the bottom of a steady descent into madness.

At the time of our 1987 visit, all of the signs of a severe thought disorder were present. Concentration was impaired; attention was limited; and his speech was rambling, frequently incoherent, and sprinkled with bizarre statements. Asked about what medication he had been given, he mentioned a yellow pill that he refused to take because "it was urine." He wanted to know if a longtime friend and supporter named Gail was the daughter of President Ronald Reagan.

Periodically during the 1987 interview he stopped talking, his eyelids fluttered, and in response to a question he reported having heard voices. Some of these voices told him that yet another death warrant in his case had been signed. He was obsessed with the 1974 attempted robbery in Ft. Lauderdale in which he had killed a policeman. He mumbled about the Red Lobster restaurant where it occurred; he inquired about "the number of black males age one to 50 who shot a policeman and didn't get a death sentence"; he referred in a vague manner to his 300-mile drive to Gainesville after the murder (where he was eventually apprehended).

But that was in 1987. Now—at least on this day in 1990—his psychotropic medication was having some effect. The surface changes were obvious. While not as tidy, he generally appeared to be in better control than he had been for several years.

By the end of our 90-minute visit, it was clear that much of the emotionalism and intensity characteristic of earlier times were subdued or camouflaged by the medications. Certainly there were unmistakable signs of the psychosis that had been periodic over the years, but it had taken on a different color. Now there was an air of resignation, passivity, apathy, withdrawal, and regression. Nothing that we said could get past the psychosis and the protective veil of psychotropic drugs.

The State of Florida tried its best for 16 years to execute Alvin Ford. After 1984 only his madness kept him alive. But at this point, in 1990, we felt it was not altogether clear how much Ford really understood or cared about living. Nothing seemed to give him even a few seconds of peace—he appeared to be totally preoccupied and uninterested in other people, current events, or daily life in the prison.

For many years the state's prosecutors, supported by the prison administration and mental health staff, maintained that Ford was not mentally ill. The state claimed that he was "malingering" or faking the symptomatology. While the prison's medical records for 1990 reveal that its mental health staff had finally admitted that there were times when Ford was psychotic (even to the point that they administered medication, to which he was responsive), the state never stopped maintaining that Ford should still be put to death.

Alvin Ford made history as the man who forced criminal justice authorities, lawyers, judges, politicians, mental health professionals, and a host of others to seriously debate the question of what types of mental illness should exempt condemned prisoners from execution and how (and by whom) these life-and-death determinations should be made. Before Alvin Ford, there was a centuries-old tradition that applied if a condemned prisoner was insane. In such cases the chief executive would intervene, exercise clemency powers, and commute the death sentence to a term of imprisonment. But in the political environment in which the modern death penalty is practiced in America, governors rarely commute *any* death sentences, no matter what special circumstances arise.[2] When Ford was denied clemency despite his psychosis by then-governor Bob Graham in May 1984, Ford's attorneys took the case all the way to the U.S. Supreme Court. In 1986 the Court decreed that the prohibition against executing the insane was not simply a tradition to be followed at the whim of the state's chief executive or pardon board—it was also a constitutional right. In short, mentally ill inmates have a constitutional right not to be executed.

The Supreme Court's ruling, however, did not end the debate. As will be discussed in Chapter 8, the Court was fragmented in its opinion, with few pairs of justices in total agreement, and the bottom-line vote of 5-4 left a bare majority in Ford's favor—not going so far as agreeing that he was incompetent, but at least accepting the argument that he had a right to judicial determination of that issue. Three majority justices, Powell, Brennan, and Marshall (the latter two opposed the death penalty regardless of circumstance) have since retired from the Court and have been replaced by more conservative voices. These changes in Court personnel could easily result in a reversal of the thrust of the *Ford* decision.

In still other ways, the contribution of the *Ford* case to the clarification of America's execution policies did not end with the Supreme Court's 1986 decision. The next questions are these: If states are to exempt the mentally incompetent from execution, what are the manifestations of mental illness that are necessary and/or sufficient for a finding of incompetence for execution? How are the states to decide who is mentally competent for execution and who is not? In the *Ford* case, some psychiatrists recognized that the inmate was psychotic, but took the position that psychosis itself does not render a prisoner incompetent for execution. In Florida (as in other states), "competency for execution" is defined not with medical vocabulary (like "psychosis" or "schizophrenia"), but as "the mental capacity to understand the nature of the death penalty and the reasons why it was imposed." Even psychotic people, so goes the argument, can have sufficient understanding to make them competent for execution.[3]

This raises the question of who should determine competence for execution. At times Alvin Ford was evaluated by psychiatrists, appointed by the governor, who were known for their proclivity to side with the prosecution, and by other psychiatrists known for their record in cooperating with the defense. Some of the psychiatrists who evaluated Ford no doubt strongly support capital punishment; other psychiatrists who were involved in the case oppose it. Are evaluations of competence for execution a product of medical skill, the politics of the examiner, or some mixture of both?

And who should make the ultimate decision of whether the prisoner is actually competent? The Supreme Court ruled that governors could continue to do so; but negative clemency decisions could be appealed to the judiciary (in some states, the judge who first hears competence claims that have been denied by the governor is the judge who initially sentenced the defendant to death). Some may argue that after investing so much time and thought in a given death penalty case, and after going on record as siding with those who believe the defendant has forfeited his life, the trial judge has a vested interest in the case, is unlikely to change his or her mind, and cannot be neutral when deciding on the defendant's competence. Even judges who have never before made decisions in the case may feel some pressure to let the death sentence stand. The validity of such arguments will become more apparent during the 1990s as the number of death-sentenced prisoners contesting their competence for execution grows.

Finally, the issues raised in the *Ford* case culminate in the still unresolved problem of what to do with those inmates who (unlike Ford) are successful in their attempts to be found incompetent for execution. Only one state, Maryland, has provisions for the automatic commutation of death sentences to terms of life imprisonment for inmates found incompetent for execution.[4] In other states, including Florida, the exemption from execution for mentally ill prisoners is *temporary*: If a prisoner is found incompetent, he is removed to a state mental hospital, treated, and—once his mental health is restored—returned to the prison for execution. As will be discussed in Chapter 10, this has resulted in controversy and outrage among many mental health professionals who might be asked to treat such inmates and criticism from the American Medical Association, the American Psychiatric Association, and several other professional organizations. It has also led to demands from more punitive sectors in society that the prisoner be treated against his will with antipsychotic medication so that his mental illness is masked and his life can be taken.[5] It is a classic "Catch-22" dilemma.

The *Ford* decision apparently means that the courts will exempt from execution only the most severely mentally ill. But the decision only clarifies what the courts would do; it says nothing about how the state's executive branch can exert its powers through executive clemency. Although the issue is not yet completely resolved, it appears that to legally qualify for execution, the prisoner only has to know the nature and effect of the death penalty and why it is to be imposed upon him—which apparently means only those prisoners with impairments relevant to understanding (e.g., delusions about being immortal; severe intellectual limitations preventing the causal connection between the crime and the execution) will be exempt. Other mental illnesses might warrant executive clemency, which can be given whenever the clemency officials (usually a governor and/or a clemency board) want—and for any reason they want, including no reason at all.

In reality, however, few exemptions from execution because of mental problems are given. Since 1972 only two prisoners have been exempted from execution because of mental illness, one in South Carolina by the courts (his sentence was commuted to life), and one temporary exemption, now retracted, given under executive authority to a prisoner in Florida.[6]

Events surrounding the *Ford* case have inspired passionate debate within the mental health professions and brought consternation to judges, politicians, and prison officials. The case raises a number of difficult questions about the administration of capital punishment—questions that involve ethics, politics, economics, the role of the courts, and the care, treatment, and management of the insane on death row.

As a result of a hearing ordered by the Supreme Court in *Ford*, in 1988 a federal district judge ruled that Ford was competent to be executed. This ruling put the judge in agreement with the governor and the original panel of three psychiatrists, selected by the governor, whose similar finding in 1984 sent Ford on his journey to the Supreme Court. The federal court's 1988 finding was appealed, and on September 18, 1990 (5 days after our prison visit), oral arguments on that appeal were heard by the U.S. Eleventh Circuit Court of Appeals in Atlanta.

We will never know how the Circuit Court of Appeals reacted to Ford's last appeal. Alvin Ford died unexpectedly (and somewhat mysteriously) on February 28, 1991, 2 days after he was found unconscious in his Florida State Prison cell. The autopsy report gave acute pancreatitis as the cause of death. Newspaper headlines proclaimed his escape from the chair. The sentencing judge, J. Cail Lee, said: "[Ford's crime] was unquestionably the most brutal crime I have ever had experience with." He lamented that Ford "never did have to answer for it. There's something wrong about that kind of labored justice."[7] The lead defense attorney on the case, Richard Burr of the NAACP Legal Defense and Educational Fund, reacted with a comment on the significance of the *Ford* case: "[I]t made the Supreme Court face up to the fact that people who live day in and day out on death row face a very heavy burden, and that burden could crush them."[8]

So, although Alvin Ford is dead, the questions raised in his appeals will continue to be debated for as long as executioners remain in America's employ. With his death, we can now look back and see what lessons can be learned. Close inspection of his case can teach much about the modern practice of capital punishment in America and the ethical issues confronted by physicians, psychiatrists, and other mental health professionals who are involved in these life-and-death decisions.

Notes

1. Camus, 1974, pp. 200, 205.

2. Bedau, 1990-1991.

3. In fact, there are virtually no legal decisions that are made solely on the basis of a medical diagnosis. There is typically a functional test required by the law that involves the question of what the individual must be able to think, do, or say to meet the minimum requirement. This principle was affirmed most recently in the *Penry* case (see Chapter 10), in which the Supreme Court refused to make mental retardation an automatic bar to the imposition of the death penalty.

4. Annotated Code of the Public General Laws of Maryland, 1987 Cumulative Supplement, Article 27, Section 75A.

5. These demands will be examined in conjunction with the discussion of the case of Michael Perry in Chapter 10.

6. These men, to be discussed in Chapter 10, are Fred Singleton in South Carolina and Gary Alvord in Florida.

7. *Sarasota Herald Tribune,* March 9, 1991, p. 10B.

8. *Sarasota Herald Tribune,* March 9, 1991, p. 10B.

3

Family Background, the Crime, and Trial: 1953–1974

Alvin Bernard Ford's family hails from Palmetto, Florida, a small town located on the Gulf Coast just south of St. Petersburg. The 1970 population of Palmetto was 7,427. Alvin was the oldest son and second child born to Connie and William Ford. The Fords spent summers as itinerant farm workers, so Alvin's birth, on September 22, 1953, actually took place in a hospital in Albion, New York, a farming center just east of Niagara Falls. Albion was the year-round home of Alvin's paternal grandparents.

The harsh environment in which Alvin was raised is common among death row inmates; such environments do not cause violence, but the odds of an infant from such an environment becoming criminally violent in adulthood are considerably higher than similar odds faced by the children of the white middle class.[1] Thus, what we see in the life of Alvin Ford is all too typical of those on death row in America today.

The plight of migrant farm workers during the 1950s was brought to America's attention by Edward R. Murrow's seminal documentary, *Harvest of Shame*. The film, produced in 1960 when Alvin was 7 years old, portrays the squalid conditions that infants, children, and their families faced while traveling along the migrant trail. Beginning in Florida in the spring and peaking in northern New York (where Alvin was born) before returning to winter quarters in Florida in late November, the farm workers usually earned only enough money to carry them to their next job. Unlike their employers, virtually all the farm workers were (and are) nonwhite, so it is impossible to understand the system without some understanding of racism. Murrow observed that Americans once owned slaves, but in the 1960s, simply rented them in the form of farm workers.

During the winter months, and year-round after their summer travels to New York ended when Alvin was age 5, his father was a self-employed construction worker. He often completed projects with the help of the entire family, and especially from his oldest son, Alvin. From all accounts, during his childhood Alvin got along well with his father. Mr. Ford specialized in cement work, and over the years he became skilled at it. Their own house, however, was shabby; it even lacked indoor plumbing. With assistance from Connie and Alvin, William Ford built a new house for the family, completing the project in 1963, so Alvin was 10 years old before he had access to running water and an indoor toilet. But soon thereafter, when he was unable to find regular work in the depressed construction industry, William's drinking problems escalated, and he no longer could be counted on by the growing family. He became belligerent and verbally abusive; at times Connie and the children were afraid of him, and occasionally Alvin found it necessary to step forward and protect them. In 1971 Connie divorced her husband. William Ford died of liver problems in 1975 at age 45.

In addition to his older sister, Gwendolyn, Alvin had two younger brothers and two younger sisters. Wilma, born in 1957, followed her older sister's footsteps into a nursing career. Norma, today a secretary, was born in 1959. Roderick, born in 1961, entered the Air Force after his graduation from high school and later decided to pursue it as a career. Alvin's youngest brother is William, who was born just before the Fords moved into the new home. Like Norma, in recent years he has been struggling with drug problems. Alvin and all his brothers and sisters are high school graduates.

Connie Ford went to night school to obtain her high school diploma and encouraged her children to achieve. Today she is employed as a domestic worker. She is religious, hard-working, and committed to traditional American values. As one neighbor described her: "She brought her children up all alone and in a Christian home. I have often wondered how a child of Mrs. Ford's could have done what they say Alvin did."[2]

In the months following Alvin's arrest for murder in 1974, there was little, if any, investigation done on his background. For example, his attorneys did not learn until Alvin's funeral in 1991 that, shortly after he graduated from high school, he had fathered a child. Few friends or acquaintances were interviewed, and none of the documentation that should be routinely assembled in death penalty cases (e.g., birth, medical, school, and social records for the entire family) was gathered. Consequently, no thorough, reliable social history of him or his family was prepared, and significant details about his life and his family's history remain undocumented. We do not know, for instance, the prevalence of mental illness in his family tree, details of the prenatal care his mother received, or information on the possibility of in-utero trauma caused by pesticides from the fields in which his mother worked.

Alvin attended Memorial Elementary School and Palmetto High School. During his high school years he was the defensive cornerback for the football team, worked as a dishwasher and cook, contributed financially to the family, and generally assumed responsibility for his younger siblings. His sister Wilma told an interviewer with the Probation and Parole Commission that Alvin was like a father to them, often protecting his brothers and sisters from their abusive father and assuming many aspects of the male head-of-household role after William Ford's departure.

Alvin's high school was predominately white; of the 137 graduates pictured in his senior yearbook, only 22 (16%) are African-American. In contrast, the 1970 census found that 30% of Palmetto's residents were African-American. Alvin took part in a number of organizations, including the Future Farmers of America, the Future Business Leaders of America, and the Science Club. At one point in high school he won an honorable mention in a state science fair. Showing an influence from the *Harvest of Shame* life that he had left far behind, in 1969 he received a Certificate of Merit from the Future Farmers of America. He was slightly above average as a student, with a high "C" grade point and a class rank at his 1971 graduation of 51 out of 152.

Alvin's high school biology teacher described him as "a very good student . . . [with] an inquiring mind. He was always polite and showed good manners." Andrew Alexander, a neighbor who had known the Ford family since before Alvin's birth, said: "His personality was always kind, gentle, respectful and obedient, and he was well liked in the community." Alvin's former Sunday school teacher, who also occasionally employed Alvin at his packing company, had this to say: "I watched him grow up. . . . A very nice person, obedient to his parents and elders of the community. . . . He never gave any trouble in any way."

A review of his elementary and high school records reveals that Alvin had some problems with his temper, but there are no records of any major disciplinary actions.[3] A friend said that fellow students in high school thought of him as likable, but "carrying a chip on his shoulders." The only blight on his high school record came when he and a friend skipped school in order to drive to nearby Bradenton to get copies of pictures of them that had appeared in the sports section of the local newspaper. For this, Alvin—but not his friend—was suspended for 3 days. Some speculated the reason his friend was not punished was because the friend was the star running back and was badly needed for the Friday night football game.

After graduation, Alvin had a more serious problem. On March 18, 1972, he and some friends stole $3,000 worth of automotive equipment from the storage building of a local moving company. Alvin's mother saw the equipment in her yard, where Alvin and his friends liked to tinker with cars, and it was she who alerted the authorities. It led to a conviction for breaking and entering and a sentence of weekend confinements followed by 4 years' probation. The offense was considered to be relatively insignificant, however, as later it was ignored when Alvin was hired as a guard in the state prison system.

Like many other teenagers in the early 1970s, Alvin experimented with some of the widely available drugs. During the summer of 1971 he dabbled for the first time with marijuana, LSD, and synthetic mescaline. At that time he was not a regular drug user, however, and he did not experience any difficulties that could be traced to drug use. Later he did. As he told a reporter at Florida State Prison in 1979:

> Drugs can alter a person's mind. I'm not gonna say you take drugs and you're gonna go out and murder somebody. I'm saying drugs will alter your normal life-style . . . The first time I ever took drugs was when I was in the 12th grade. A friend—I thought it was cool, just like cigarettes. It led to something and something else. My mother is very religious, strictly religious. Somehow when I got on drugs, she didn't know how to handle me. My family came to me with the problem. That pushed me further back. I eventually ended up on the street.[4]

Alvin's use of drugs later escalated, and it led directly to the crime that put him on death row.

Alvin had worked for some time at the Red Lobster restaurant in Bradenton. He was a decent worker; at one point his work was good enough to place him on a team of employees that traveled across several states to open new restaurants and train the newly hired staff. In 1973, when an acquaintance of Alvin's invited him to go up to Gainesville to help open a new restaurant ("The Italian Fisherman"), Alvin decided to accept the opportunity, leave the Red Lobster, and, for the first time, move out of his family's home. Gainesville, 150 miles to the northeast, not only offered better job prospects, but, as home to the University of Florida, it was an exciting town for young adults. At the Italian Fisherman Alvin quickly became the assistant manager, taking responsibility for handling receipts and supervising other employees.

He was working long hours, making $190 per week and 2% of the profits, not bad for an 19-year-old at that time and place. He would always send a portion of each paycheck home to Palmetto to help support his mother, siblings, and daughter (who lived at times with Connie Ford, and, for almost 2 years, with his older sister). But problems developed around his inability to handle the increasing book work and the reconciliation of two cash registers. Dr. David Taubel, a psychiatrist who interviewed Alvin in 1974, discovered that Alvin had dyslexia, causing difficulty in handling numbers and significant stress and frustration. Records from the Italian Fisherman that are found in the Department of Corrections files indicate that Alvin was a "good worker but [has] several undesirable character traits, and he is not eligible for rehire." In October 1973, after 7 months of employment, he left.

Alvin next worked as a salesman in a paint store, but left after a few weeks with complaints about the lack of responsibility. Shortly thereafter, on February 15, 1974, he was hired as a guard at Union Correctional Institution in Raiford, the state's largest maximum security prison, 40 miles north of Gainesville. The prison is within sight of Florida State Prison, which houses Florida's death row, although the institutions are in different counties and cities. The proximity did not act as a deterrent.

Early 1974

By the spring of 1974, Alvin was having major troubles. His drug use was escalating. He was arrested for going around a police barricade, for speeding, and for writing bad checks. A more serious charge came in March 1974, when he was picked up for the robbery of the same Red Lobster restaurant in Bradenton at which he had previously worked. A witness first identified him from pictures, but when she was later unable to do so in a lineup, Alvin was released after 20 days in jail. One month after his arrest and consequent loss of his job, he convinced officials at the prison that the arrest had been a mistake, and so on April 26 he was rehired.

He liked the idea of working in law enforcement and began to plan a career in corrections. This led to his application for a program in officer training at Santa Fe Community College in Gainesville. Hoping to matriculate, he asked his mother, a talented seamstress, to make a new pair of pants for him. But soon after he enrolled in classes and purchased books, the idea collapsed. The commute from Gainesville to Raiford—40 miles each way— was taking its toll on his car, and the mechanical problems caused him to miss work. His supervisor at the prison, however, refused to accept the excuse, telling Alvin, "You're putting me on. You're joking. You just don't want to come to work."[5] On June 10, Alvin was fired.

Alvin was depressed and restless. No job. No money. He had let his family down. With no job, his hopes for college were gone and his car had been repossessed. At one point in early 1974, a Gainesville vocational rehabilitation counselor referred Alvin to a psychiatrist for treatment for depression. As psychiatrist Jamal Amin later observed, Alvin had "an increasing overwhelming sense of failure and disappointment over his inability to be successful in college or his jobs as a prison guard or restaurant manager."[6] His use of cocaine had moved into the $300 per week range and he began selling drugs to support the habit. He was dealing with a 26-year-old Jacksonville man named Henry Edward Robinson, who later was involved with Alvin in the Ft. Lauderdale murder. The drug deals were usually in amounts of $2,000; each resale netted Alvin about $600, a portion of which he sent to his family.

During this period, Alvin was so depressed that he was not only trying to medicate himself with cocaine, but also thinking about death. For one thing, he purchased a $25,000 insurance policy, naming his mother as beneficiary. This may have resulted from thoughts of suicide. A friend of Alvin's from Palmetto hand-delivered the insurance policy to Mrs. Ford, but after a short while it was canceled for lack of payment.

Alvin's periods of depression were broken by periods of mania. A psychiatrist, Dr. David Taubel, testifying at Alvin's trial, described his condition at this time as follows:

> Then a rather strange thing happened. He didn't recognize it as strange but I sure recognized it as strange. This man's behavior pattern suddenly reversed itself and instead of being an essentially responsible person who worked hard, long hours, was rewarded with good pay and responsible jobs, he suddenly became a real fat cat in Gainesville. He is swinging. Man, but is he swinging. He is going horseback riding in the morning. Now, that is a bit unusual. He's got a lot of girl friends. Doesn't have any men friends, except one man at the University of Florida that he is close to. But women, horseback riding, cars, out all night, spending a lot of money. He is acting, I said to myself—he didn't say this to me—he is acting as if he were eating, drinking and being merry for tomorrow you may die. He is acting as irresponsibly as all get out.[7]

In retrospect, the case can be seen as a harbinger. In 1974 cocaine was widely seen as a "harmless" drug, but in the two decades since, we have learned that the drug can be highly addictive, and robberies (and spur-of-the-moment murders committed while drugged) to feed the habit are common. Obviously, Alvin's life-style could not be sustained for long.

July 1974: The Red Lobster Murder

The crime occurred only a month after Alvin was fired from Union Correctional Institution, and when the country was captivated by the release of the "Watergate Tapes" and the hearings to impeach President Richard Nixon. On Friday, July 19, 1974, 20-year-old Alvin Ford left Gainesville, headed for Jacksonville in a dark green Volkswagen borrowed from a friend, Louise Mazik. There he rendezvoused with George Angelo DeCosta, age 25, and Alvin's drug-trading acquaintance, Henry Robinson. He had known these men, both of whom were older and more urbane than Alvin, through the drug trade, although only for a matter of months. The three of them drove back through Gainesville and on to Ft. Lauderdale, where they planned to buy some cocaine for subsequent resale. The 300-mile trip was uneventful, except for a speeding ticket received by DeCosta.

At a turnpike exit in Ft. Lauderdale, an acquaintance of Ford's, Alvin Ray Lewis, age 21, was waiting for them. They followed Lewis to his home, had something to eat, and eventually checked into the Town and Country Motel. Lewis registered for the room, giving a false name and Miami address, but then went back to his own home for some sleep.

Sometime during that Saturday evening, plans were made to rob a Red Lobster restaurant—possibly two Red Lobster restaurants—with the goal of securing enough cash for the impending drug deal. It is not clear from the record whose idea it was, who did the planning, or if very much planning was involved at all. It was left that Lewis would come by the motel around 8:00 a.m. Sunday morning, July 21.

After meeting at the motel and numbing their fears with cocaine, the four men rode past a Red Lobster on Route 441 and then

on past a second one at 5950 North Federal Highway. They chose
to rob the latter. Ford and Robinson were in the Volkswagen,
which they parked at a nursery several blocks from the restaurant,
ready for use as a getaway car. DeCosta and Lewis, riding in a blue
1968 Chevrolet that belonged to Lewis's uncle, then picked up
the other two men for the short trip to the restaurant.

They approached the restaurant shortly before 9:00 a.m., just
as the workers were beginning to prepare for the 11:00 opening.
All four men had stockings or ski masks to pull over their heads.
DeCosta and Lewis, armed with a .22 rifle, waited in the car. Ford
and Robinson carried handguns—one a .38 revolver borrowed
from a neighbor of Robinson's, the other a .357 magnum purchased by DeCosta. Apparently the plan was for DeCosta and
Lewis to enter the restaurant a few minutes after Ford and Robinson in order to help tie up the staff. Whatever the plan, the
robbery was badly bungled.

Ford and Robinson, faces covered with ski masks, then approached the restaurant. A custodian taking garbage through the
back door was stopped and forced at gunpoint back inside. Some
of the workers were tied up, and one locked himself in a small
office. The manager, Norman R. Phillips, was struck on the head
and his glasses were damaged, causing him difficulty in opening
the safe. One of the cooks pried open a door and ran out to flag
down a car, but she was stopped by the robbers and brought back
into the restaurant. Meanwhile the custodian bolted away, ran
three blocks, and called the police.

Ford had not yet taken the money (some $7,500) from the safe
when he heard a banging on the back door—"Man, the police are
coming. Let's get out of here. Let's get out of here." Robinson was
quicker than Ford, and he sprinted to the already moving Chevrolet,
joined his companions, and the trio sped away—leaving Ford behind.

Abandoned, Ford panicked. As he tried to leave by the rear door,
he saw a policeman, Dimitri Walter Ilyankoff, approach with a
clipboard in hand. Apparently Ilyankoff had not understood that
a robbery was in progress, as he failed to follow standard police
procedures and wait for backup officers before entering the
building. Ford shot him twice in the abdomen and rushed out the
door. Ilyankoff used his portable radio to call headquarters. "I'm

shot. Help me. I'm shot. Help me. I'm shot. Help me."[8] Meanwhile, Ford decided to flee from the scene in the police car. Finding no keys in it, Ford reentered the building, yelled for Ilyankoff to give him the keys, and in a state of panic shot the officer in the back of the head with a .38-caliber "Saturday Night Special." Within 20 minutes after arriving at Holy Cross Hospital, Officer Ilyankoff was dead.

Meanwhile, Ford grabbed the keys and made his escape in the police car, transferring to the Volkswagen that had been parked a few blocks away. A passerby spotted him, jotted down the license number of the Volkswagen, and soon the police had traced the ownership.

Three hundred police officers, aided by K-9 dogs, quickly joined the search for the killers. DeCosta was arrested within an hour of the murder; he had attempted to elude arrest by jumping out of his car at a roadblock near the restaurant, but the dogs found him hiding in some nearby bushes. Lewis was arrested at 8:30 that night when the authorities found the getaway car parked in front of his Ft. Lauderdale home. The fourth bandit, Henry Robinson, eluded the police for 3 months before being apprehended in Guatemala.

Too panicked to think clearly, Ford drove directly back to the two places where he would most likely be picked up—his mother's house in Palmetto, almost 200 miles northwest, and then on to Louise Mazik's apartment in Gainesville, an additional 150 miles to the north.

Dr. David Taubel, who interviewed Ford one week after his arrest, reported the following:

> I asked him, "Did you think of escaping? Did you think of assuming a disguise, of going somewhere? Did you realize that lots of people get away with crimes in this country and are never caught? You can go to Mexico, the Bahamas. You can become a farmer in Kansas. Who knows? There are lots of places where you can go where nobody can catch you. Did you think of doing this?"
>
> No, he hadn't even thought of it.
>
> "What did you think of doing?"
>
> "I went home to see my mother."

He drove to Palmetto to see his mother. She was working, so, instead, he saw his girlfriend, visited for a short while, went to Gainesville . . .

I asked him why. "Did you not think that the police would surely believe you were in one of these two places; the most likely place to look for you in one of your two homes?"

Yes, he did not care. He didn't care.[9]

The police, having traced the ownership of the car Ford was seen driving, arrested him in Gainesville about 12 hours after the murder. The authorities quickly secured a small plane and flew him back to Ft. Lauderdale for arraignment.

Meanwhile, Connie Ford had spent her day attending a 50th wedding celebration for some friends in Sanford, Florida, 100 miles northeast of Palmetto. As she remembers it today, all day long she had anxiety attacks and feelings of dread that told her she had to get home to her children as soon as she could. Even before the party began, she started telling her companions that she had to return home. During the dinner, she ate quickly and waited on the porch for the others to finish. When she was finally able to leave, she sped back to Palmetto. Shortly after her arrival, Louise Mazik called from Gainesville to tell her of Alvin's arrest.

While being transported back to Ft. Lauderdale, Ford confessed to participating in the robbery but denied the shooting. He claimed that when he refused to talk, one of the officers threatened to "push this nigger off the plane," and that later he was kicked while in the squad car and that his toes were stomped on. Codefendant DeCosta was so badly beaten on the day of his arrest that Ford did not recognize him. (The police said his cuts and bruises came from his attempt to hide in some bushes and from fragments of buckshot the police fired into the hole in which he was hiding.)

Officer Walter Ilyankoff, age 40 and a 15-year veteran on the force, was survived by his wife, Maryanne, and an 18-year-old son, William. He was the first Ft. Lauderdale policeman ever to be murdered while on duty. The community was shocked and outraged. Although the atmosphere would have been tense no matter what the races of the defendants and victim, the fact that the defendants were African-American and the murdered officer was white fanned the flames of outrage. On July 23, less than 48 hours after the murder, the editorial page of the local newspaper carried a cartoon, titled "A Life For A Life," which had unmistakable racist overtones. It showed a black ape-like person (labeled "killer") pointing a pistol with two barrels: One pointed away from him and the other pointed toward him.[10] On the front page of the local section there was an article headed "I'm Glad I'm Not A Cop." It described being a cop as "the most thankless, dangerous job in the world," and described Ford as "some piece of human garbage," a "murderous thug," "a sadistic savage," and a "bloody-handed jerk."[11] The reporter who wrote this article, George McEvoy, later covered Ford's trial for the newspaper.

December 1974: The Trial

Robinson fled to Guatemala, where he was arrested in October and returned to Ft. Lauderdale for trial. In April 1975 he was convicted of first-degree murder and given a life sentence. Lewis and DeCosta were originally charged with first-degree murder, but these charges were reduced to second-degree through plea negotiation. Just before Ford went to trial in December, they were allowed to plead *nolo contendere* and were given life sentences in exchange for testifying for the state against Ford.

Ford's trial on first-degree murder charges began in Ft. Lauderdale on December 9, 1974. Presiding was Judge J. Cail Lee, a 50-year-old alumnus of the University of Florida and the University of Miami Law School. In 1970 Judge Lee headed the Broward County campaign for gubernatorial candidate Reubin Askew; and Askew, after he was elected, appointed Lee to a vacant seat on the Circuit Court in 1971. Judge Lee was elected to a full 8-year term in 1972.[12]

Because of the possibility of contradictory defense strategies, the public defender's office could not handle the cases for each of the four suspects. Therefore, the court appointed a private attorney, Robert T. Adams, Jr., to handle the defense. Adams, a former prosecutor who occasionally calls himself "Friendly Bob Adams" (after an advertisement by Household Finance Corporation), was a 1954 graduate of the University of Miami Law School. The county paid him only $1,500 for the defense, and therefore he had no resources to investigate, prepare, or present the case. It was not a stellar defense.

The trial began with a false start. In a court recess during jury selection, Judge Lee was asked a question by a 16-year-old Pompano Beach high school student: "Why does that man have those things on him?" (referring to the shackles around Ford's legs). None of the court officials had paid much attention to the shackles, but they were clearly visible to the 21 prospective jurors.[13] Because shackles could prejudice the jury by conveying the image that Ford was an excessively high danger and escape risk, the judge said he had expected the defense attorney to raise an objection. But after the student's question, the judge waited no longer for Adams to protest: He promptly dismissed the jury panel on his own initiative and ordered the removal of the shackles.

When jury selection began anew, Adams failed to challenge the dismissal by the prosecution of 12 jurors who expressed reservations about the death penalty. Those who firmly oppose the death penalty are not allowed to sit on juries in cases in which the punishment may be death (the state fears that the jurors' antipathy toward the death penalty might lead them to vote for acquittal), but conscientious defense attorneys always object when these jurors are dismissed. In order to dismiss potential jurors on these grounds, it has to be shown that there are *no* cases in which the juror would *ever* vote for death.[14] Potential jurors are allowed to say that they will be especially careful in a death case, but they cannot say they would *never* vote for death. The job of the defense attorney is to help the juror think of at least one scenario in which he or she would at least *consider* death. In the Ford case the dozen citizens dismissed from the jury pool unquestionably had some reservations about the death penalty, but whether their opposition was firm and universal is unknown, because they were sent home before it could be ascertained. Eventually, an all-white jury of 10 men and 2 women was selected.

The feelings in the community were strong; there was a substantial amount of pretrial publicity, and most citizens wanted both a prompt conviction and a severe penalty. A number of police officers attended the trial. Trial judge Lee acknowledged the atmosphere, but refused to sequester the jury. He stated that "There are emotional attitudes, political implications. But this isn't Watergate.[15] Three persons were struck from the jury panel because they were firmly convinced that Ford was guilty, a number that was characterized as unusually high. During the trial, two tires on defense attorney Adams's car were flattened when someone kicked out the valve stems while the car was parked outside the courthouse.

The unsuccessful attempt to have the jury sequestered was made because of the pervasive atmosphere of prejudicial publicity in general, and three items in the morning newspaper in particular. These included a reference to Ford's having "executed" the deceased, a reference to the incident involving the shackles, and an editorial critical of the court staff for allowing the shackle incident to have occurred. The inflamed publicity continued to be an issue raised by the defense throughout the trial, but Judge Lee always denied relief.

Once testimony began, Lewis and DeCosta told the jury about the events leading up to the attempted robbery and murder. Others described the chaos within the restaurant, sometimes with minor contradictions and inconsistencies. For example, star prosecution witness Barbara Buchanan, an employee of the Red Lobster, stated that she had seen the last shot fired, but before trial she had identified DeCosta as the one who shot the police officer, and she was confused about the weight, height, and clothes worn by the murderer. She admitted that she had "given many different stories."[16]

The trial failed to reveal a clear picture of events prior to the murder—who planned it, who obtained what guns, and so on. At one point state attorney Michael Satz was so frustrated with DeCosta, his own witness, that he tried (and failed) to have him designated as a hostile witness so the witness could be "impeached" or discredited. Over the months since the murder, DeCosta had given at least five different versions of events. There were similar problems with Lewis's testimony.

It took the state 5-1/2 days and 31 witnesses to complete the presentation of its case. Ford's defense, which at best can be characterized as weak, then began. Ford did not take the stand to testify on his own behalf, and he was not particularly communicative with attorney Adams. He seemed to place greater trust in his codefendants, even though two of them had already turned state's evidence. Ford had some anxieties about Adams, somehow having gotten the mistaken impression that Adams was the father of a police officer and therefore unsympathetic toward his case. (Adams was the son of a police officer, and he was also a former FBI agent. To this day, an autographed picture of J. Edgar Hoover hangs in his office, now located in Marianna, Florida.) Whatever the reason, the relationship between Ford and his attorney was always somewhat distant. And the defense phase of the trial ended quickly, because no defense witnesses were called.

In closing arguments, Adams could not maintain that Ford was uninvolved in the crime (for one thing, Ford's fingerprints were found in the slain officer's squad car). Instead, in a 75-minute presentation, he argued that because of extreme mental and emotional disturbances, Ford had an impaired capacity to appreciate the criminality of his conduct. Adams asserted that because of the lack of premeditation, Ford should not be treated more severely than his crime partners, who stood convicted of second-degree murder.

Prosecutor Satz took only 15 minutes for his closing arguments. He described the crime as cold and ruthless. "I characterize this as an execution. He didn't do it out of fear, out of a sense of survival. It was an execution."[17]

Then, after 7 days of trial, the case went to the jury. It took them only 2 hours to return with a verdict of guilty of first-degree murder.

In capital trials in Florida, as in other states, there are two phases: a determination of guilt, followed by more arguments and witnesses and a deliberation on a recommendation of whether the defendant should be sentenced to life or death. Unlike most other states, in Florida the jury's decision is not binding; the court may overrule a recommendation for life and impose a death sentence. This "override" by judges of juries' life recommendations has occurred in only a handful of cases in Indiana and Alabama (the only other states that allow it), but in more than 135 post-*Furman* cases in Florida, through 1992.

In coming to the life-or-death decision, judges and juries must consider both aggravating and mitigating circumstances. The aggravating circumstances increase the suitability of the death penalty for those convicted of first-degree murder; the mitigating circumstances decrease it and support a punishment of life imprisonment. If the death penalty is not imposed, the only other possible sentence is life imprisonment, which in Florida is defined as at least 25 years in prison before parole eligibility.

During the sentencing phase, the state argued that several aggravating circumstances were present:

1. Ford created a great risk to many persons (not only at the scene of the crime but in speeding away).
2. He committed a capital felony while he was engaged in another felony—a robbery.
3. He committed a felony while attempting to avoid arrest.
4. The murder was committed for pecuniary gain.
5. He disrupted and hindered the enforcement of laws.
6. His crime was especially heinous, atrocious, or cruel.
7. When the murder was committed, Ford should have been under imprisonment for the robbery, and hence he was under a sentence of imprisonment when the murder was committed.
8. Ford had been convicted of a previous felony (breaking and entering) and had admitted that he sold narcotics, both of which threaten the safety of the general public.

Very little evidence was presented to the court regarding mitigating circumstances. Defense attorney Adams put on three witnesses—Ford's mother, Connie; his girlfriend, Verna Sanders; and Dr. David Taubel, the psychiatrist.

During the penalty phase of a capital trial, the defense is permitted to present testimony on any aspect of the defendant's character and background that might support a sentence of life rather than death. Nonetheless, Ford's jury heard nothing about the devastating poverty and racism that surrounded his early years, nor about his admirable struggles to overcome these obstacles. At the very least, a complete social history of the defendant needs to be compiled in all death penalty cases, and testimony from friends, family, and acquaintances is needed to help the jury understand the defendant as a human being.[18] Because no social history was ever compiled in this case, the jury learned little about him.

Mrs. Ford testified that Alvin tried to take over for his alcoholic and abusive father by being extra-helpful to his siblings. After leaving home he continued to write and send money. She confirmed that he had taken out an insurance policy in the summer of 1974, designating her as beneficiary. She later told us that throughout the trial, she had been praying that God would take her life instead of her son's.

Verna Sanders, by then a student at Florida A & M University in Tallahassee, had known Alvin for many years. (At one point, Alvin thought of asking her to marry him, but Verna's parents disapproved of their relationship.) She told the jury that Alvin was a popular and generous person who was liked by everybody. She also spoke of his concern for his brothers and sisters. Verna was to remain close friends with Alvin until his death.

Finally, the psychiatrist, Dr. David Taubel, testified. His analysis was shallow at best and, in the eyes of some attorneys who later worked on the case, manifested a subtle, if unintentional racism:

> He is the oldest son in a family of six, a black family of perhaps better than average ability and more drive for success and achievement than I would estimate the average black family to have had.
>
> He comes from a family that is overstriving beyond their means to achieve and accomplish. He took the father's role as a young man, became the responsible male in the family. One has to realize that in the black culture a responsible male is not the same thing, is not as common as in the white culture, by any means, but he took that role. He wanted the role. He accepted it.

Dr. Taubel attempted to help the jury understand Ford's criminality—not to excuse it, but to show that his lack of premeditation or prior history of violent criminality made life imprisonment the fitting punishment:

> He did quite well in [the white culture] but he didn't have all the ability to handle it because he has, I think, a Dyslexia, and he can't handle the arithmetic. He can't handle the reading and writing as adequately as a man of his intelligence or as adequately as a man would have to do in the types of jobs that he tried to handle, that he aspired to. He became frustrated at progressive failures that he

couldn't handle. He didn't understand why he couldn't handle things. He got more frustrated, more angry, got depressed and pretty soon he acted as a man who wasn't going to live much longer and said, "Well, the hell with it. Eat, drink and be merry for tomorrow I will die," and from that point on his life led to the conclusion that we see in this courtroom. That is the way I see his life.

On the other hand, it was clear that Dr. Taubel believed that Ford had the potential for rehabilitation:

Q: Doctor Taubel, one last thing. What about a hope for the future of Alvin Ford?

A: Well, I wouldn't want to say what my personal feelings would be. I want to be a psychiatrist, a professional. Is there a possibility of rehabilitation of this man, is that what you are asking? Yes, I would say that the man has the potential for rehabilitation. That is a guarded opinion. It would have to be over many years but he does have the potential. He has the intelligence. He has the background. He has the ability to receive the insight.[19]

The penalty phase testimony, from start to finish, took only one morning. The jury then again went into deliberations. Significantly, on an initial straw vote, the jurors were divided 6-6 on their life-or-death recommendation. But on the second vote a 9-3 majority settled on a recommendation of death.[20] The deliberations were completed in an hour.

Sentencing day was January 6, 1975. No one was surprised when Judge Lee pronounced sentence: death in Florida's electric chair. "Alvin Bernard Ford, I sentence you to be held in close confinement until a date has been set for your execution, and upon that date you shall be put to death in the manner prescribed by law—namely, execution. May the Lord have mercy on your soul."[21] Judge Lee acknowledged that Ford's comparative youth might be considered a mitigating circumstance, but it was not sufficient to justify life. He found all eight of the aggravating circumstances argued by the state (a finding to be challenged on appeal), and nothing in mitigation. Later, he acknowledged that he had some strong feelings:

I am not saying that every person who takes another's life should be executed. But there is a species of human animal that does not deserve to live in the company of civilized man and men of good-will.[22] . . . This particular case was the only one in which I ever imposed the death penalty. You can be assured that I did not do it lightly. The facts of the case allowed no other sentence.[23]

It should also be noted that defense attorney Adams said in court that he had been contacted by the prosecutor regarding the possibility of exchanging a guilty plea for a sentence of life imprisonment. Thus at some early point in the process, the prosecutor obviously thought that the case did not necessarily call for the death penalty.

As he was leaving the courtroom, Ford slipped a note to George McEvoy, the reporter for the *Ft. Lauderdale News* who had covered the trial and had referred to Ford as human garbage and in other derogatory terms. The rambling note read:

> In a world plagued by racial hatred, religious bias and political rivalries, it teaches the "in spite of" kind of love. That's the kind that respects another person and shows no concern about his needs "in spite of" his hangups, his political beliefs, his racial or national origin, his attitude, his family background.
>
> Only bigots let these things prevent them from helping a person in need.
>
> You have to be little to belittle. Check it out for yourself. And the talk about drugs, it's our oppressors that make them!! Put that in *The News*.[24]

The note lacks clarity, but it does show that Ford felt the sting of the biased reporting. Despite its ambiguity—or perhaps because of it—the note was printed on the front page of the *Ft. Lauderdale News* the next morning.

In an interview with a psychologist 11 days after entering prison, Ford showed that he still had not come to grips with the reality of his predicament. He told the psychologist that he planned to appeal his case, enter college, and become a correctional counselor. That, of course, was not to be.

Notes

1. For other life histories of death row inmates, see Miller and Miller, 1989.
2. This and the following statements relating to Ford's early years were drawn from the files of the Office of Capital Collateral Representative (CCR), Tallahassee.

CCR is a state-funded law office that handles appeals for death row inmates after their initial appeal is denied by the Florida Supreme Court and the U.S. Supreme Court.

3. Florida Parole and Probation Commission, Presentence Investigation, January 6, 1975.

4. *Bradenton Herald,* November 5, 1981, p. 1.

5. Trial transcript, *State of Florida v. Ford,* No. 74-2159A, December 18, 1974, p. 1333.

6. Report of Jamal A. Amin, M.D., August 21, 1981, p. 3.

7. Trial transcript, p. 1334.

8. Trial transcript, p. 105.

9. Trial transcript, pp. 1336-1337.

10. *Ft. Lauderdale News,* July 23, 1974, p. 10.

11. *Ft. Lauderdale News,* July 23, 1974, p. 1B.

12. *Ft. Lauderdale News,* April 19, 1976, p. 1.

13. Trial transcript, pp. 105-110; *Ft Lauderdale News,* December 10, 1974, p. 1.

14. The standard is given in *Wainwright v. Witt,* 469 U.S. 412 (1985), p. 424. The standard for determining when a prospective juror can be excluded from jury service for cause is "whether the juror's views would prevent or substantially impair the performance of his duties as a juror in accordance with his instructions and his oath."

15. Trial transcript, p. 28.

16. Trial transcript, p. 1241.

17. Trial transcript, p. 1263.

18. Andrews, 1991.

19. Trial transcript, p. 1328, 1338-1340.

20. *Ft. Lauderdale News,* December 18, 1974, p. 1.

21. *Ft. Lauderdale News,* January 6, 1975, p. 1.

22. *Tallahassee Democrat,* April 20, 1986.

23. *Ft. Lauderdale News,* November 26, 1981, p. B1.

24. *Ft. Lauderdale News,* January 6, 1975, p. 1.

4

Anticipating and Enduring the First
Death Warrant: 1975–1981

The doors of Florida State Prison at Starke closed behind Alvin Ford on January 9, 1975. Soon he was using a prison nickname, "Sherlock," which Ford told a friend was a name "given to [him] by a girlfriend on a rainy night."

He was processed in the standard way for all newcomers to the prison—given interviews, a physical examination, psychological evaluations, and various achievement tests. The prison psychologist calculated that Ford had an IQ of between 80 and 89; achievement test scores placed his functioning at the fourth grade level in math and at the eighth grade level overall. These scores were lower than would have been expected from Ford in light of the relatively high-level jobs he had tried to hold when he was helping to support his mother and siblings—and, after all, two-thirds of his high school classmates had graduated with lower grade point averages. It is possible, of course, that the achievement tests were unreliable due to problems of administration, Ford's dyslexia or unwillingness to cooperate, or the depression that had clouded his life over the previous year.

In Florida, as in virtually all other death penalty states, condemned inmates are housed in small individual cells; the ones in
Starke measure 54 square feet. In the cell are a bed, a combination
toilet/sink, and the most cherished furnishing, a small black-and-
white television set. (In other states, it is common for the televisions to be outside the cell in a hall, there to be shared by several
prisoners.) Some refer to the televisions as "electronic pacifiers,"
since without them the inmates would have precious little to do
with their time and might become disruptive. Those prisoners
with families or friends who can afford it can also have a radio
and headphones, which serve as the best vehicle through which
to escape the constant noise of the prison surroundings.

Few exits from the cell are possible: There is no access to a
gymnasium, library, or religious services, and meals are served in
the cells. In good weather the inmates—a dozen at a time—are
"exercised" in a small prison yard, twice a week for a 2-hour spell.
In addition, every other night the inmate may stick his arms
behind his back and through the cell bars, be handcuffed, and
then, after the door is opened, be led down the tier for a 5-minute
shower. The only other exit is when the prisoner has a visitor, legal
or social. Hence, death row inmates are essentially confined to their
small cells for an average of more than 23 hours per day. No access
to a phone is possible unless there is a life-and-death emergency, and
no one, not even attorneys, may call in and leave messages.

Inmates may receive packages four times a year from family or
friends; what is permitted is highly restricted (e.g., no food or
books). Occasionally a cart appears at the cell door with a few
library books on it that the prisoner is permitted to borrow. In 1992
new regulations were imposed on books: Now they may be obtained
only if ordered directly from publishers (paperbacks only), and a
maximum of 10 books is permitted in the cell at any one time.

The guards keep their distance; most are fair but a few can be
extremely unpleasant. Tension is never far from the surface, and
in the effort to keep emotional distance, the inmates are regularly
dehumanized. The prison staff generally treats inmates like objects to be stored or like caged animals. For example, the men do
not take showers or go for exercise, they are "showered" or
"exercised."[1] Mealtime is called "feeding."

Ford's first year on death row was a relatively quiet one. A note in his records after 2 months reads "Adjusting to quarters and inmates on R-Wing. Not a disciplinary problem nor does it appear that he will be one." He spent most of his time writing, oil painting, lifting weights, drafting grievances for fellow inmates who could not write, working on his appeal, and reading. As is common on death row, he spent substantial amounts of time sleeping, especially in the summer when the midday heat and lack of ventilation regularly make the temperatures unbearable. Many men become night owls during the summer, as the temperature becomes less oppressive after midnight.

Whenever an inmate violates a prison rule, there is a formal procedure that, at the will of staff members, can be invoked. To do so, the staff member fills out a form detailing the objectionable behavior (a Disciplinary Report, or "D.R."), and obtains statements from witnesses. The inmate is told of his rights and is given an opportunity to appear before a Disciplinary Committee (composed of prison staff members), which adjudicates guilt and determines punishment. The punishment usually consists of a loss of gain time ("LGT")—which is not of much significance for a death row inmate unless his death sentence is eventually commuted—or disciplinary confinement ("D.C."). The latter is important because it means that the inmate is restricted to the cell, with no outside exercise, no television, a removal of personal property from the cell (e.g., books), and no visits. Each D.R. is reviewed and signed at the central office of the Florida Department of Corrections.

By the end of his first year in prison, Ford had his initial D.R. It was given for destroying state property—for tearing a pair of pants that were too tight in the waist for him to wear. Ford claimed that the "runner" (a non-death row prisoner who brings food and other necessities to the cells of condemned inmates) had told him to do it so that the clothing room would quit sending that size to him. For this he received perfunctory punishment: a loss of gain time.

After his first year, Ford did not remain acquiescent. Over the next 2 years there were a number of verbal altercations with the staff, and to a lesser degree with other inmates. The disciplinary reports slowly accumulated and included such infractions as verbal disrespect, failure to cooperate in the daily prisoner count (in which the prisoner is required to step to the front of his cell and recite his prisoner number), arguments with guards over whether his haircut was "regulation" (a common conflict between white guards and African-American prisoners), and his insisting upon an African-American barber. There was a fight with an inmate who was "saying bad things about me" (perhaps a sign of growing paranoia). One entry in his record noted "boisterous and at times rebellious, which is shown in his refusal to eat his meals at times."

But the annual progress report written in the fall of 1977, when Ford was approaching the end of his third year in prison, indicated that things had settled down. It was noted that he was receiving "average" quarterly reports and was not considered to be a problem inmate. The evaluation team observed that he had a good attitude during their interview and responded well to team questions. "Inmate Ford has made a good adjustment and has accepted his death sentence. However, he does hope to appeal and have his death sentence overturned." A year later, the classification team came to a similar conclusion: "The team feels that [Ford] will try to maintain a good adjustment in the near future and not present any problems."

During these early years Ford had a variety of medical problems, but the lack of adequate health facilities in the prison meant that he never had a thorough physical exam, so the precise nature of these problems cannot be determined.[2] Some of Ford's complaints were dismissed by the medical staff (just as in later years, according to Ford's attorneys, the medical staff ignored or discounted signs of his psychosis) as psychosomatic, stress-related problems, such as pains in his stomach and knees. Ford also developed a skin problem (vitiligo), and when the prison failed to provide any treatment for it, he filed a number of grievances. The prison doctors eventually gave him the lotion he needed, as well as a full upper G.I. evaluation and X-rays of the knees.

Ford's family, particularly his mother and older sister, Gwendolyn, stayed in close contact during this time, writing often and visiting approximately once a month. All of his siblings visited at least occasionally, as did his girlfriend, Verna Sanders. The family visits involved leaving Palmetto about 5:00 a.m. for the drive to Starke and not arriving back home until 14 hours later. Death row prisoners in Florida can receive up to three "social" visitors for a maximum of 6 hours per week, either on Saturday or Sunday (there are fewer restrictions on legal visits). The visitors must go through an elaborate process to be put on the inmate's visiting list and, once at the prison, must show identification, allow themselves to be searched, and pass through the metal detector. The prisoner, meanwhile, is handcuffed behind his back when moved to the visiting room, but once there is unrestrained.

A death row visiting "park" is set aside in the prison; it is a former cafeteria in which inmates and their visitors can freely talk. In it are 30 tables, each with four stools attached to it. Depending on the mood of the guards, prisoners and their families can occasionally chat with other prisoners and their visitors. For at least the past 20 years, no incidents of violence have marred the amicable atmosphere in the visiting park.

But especially in the summer heat and especially for older people, visits in the un-air-conditioned, smoky room, sitting on stools without cushions or backs, can be draining. It is extremely difficult to maintain a regular pattern of visits year in and year out, and it is not uncommon for the frequency of visits to decline. This happened to Ford. By 1981 he was receiving few visitors, although both he and his family reported that this was due primarily to economics and not to any lack of concern.

On May 25, 1979, Florida executed John Spenkelink, a white drifter who had killed a traveling companion in 1973. Unlike Gary Gilmore, executed 28 months earlier in Utah, Spenkelink continued to appeal his death sentence up to the very end. Because he was the first post-*Furman* inmate in America to be executed without abandoning his appeals, his execution gave added meaning to being on Florida's death row.

With the Spenkelink execution, the nation knew that Governor Bob Graham was serious about using Florida's electric chair. It would be more than 4 years before Florida's next execution, but the Spenkelink message was clear: The death penalty would no longer be an idle threat. Until then, there was a feeling that the citizens of Florida may have had more tolerance for imposing death sentences than for actually carrying out executions. Not so. There was no backlash against Governor Graham for the Spenkelink execution; in fact, as Graham was to demonstrate (through his reelection as governor and two later victories in U.S. Senate races) and many other politicians were quick to learn, supporting the executioner became an effective method of attracting votes.

At one time Spenkelink had been in a cell adjacent to Ford's, and the two had become friends. This is one of the more difficult aspects of death row confinement: Not only is the prisoner to be killed, but before he is killed, the state takes the lives of some of his closest friends. The psychological pressure grows with each execution; the prisoner realizes that his own date with the executioner is growing closer and more certain. What went through Ford's mind during that period will never be known, but with some imagination it is possible to understand a bit of what he and other death row inmates must have been thinking, sitting in their cells and contemplating the day when the death squad would come for them.[3]

Some citizens unfamiliar with prisons believe that death row inmates are escaping punishment while their death sentences are being appealed. The reality suggests otherwise: America's death rows are designed to make their residents miserable, and they are highly successful at achieving this goal. Camus is among those who have argued that the public is unaware of the extent of misery on death row and the horror of executions. In his words, "It would be harder to execute men one after another, as is done in our country today, if those executions were translated into vivid images in the popular imagination. The man who enjoys his coffee while reading that justice has been done would spit it out at the least detail."[4]

The inmates' families must also deal with the shame and uncertainty of death sentences. In fact, the death penalty can punish the inmate's family almost as much as it punishes the inmate himself.[5] Connie Ford expressed it in these words in a letter to attorney Larry Wollan:

[H]e is my son. He is the second child and the first boy born to me. I brought him up in the Sunday School and church, as I did all of the rest, and I never dreamed it would be in him to do such a thing, as parents always try and do all that they can possibly do for their children. We were poor, as far as money was concerned, but we were rich in love as a little family.[6]

Ford's situation was extremely difficult for Mrs. Ford to accept, just as it would be for any other mother with a child in his position. She coped with it in part by strengthening her religious convictions.

For the inmate and his loved ones alike, it is the chronic uncertainty that is perhaps the most difficult aspect of death row confinement. "Torture through hope alternates with the pangs of animal despair."[7] There are plenty of reasons to hope; in the past 20 years about half of all death sentences that have been reviewed by appellate courts in the United States have been reduced to terms of imprisonment,[8] and less than 5% of all death sentences imposed have actually been carried out.[9] The family members often find themselves in a position of wanting to do something—anything—that might help their loved one, but again and again they are faced with the cold realization that their family member is in very serious trouble and that there is virtually nothing that they can do about it.

On the legal front, things in Ford's case moved slowly. There was little court action during his first years in prison. A "direct appeal" was made by trial attorney Robert Adams to the Florida Supreme Court (the Florida Constitution mandates that all death penalty cases skip the intermediate appellate courts and go directly to the state's highest court in Tallahassee). The appeal raised several issues: alleged juror misconduct in some statements made at a racetrack during the trial, the right to counsel while being questioned on the plane following the arrest, a challenge to the constitutionality of the death penalty, the failure to sequester the jury, the manner in which aggravating and mitigating circumstances were handled by the court, and the trial court's refusal to allow recall of an eyewitness for further cross-examination. No claims of racial discrimination were raised.

On July 18, 1979, the court rejected these allegations and affirmed the conviction and sentence.[10] The only positive finding for Ford was the ruling that two of the eight aggravating circumstances used by Judge Lee to justify the death sentence were not supported by the evidence, and a third was a duplication. In September the same court rejected a defense request for a rehearing.

Meanwhile, Ford began to deteriorate. What his defenders later interpreted as possible signs of a growing mental illness, however, were characterized by the prison as disciplinary issues, not medical problems. He was irritable and anxious. In 1980 the classification team found him to be argumentative and, overall, to have a poor attitude. A year later he was in better control, displaying "a polite and mature manner." Nonetheless, some of those who knew Ford and were working on his case began to wonder about his mental stability.

Ford also found himself without an attorney. In July 1979, 5 days after the Florida Supreme Court denied the direct appeal, Robert Adams wrote to Ford and gave him addresses of five organizations (e.g., ACLU, Southern Poverty Law Center) that Adams thought might be able to take over the case. Because the decision of the Florida Supreme Court had to be appealed immediately to the U.S. Supreme Court, Adams's departure from the case came at a very bad time.

The case then fell into the hands of volunteers, as especially at that time there was little money and virtually no encouragement for attorneys to work on capital cases in Florida. For the first decade after Gary Gilmore's execution in Utah in 1977, a low-budget Tallahassee organization called the Florida Clearinghouse on Criminal Justice was virtually all that stood between the executioner and scores of Florida death row inmates. Led by a talented and dedicated community organizer named Scharlette Holdman, one of the primary tasks of the Clearinghouse was to recruit volunteer attorneys to take the cases of condemned prisoners in Florida. The Clearinghouse's task was overwhelming. When Holdman's dogged efforts to attract volunteer attorneys to a case failed, death row prisoners were left without any legal representation.

So, the task of drafting the petition for *certiorari* (a request for the Supreme Court to hear the case) fell to Deborah Fins, a 1978 graduate of Columbia Law School who was just completing her first year of work with the NAACP Legal Defense Fund in New

York. The Legal Defense Fund, which had masterminded the litigation leading to the 1972 *Furman* decision,[11] was, at the time, trying to find attorneys to cover death penalty emergencies throughout the United States, particularly in the South. Fins was responsible for Florida.

Given the small rate at which the Supreme Court accepts cases for review, no one was surprised on April 14, 1980, when the Court denied the petition asking it to review the Florida Supreme Court's decision in *Ford*.[12] While Fins did not have the resources to take the case further on her own, she remained as a consultant on Ford's defense team for the next 10 years.

Another year passed before Holdman and Fins found an attorney to handle the case. They found an excellent one. In the late spring of 1981, Holdman convinced Laurin A. ("Larry") Wollan, Jr., a professor of Criminology at Florida State University, to handle the appeal. He never received a cent for his work. Wollan, a 1962 graduate of the University of Chicago Law School and an occasional supporter of the death penalty, had visited the Clearinghouse to get a minor research question answered, and when Holdman learned that he was an attorney, she convinced him over several months to take the case. Wollan had served as a state's attorney in Illinois and had spent 4 years with the U.S. Department of Justice before joining the Florida State University faculty in 1976. His background (prosecutor) and politics (death penalty supporter) did not make him the type of person who normally becomes involved in death penalty defense work, but, as a man of compassion and valor, he was drawn to the special aspects of Ford's life and case. He volunteered his services on the condition that other attorneys, more experienced in this area of law, would also be available. His first meeting with Ford was at Florida State Prison on May 14, 1981.

During the summer of 1981, Wollan and the Florida Clearinghouse on Criminal Justice pooled their meager resources and worked together to prepare a clemency application. Although specific procedures vary, every state with the death penalty provides the right to appeal for clemency. It is a matter of grace and mercy, not based on legal grounds, and there are virtually no restrictions that limit when clemencies can be given. In Florida, for clemency to be granted, the governor and three additional members of the seven-member state cabinet must concur. Commuted sentences are reduced to life imprisonment.

At the time there was strong hope that the governor would intervene and commute the sentence to life imprisonment, but Wollan, Holdman, and their volunteer helpers knew that only a high-quality clemency application could make that happen. As a result, although by today's standards the clemency application they prepared was unsophisticated, in 1981 it was the most comprehensive of any clemency application that had come before the governor and the cabinet in the preceding decade.

As a first step, Wollan and the Clearinghouse arranged for an interview between Ford and a Harvard-trained psychiatrist, Dr. Jamal Amin. The goal was to examine Ford's mental status and to get a more complete life history than had been obtained at trial. In the light of subsequent developments, the mental status examination conducted by Dr. Amin in August 1981 merits attention; it concluded that Ford showed no signs of serious mental disorder:

> Generally friendly. Good rapport and repeatedly expressed satisfaction at seeing a Black psychiatrist [Dr. Amin, now deceased, was African-American]. Appropriately dressed in neat prison clothing. Normal facial expressions. Poor eye contact consistent with feelings of shame. His speech was productive. Thought content examination revealed no overt thought disorder at the time of the interview.
>
> He was oriented to time, place, and person and situations and had good contact with reality. Recent memory was intact but remote memory appeared somewhat impaired. He appears to be of above average intelligence. He wept openly during parts of the interview. He repeatedly expressed his sorrow and regret about his actions and his affect was consistent with these feelings. His mood was one of despair and worthlessness.[13]

This observation challenges one erroneous stereotype of death row inmates: They are often viewed as unable to feel remorse. However, with time to grow up and to reflect on their criminality, most death row inmates struggle to deal in some way with their shame, guilt, and the seriousness of their crimes.[14] To be sure, some do a poor job with this task, but Ford was not among them.

The folder of materials submitted in support of Ford's plea for clemency included Dr. Amin's five-page report; it also contained pictures of Ford as a child; supportive statements from family, neighbors, former school teachers, and employers; and a petition requesting clemency signed by more than 300 Floridians (primarily from Palmetto and Bradenton). Included was a letter in support of clemency from noted pro-death penalty scholar Walter Berns, then with the American Enterprise Institute.[15] Berns went to great length to say that he felt John Spenkelink's death sentence was unwarranted, and because he trusted Larry Wollan's judgment that Ford's crime was less heinous than Spenkelink's, he wrote "I trust your judgment concerning the person you are representing and I hope you can persuade the governor to commute his sentence."[16]

Robert Adams, the trial attorney, wrote a letter in support of clemency, saying, "I hope that leniency can be given him. He has appeared to me to have a sense of morality and decency that should not be overlooked."[17] A volunteer with the Florida Clearinghouse examined Ford's prison records and D.R.s, and described Ford as having "a strong sense of justice and fairness, willing to put himself to considerable inconvenience by consistently and thoroughly reporting problems at the prison through channels provided by law."[18] Connie Ford, accompanied by several Tallahassee citizens, personally appeared before cabinet aides to beg for her son's life. On the other hand, police officers and citizens of Broward County (Ft. Lauderdale) presented a petition to the governor and cabinet containing 337 signatures, asking that clemency be denied.

From 1925 to 1965, 21.3% of those condemned to death in Florida had their sentences commuted to life in prison.[19] But clemency has been a rarity since then, both in Florida and throughout the nation.[20] Post-*Furman* clemency hearings have become essentially a perfunctory ritual that precedes the day when the governor signs the death warrant. Today's governors typically say they believe that the legal system gives an inmate sufficient opportunities to invalidate unwarranted death sentences, and so they are reluctant to go against the conscientious decisions of prosecutors, jurors, trial judges, and a host of appellate judges.[21] In 1986 outgoing New Mexico Governor Toney Anaya took a rare stand against this trend when he commuted to life terms the sentences of all five inmates then on New Mexico's death row. In the two decades preceding December 1992, only 65 other death row inmates in America have had their sentences commuted to terms of imprisonment.[22]

Under Florida Governor Bob Graham (1978–1986) there were 225 clemency hearings, but death sentences were commuted for only six inmates, and each of these clemencies was granted early in his first term as governor. They were granted primarily because of doubts concerning the defendant's guilt or culpability for the crime. Clemency was not granted, even once, during the 4 years that Bob Martinez was governor (1986–1990), nor during the first 2 years of Governor Lawton Chiles's administration, which began in January 1991.

On October 7, 1981, Governor Graham and the cabinet held public hearings on Ford's appeal for clemency. Prosecutor Michael Satz presented the case for the state, while Larry Wollan argued the case for the defense. The routine followed in these proceedings is that only decisions to grant clemencies are formally announced. Negative decisions, like that in Ford's case, are announced only by the signing of a death warrant. On November 4, Governor Graham signed death warrants for Ford and a second prisoner, Amos King. The procedure in Florida is for the governor to set the week of the execution, and for the superintendent at Florida State Prison, then C. E. "Sonny" Strickland, to set the specific date and time. Their dates with the executioner were scheduled for 7:00 a.m., December 8, 1981.

Life Under A Death Warrant

The death warrants brought into play a number of procedures and rituals that have evolved over the years to govern virtually every movement made by an inmate in the weeks preceding execution. In Florida, the month or so of an active death warrant is controlled by rules that are spelled out in a Department of Corrections policy memorandum titled "Staff Responsibilities and Special Procedures for Inmates with Death Warrants."[23] The document's detail demonstrates that today's executions are carried out with a goal of precision. Nothing is left to chance.

After a warrant is signed, the inmate is placed on what is called "death watch," and special restrictions apply. The memorandum covers predictable issues that may arise during death watch, such as handling of visitors, contact with the media, security measures, and access to attorneys. While on death watch the inmate may continue to receive periodicals, but new subscriptions are not permitted. Disciplinary reports may be written but processing is postponed. The inmate is under 24-hour observation in the special death-watch cell, ostensibly to prevent suicide. Colin Turnbull, one of the world's foremost anthropologists, speculates that this ritual actually serves the purpose of preparing guards to move from protecting prisoners to killing them.[24] The ritual also guarantees that the prisoner becomes secondary to the meticulous steps of the ritual itself.

The document also specifies the step-by-step details of how to prepare for and carry out an execution. On "execution day minus five" the electrician tests the electric chair and the nearby phone. On "execution day minus four" the inmate is measured for a burial suit and is asked for written instructions detailing funeral arrangements and property dispersal. After a day of no preparatory activities, on "execution day minus two" all the equipment is again tested. The same happens again the next day, which also includes an "execution squad drill." The inmate's final visit, behind glass, lasts from 8:00 p.m. until midnight.

Finally, the day of death arrives; in Florida, executions are usually scheduled for 7:00 a.m. At midnight, the prisoner is permitted to have an hour-long, closely guarded "contact visit" with his family, which ends, as can easily be imagined, with agonizing good-byes. A minister or spiritual adviser is permitted to sit outside the inmate's cell from 1:00 a.m. until 5:30 a.m. After he or she leaves, the prisoner's head and right leg are shaved to facilitate contact with the electrodes, and he is permitted to take a final shower. He then dresses: slacks, a white dress shirt, undergarments and socks (no shoes). The suit coat is not to be worn until after the body is lifeless. At 6:50, the top of his head and the side of his right leg are smeared with a gel to aid conductivity. At 6:56, the inmate and his "escorts" enter the execution chamber, with the inmate locked in special wrist restraints that will be used by the escorts to break his bones if he should resist the execution. By 7:00 a.m., the man is seated, strapped tightly, and ready to begin his final statement. Eight or 10 minutes later, he is dead. After the body cools a bit, a physician listens for a heartbeat and confirms that the process has been successful. The witnesses (who are given a light breakfast before the execution) file out of the viewing area while the body sits lifeless in the chair.

Those working with Ford during the week preceding his scheduled death reported that he needed constant reassurance that he would not be executed. While to this day no Florida inmate has been executed on his first death warrant, that pattern is not a guarantee, and in 1981 there was not much of a history on which to base confidence in getting a stay.

On November 25, Ford's request for a stay of execution was heard in Ft. Lauderdale by the judge who had presided over his original trial, J. Cail Lee. In the years since Ford had last seen him, Judge Lee had encountered problems of his own, and as a result was authorized to hear only civil cases. He had been arrested at 5:30 a.m. on Easter morning 1976, for public indecency when a Ft. Lauderdale police officer found him having sexual intercourse in the front seat of an automobile parked outside a local tavern.[25] The police officer was summoned to the scene by a resident of a nearby condominium, who became concerned when the emergency lights on Judge Lee's car continued to flash for 30 minutes. To make matters worse, Judge Lee's partner in the car, Patricia Rose Byers, was not his wife. Judge Lee and Mrs. Byers were each released on $1,000 bond, and Judge Lee voluntarily suspended himself from the bench. According to Mrs. Lee, the judge then immediately left town. His suspension was made formal by the Florida Supreme Court on May 21,[26] and in August, after the judge told the court that he had not had any alcohol for 90 days, he was issued a public reprimand and prohibited from exercising jurisdiction in any criminal case without the express approval of the chief justice of the Florida Supreme Court.[27]

But he still retained authority in the Ford case. Judge Lee heard allegations by defense attorneys Larry Wollan and James Eisenberg that ineffective assistance of Ford's attorney at trial, Robert Adams, led to the conviction and death sentence. Nine jurors had voted in favor of death. Had only six (or fewer) voted for death, the jury's recommendation would have been for life, which would have forced Judge Lee to show especially strong reasons for imposing a death sentence. Hence, Ford's attorneys took the position that errors by attorney Adams had lost the votes of the three crucial jurors. In addition, they claimed that Adams "did not take pre-trial statements from the prosecution's two chief witnesses, cross-examined an eyewitness improperly and didn't see that jurors were instructed properly."[28] The defense also raised issues concerning jury selection, jury instructions, the admissibility of Ford's "confession," and the standard of proof required at the sentencing stage. After hearing 5 hours of arguments, Judge Lee denied the claim, telling the courtroom audience, "The facts of the case allowed no other sentence."

Judge Lee's findings were appealed to the Florida Supreme Court. On December 4, that Court unanimously denied relief and a stay of execution. They found that only one of the issues—ineffective assistance of counsel—was properly raised, and that the other four issues should have been raised by Adams in the initial appeal.[29]

The case then went before U.S. District Court Judge Norman C. Roettger, Jr., (pronounced "Rut-ger"), a 51-year-old Republican appointed to the bench in 1972 by President Richard Nixon. Judge Roettger was to become a major actor in the case. In 1992 he was described in the *National Law Journal* as "well known among local lawyers for his crusty demeanor, his off-the-cuff quips, his hunting trips in Montana and his habit of wearing jeans under his black robes."[30] Ford was brought from Starke to Ft. Lauderdale for the hearings, which took place on a Friday evening, Saturday morning, and Monday preceding the Tuesday execution date. Prosecutor Michael Satz again handled the case for the state.

It was at this point that a new volunteer attorney joined Ford's defense team. He was Richard Burr, then based in Tennessee with the Southern Prisoners' Defense Committee, an organization concerned with human rights issues in the South (and now based in Atlanta under the name Southern Center for Human Rights). Burr later joined the public defender's office in West Palm Beach, and is today the director of capital litigation for the NAACP Legal Defense Fund in New York. Burr had come to Florida to write a manual that would give step-by-step directions to defense attorneys on how to appeal a capital case, and he was using Ford's as an example. When he learned more about the case, however, he made the decision to join the defense team and quickly became the lead counsel. Burr and Wollan were to stay on the case until the very end; Ford's defense team also grew to include the dedicated minds of Craig Barnard, Richard Jorandby, and Susan Cary, all from the public defender's office in West Palm Beach.

At the Ft. Lauderdale hearings, Dr. Amin testified that Ford had begun using drugs to self-medicate his depression, which in turn was caused by his inability to hold a job that would allow him to send money to his mother and family. To substantiate the claim of ineffective assistance of counsel at trial, Burr questioned trial attorney Robert Adams for an hour and a half. Judge Roettger later called the criticism of Adams's performance "Monday-morning quarterbacking."[31] Burr also questioned the trial court's finding that the murder was "heinous, atrocious or cruel," which was one of the aggravating circumstances used to justify the death sentence. To support this contention, a pathologist testified that Officer Ilyankoff would have gone into shock within a minute or two of the firing of the first bullet, and therefore felt very little pain. Judge Roettger said, "I think it would have been an insult of the jury's intelligence to present this matter and say that it was not heinous, atrocious or cruel. Just as it insulted my intelligence."[32]

Before Judge Roettger could issue his formal ruling, however, a three-judge panel of the Eleventh Circuit Court of Appeals in Atlanta—a higher court—issued a stay of execution. In those days (before Fax machines), as the execution dates grew close, papers were often filed with appellate courts even before the lower courts issued their findings. The participants were still in Judge Roettger's Ft. Lauderdale courtroom, awaiting his decision, when the word from Atlanta was received. At the same time that Judge Roettger announced the stay had come, he also announced that he was rejecting Ford's appeal. (Apparently Judge Roettger had phoned the appellate court during a recess and told them that he planned to deny the appeal, and the Circuit Court judges acted so quickly that news of their stay actually arrived in Ft. Lauderdale before Judge Roettger publicly announced his decision.) Judge Roettger was not timid about denying the appeal: "This case has been delayed far too long. A crime as heinous and reprehensible as in this case should have had the execution carried out a long time ago. Society deserves no less."[33] For Ford it was a close call: The stay came at 4:45 p.m., December 7, only 14 hours and 15 minutes before his scheduled execution. The case was to return to Judge Roettger's courtroom several more times during the next 8 years.

Notes

1. For an outstanding discussion of dehumanization on death row, see Johnson, 1990.

2. Ford's experience with prison health care is not unique. In 1972 a life-sentenced prisoner in Florida, Michael Costello, filed a class-action federal law suit because of the poor quality of prison health care. The suit successfully argued that the living conditions in general and the poor quality of health care in particular constituted cruel and unusual punishment. The suit resulted in a comprehensive overhaul of prison health care, as well as changes in food preparation and diet, fire safety, and crowding. Because the mandated changes were not fully implemented, the suit was not settled until 1990—21 years after it was filed. *The Miami Herald*, December 13, 1990, p. 14D; *Palm Beach Post*, February 14, 1989, p. 1A; *St. Petersburg Times*, March 6, 1993, p. 1B.

3. See Bluestone and McGahee, 1962; Gallemore and Panton, 1972; Johnson, 1979.

4. Camus, 1974, p. 187.

5. Radelet, Vandiver, and Berardo, 1983.

6. Letter to Laurin Wollan, June 28, 1981.

7. Camus, 1974, p. 200.

8. Greenberg, 1982; Tabak and Lane, 1989, p. 69, note 169.

9. NAACP Legal Defense and Educational Fund, Inc., "Death Row, U.S.A." (Winter, 1992).

10. *Ford v. State*, 374 So.2d 496 (1979).

11. See Meltsner, 1973.

12. *Ford v. Wainwright*, 445 U.S. 972 (1980).

13. Report of Jamal A. Amin, M.D., to Laurin Wollan, August 21, 1981.

14. Exceptions to this pattern include defendants who are mentally ill (e.g., sociopaths) or mentally retarded; those who claim the murder they were convicted of was done in self-defense; and those who are innocent.

15. See Berns, 1979.

16. Letter to Laurin Wollan from Walter Berns, September 18, 1981.

17. Letter to Laurin Wollan from Robert T. Adams, September 24, 1981.

18. Memo to Laurin Wollan from Margaret Vandiver, undated.

19. *The Miami Herald,* July 12, 1988, p. 1.

20. Bedau, 1990-1991.

21. United Press International survey reported in the *Florida Flambeau* (Tallahassee), June 9, 1987, p. 1.

22. This figure is deceptive because it includes Texas, where 36 death sentences were commuted to life by gubernatorial action between the time of the *Furman* decision in 1972 and mid-1992. However, these commutations were done for administrative convenience, not because of mercy. All the commutations followed orders by appellate courts that vacated the death sentences, and the commutations were done by the governor to save the trial courts' time (Radelet & Zsembik, 1993).

23. See Florida State Prison, "Execution Guidelines During Active Death Warrant." The document contains Florida State Prison Institutional Operational Procedure No. 34 (revised 11-1-83), "Staff Responsibilities and Special Procedures for Inmates with Death Warrants." See also *St. Petersburg Times,* May 1, 1985, p. D1.

Other states using the death penalty have similar manuals. See, for example, Commonwealth of Virginia, Department of Corrections, "Institutional Operational Procedures 426" (June 25, 1984); South Carolina Department of Corrections, "Execution Procedures" (No. 1500.31, August 13, 1984).

24. Turnbull, 1978.

25. *Ft. Lauderdale News,* April 19, 1976, p. 1.

26. *In re Inquiry Concerning a Judge,* 333 So.2d 22 (1976).

27. *In re Inquiry Concerning a Judge,* No. 76-13 (J. Cail Lee), 336 So.2d 1175 (1976).

28. *Ft. Lauderdale News,* November 26, 1981, p. B1.

29. *Ford v. State,* 407 So.2d 907 (1981).

30. Resnick, 1992.

31. *Florida Times Union,* December 8, 1981, p. B1.

32. *Florida Times Union,* December 8, 1981, p. B1.

33. *Ft. Lauderdale News,* December 8, 1981, p. 1B.

5

Psychological Deterioration
and the Road to the Supreme Court:
1982-1986

On the surface, when the stay of execution came in December 1981, Alvin Ford appeared to be mentally intact. Since the competence of his trial attorney was at issue during the hearings before Judge Roettger, Prosecutor Satz called Ford to the stand and asked if he was satisfied with his current representation. Ford responded appropriately: "I'd like to say that I don't know much about legal proceedings."[1] During the death warrant he continued his regular correspondence with family, friends, and new acquaintances. In notes to high school students he encouraged them to work hard and get better grades. Concerned about his younger brothers, he suggested that Roderick continue to pursue a career in the military "because I don't want to see him come the way I did." In a variation on the movie *Scared Straight*, he had other inmates talk to his brother William. "I let some of these guys talk to him that's here, you know, that's been here, that got 40, 50, 200 years, telling him about what this place is about."[2]

According to friends, however, the last days of Ford's death warrant were especially difficult. Amos King, who had his death warrant signed at the same time as Ford's, had received a stay some days earlier, intensifying Ford's anxiety. Ford's extensive correspondence is invaluable in documenting the content and course of the deterioration in his thinking. On December 1, 1981, during the death warrant, he wrote a letter to Gail Rowland, a Tallahassee homemaker and columnist with the *Tallahassee Democrat* who had worked closely with Ford in her (mainly volunteer) role as a paralegal at the Florida Clearinghouse on Criminal Justice. By then Gail was his closest friend. It was a conventional letter, expressing thanks for her work on his behalf, commenting on her family, and so on. It contained nothing unusual or bizarre. But a letter sent to Rowland 4 days later was a different matter. Ford's mental status had collapsed. The letter conveys his mental status as well as any psychiatric vocabulary:

Dear Rowland:

Thought I would write about WJAX, and the staff at 95X-FM, who I had informed you, have been talking to me, the pass few weeks.

I wrote and informed them, their names will go in my file, so send Fins Esq., Hill Esq., a copy of this letter. Please send Hill Esq., a copy of the letters concerning death watch.

Well a friend Clyde Holmes, use to call 95X (WJAX) and ask Otis Gamble to play different songs for me. [Holmes, an oddly named woman in her 50s, had a history of befriending men on death row]. This went on for months.

I would tell Holmes, to give Otis Gamble a message (he calls himself "the Greatest," the name I gave him, but usually Gambini) which would be a message in a joking manner.

Then Gambini would get on the radio, and tell me, what he would do to me, by his being 6'4", and 230 pounds. So I would send a message I lift 400 pounds easy. So this is how it started.

Then the guy who does the news, Scott, would get on and talk about 400 pounds. So for whatever, I had sent the message, they would let me know, they got the message. All this was in kidding.

I never wrote the radio station until a few days after the warrant was signed. This guy Scott got on the radio, and was asking could I talk, "What's the matter with you can't talk," so I wrote.

From the time prison officials gave me the radio, Scott had been selling out, so much so. I couldn't let him get the last word in. So Scott and Gambini has kept me laughing.

The guards know, they talk to me over the radio. Scott gets on the radio 5:30 A.M. in the mornings and says, "is he up, wake him up," and the guard wakes me up, and I say, "Damn Scott is talking that crazy shit, this early in the morning."

The lady who does the news, Peggy, kids me because I kid her. Then while doing the weather, tell me no good news. She calls Bob Graham the "gritch" (spell wrong) that stole X-mas. They tell, all sorts of stories. Funny ones.

Then there's a lady named Destiny. Who takes over where they leave off, she said her name was Gail Adams the other night.

The people at the radio station has really made the situation more easier. They told me good luck, before the hearing Friday. Peggy, the newslady said she hadn't heard anything about 5 P.M., asked had I one day I could hear them, turning the pages of the newspaper, someone would ask "any good news," the other "I don't see anything."

They the four people have said, so much over the radio, to me. They told me it was (11) secretaries typing the weekend after the hearing was denied in Ft. Lauderdale, and so many other things I can't even begin to write. So I thought I would like in the file, they were special people to me. They say, they will be with me, until 8 December 81. So I would like to have this in the file, if ever its read, by others.

Thank you. Alvin B. Ford

This was the first of a number of letters referring to a Jacksonville radio station, WJAX, and an elaborate set of delusions associated with it. These letters were followed by the rapid appearance of other delusions, and both auditory and olfactory hallucinations. Ford thought that the Ku Klux Klan was holding his family hostage in the prison, that personalities at the radio station were controlling his thoughts, that he was Pope John Paul III, and that bodies were being encased in the concrete beds in the prison. He then moved on to grandiose ideas of power and control—that he had the power to free American hostages and to replace prison officials and Supreme Court judges. He began to distrust the people who had been his friends and supporters, eventually refusing to see them.

The following extracts come from a letter written September 11, 1982, to attorney Deborah Fins:

Dear Fins Esq.:

Thank you for your letter of 22 July 82, as of this date, I still want my files closed to Doug Magee [a writer] and no one is to have access other than lawyers.

Also, I do not in any way, want Dr. Amin, or Gail Rowland, associated with my case in any manner as of this date. . . .

My situation needs a solution, as soon as, humanly possible. I have been threatened 24 hours a day, for the pass three months, by guards and Bill Wilkinson of the KKK. He has been working here, under the name of Officer McKenzie, Q-Wing.

When you do, visit again bring a tape which can play six to eight hours. There's so much has happened, until I don't know where to start.

My life is in danger, by these guards and the KKK, and Owl Society or organization, plus this labor union, you should be receiving, copies of letters, to this effect.

They put me on DC for quite some time, for no reason. Just got some stamps . . .

Things have been the same continuous hounding. They are at my door now and in the pipe alley at the cell, vent.

The story is too long to write, but it's the truth. A lady is being held in the pipe alley on Q-Wing, third floor, behind the cell, I'm in.

As soon as I got back to Q-Wing, I was told Crooks, is to murder me on R-Wing or S-Wing, and either make it look as a suicide, or murder. This lady has been held in the pipe alley since, well about two months, being raped by guards as well as prisoners. This is the reason, I haven't gotten very much help. Guards are allowing prisoners to rape this lady, to keep things quiet, and no one knows she is in this prison.

While on S-Wing, guards have tried to ease my door open in the A.M. hours. Luckily, I was not asleep, 3:30 A.M., because this plantigraph was waiting to enter the cell with a knife and hatchet, this is the truth, whole truth, and nothing but the truth, so help me God.

. . . the plan was to run me insane and make me commit suicide. Channel 4 of Jacksonville has been helping. Keeping the guards from killing me. The evidence, I wrote to Jim Smith, State Attorney General, concerning that book was written over the cell walls of Q-3-West-#, the cell I'm in now. (That evidence on the book, was removed from my cell, from S-Wing in the month of July 82).

So my life is in danger, and need help. Please send a copy of this letter to the FBI, as soon as possible, and contact, other lawyers.

Sincerely, Alvin B. Ford

cc: CIA-FBI
Directors
Washington, D.C.

Preoccupation with the fear that his family was being held hostage within the prison was a major theme of Ford's letters for the next 2 years. In addition to confirming this delusion about his family, they give us a good picture of his rambling, disturbed thinking. The following is from a letter to his grandmother, December 5, 1982:

> I know that you are inside this prison, behind my cell. I have been wondering, how you got in this prison, also with Mother, Gwen, and the other relatives.
> Put your trust in God, don't write and tell me lies . . .
> I won't be having any visits, until all my relatives, are safely out of this prison, one way or the other. I know now about the relatives, as well as the outside world, so trust in God.

And from a letter to his mother, May 8, 1983, comes this:

> Here is a list of people trying to help, and there's many more. This postage stamp, showing the mail is illegal, or no stamp on the mail, stealing money from the U.S. Government. This has been done some 315 days, stealing the mail from my cell door, then taking it, to the pipe alley on N-Wing, S-Wing, R-Wing and Q-Wing.
> The world knows you are here and been hostage with your family since July, 1982.
> Hopefully you are well. You have been 315 days inside Florida State Prison, with [the names of 315 people are then listed].

The use of the number "315" may not be coincidental. Ford was then facing 315 days of disciplinary confinement.

On November 28, 1983, he wrote this letter to his mother:

Dear Mother,

> It has been awhile, since I wrote, but there is no need, with this government, or rather this state, having so many problems.
> Couldn't imagine this state, and the U.S. government could be so, corrupt. Also, the other countries of this, universe. Excuse the above

mistakes, rushed and making notes for the service. If my aides, were at hand, the mistakes would have been cleared. So overlook them.

Expect some lawsuites [sic] about this letter so, to all, concerned, be well informed.

If you can send some money and stamps, say whatever, you can, I have asked Wife I, Brition, she said $400.00, Wife 2 $500.00, Sandra Wife 3 said $1.00, Wife 4 said $300.00, Wife 5 $600.00, Wife 6 said $20.00, Wife 7 $100.00, Wife 8 (no reply) Wife 9 said (its a damn insult) Wife 10 said, (No comment).

Also send stamps, they're 30 cents so, listen you take care. Laugh God won, Daniel won, page 7 one 2 one, 6 one fort note D won, right one wrong one, wrong one right one. D one 3 one 1/2 one, years one.

Can't imagine people can try, what they have. Need anything. No never, as long as my family and wife are safe.

Rushed so the letter, should be review by reporters, mistakes? Note private. Aides tapes etc. . . . Take care.

Love you, Sherlock

Ford's relationship with his family had by then been turbulent for more than a year. On October 24, 1982, Ford's mother, along with his sister and niece, came to Starke for a visit. They left the prison bewildered and upset. Mrs. Ford was certain that something was wrong with Ford's mind: "He was distant from me and my daughter and her child. Said we were not his family."[3] Subsequent to this contact, Ford refused to see his mother and rarely wrote to the family, and Mrs. Ford's letters to him were returned stamped "refused to accept letter."

But during this period he turned out a torrent of letters, many of them 20 pages long. In another departure from his first years on death row, he completely stopped reading legal papers in his case and totally lost interest in it.

Not surprisingly, the defense attorneys and the Florida Clearinghouse on Criminal Justice became increasingly concerned about Ford's mental condition. They were also growing more concerned about his legal status: In April 1982, the Eleventh Circuit dissolved Ford's stay of execution,[4] although a rehearing was granted 2 weeks later. The appeal was eventually denied on January 7, 1983.

In June 1983, at the request of defense attorney Burr, Dr. Jamal Amin, the psychiatrist who had evaluated Ford in the summer of

1981, was again asked to prepare a written assessment. But as noted in the letter above, Ford had come to believe that Dr. Amin was conspiring against him (along with the KKK and others), and so he refused to meet with the psychiatrist. This forced Dr. Amin to base his report on his four previous interviews with Ford (the most recent of which was in August 1982), a review of taped conversations between Ford and his attorneys, letters written by Ford, and prison medical records. His findings on Ford's mental status included:

1. During the last psychiatric evaluation—the examiner was impressed with the feelings of "emotional distance" and an inability to establish a previously on-going empathic rapport.
2. Affect and moods are no longer appropriate or adequate to Mr. Ford's present situation indicating some disturbance in the regulation of his affect or emotions.
3. The content of Mr. Ford's speech increasingly leans toward the symbolic, the esoteric, and the abstract.
4. Episodes of the abrupt blocking of the stream of thought when Mr. Ford ceases to speak in the middle of a sentence.
5. Mr. Ford has difficulty in organizing his thoughts by the usual rules of universal logic and reality. His associations are loose, his attention span is diminished, and he appears unable to prevent the intrusion of irrelevant material into his thought processes.[5]

Dr. Amin went on to document the presence of delusions, hallucinations, and suicide ideations. He concluded that Ford had very little insight into his emotional problems, and that he went to great lengths to deny mental illness. The bottom line: Dr. Amin thought that Ford's initial intermittent psychotic episodes were now sustained. "Mr. Ford is now suffering from a severe, uncontrollable, mental disease which closely resembles Paranoid Schizophrenia With Suicidal Potential. This major mental disorder is severe enough to substantially affect Mr. Ford's present ability to assist in the defense of his life."[6] (Tragically, Dr. Amin was murdered in his Panama City home in June 1984.)[7]

In the autumn of 1982, Ford began to threaten to drop his appeals and ask to be executed. At one point he did so because the prison authorities had confiscated his radio. On December 17, he wrote to defense attorney Burr and expressed alarm because he believed that after a mid-December visit at the prison, Burr had been taken hostage. Burr replied on December 28, reassuring Ford that he was not a hostage, and asking that Ford quit saying he wanted to dismiss his appeal.[8] But Ford was unmoved. He sent two very disorganized letters to Governor Bob Graham, asking for help because his family was being held captive in a pipe alley (the corridor through which the plumbing in the prison runs), explaining that he had joined the KKK as Governor Graham had suggested in order to save the family, and expressing a number of other delusions.[9] In April 1983, Ford sent a handwritten note to the U.S. District Court: "The petitioner prays that the [court-ordered delay] be dissolved and final disposition of this case, execution of the sentence of death, be carried out. There will be no stay of execution request . . . Petitioner prays no court shall entertain such a request. Petitioner requests that all appellate proceedings cease."[10] These remarks, taken by themselves, look coherent; it is almost certain that Ford had assistance from other inmates in drafting them.

That request found its way into the newspapers. Burr was quoted as saying that he had an ethical obligation to represent Ford and to make a judgment of whether Ford was competent to make such a decision.[11] In reality, Burr's concern about Ford's mental health was growing. He told the Florida Clearinghouse that he was considering asking the prison for permission to spend several consecutive days with Ford "to create a different environment," in hopes of gaining a better understanding.

The following letter to Gail Rowland in the fall of 1983 reflects just how disorganized Ford's thinking had become:

Star Note 2

> Dear Rowland:
> I have a new goal (Packman) A new trial. I didn't kill a policeman.
> So No, one can eat or drink until, someone Come here, with lawyers and reporters, a World Wide, press conference.
> Then rush me to a hearing to be released, on my word.
> No one, shall ever eat again until, I'm free, Pack-man.

> So, try have everyone, try, and call CBS, NBC, ABC, and the world press, international.
>
> Take a sample, Death Total_____

Sincerely
Alvin Bernard Ford
P-2-South-5.

By November, Ford was talking gibberish in a fragmented, code-like fashion. To assess his competence, the defense brought in Dr. Harold Kaufman, a psychiatrist from Washington, D.C. Dr. Kaufman recorded the following sample of Ford's nonsensical babbling from his visit on November 3, 1983:

> The guard stands outside my cell and reads my mind. Then he puts it on tape and sends it to the Reagans and CBS . . . I know that there is some sort of death penalty, but I am free to go whenever I want because it would be illegal and the executioner would be executed . . . CBS is trying to do a movie about my case . . . I know the KKK and news reporters all disrupting me and CBS knows it. Just call CBS crime watch . . . there are all kinds of people in pipe alley bothering me—Sinatra, Hugh Heffner, people from the dog show, Richard Burr, my sisters and brother trying to sign the death warrants so they don't keep bothering me . . . I never see them, I only hear them especially at night. I won't be executed because of no crime . . . maybe because I'm a smart ass . . . my family's back there (in pipe alley) . . . you can't evaluate me. I did a study in the army—a lot of masturbation. I lost a lot of money on the stock market. They're back there investigating my case. Then this guy motions with his finger like when I pulled the trigger. Come on back you'll see what they are up to—Reagan's back there too. Me and Gail bought the prison and I have to sell it back. State and federal prisons. We changed all the other countries and because we've got a pretty good group back there I'm completely harmless. That's how Jimmy Hoffa got it. My case is gonna save me.[12]

Dr. Kaufman concluded that Ford was "suffering from schizophrenia, undifferentiated type, acute and chronic. . . . The possibility that he could be lying or malingering is indeed remote in my professional opinion." Dr. Kaufman further concluded that while

Ford understood the nature of the death penalty, he no longer understood why it was to be imposed on him, and hence he was mentally incompetent for execution.

On November 30, 1983, Florida saw its second post-*Furman* execution. The inmate was Robert Sullivan. Again, Florida death row inmates and their families were reminded that the state was serious about pushing for executions and that more were to follow shortly.

Relations With the Prison Staff

In the 2 years following Ford's first death warrant, he clearly moved into a psychotic condition, unable to communicate in a sustained way with even his family and closest friends. His decline was also reflected in his behavior within the prison; he received more than 100 disciplinary reports.

Ford's file in the Florida Department of Corrections consists primarily of a 6-inch-high stack of these reports. Also in the files is an annual progress report, summarizing the year's activity, which was prepared for Ford each fall. These reports show how the institution operates, and also correctional officers' perceptions of Ford's condition.

These reports are prepared by the guards and reflect only their perspective. We do not know to what extent Ford's behavior was influenced by hassling on the part of the guards (or vice versa), or prompted by particular relationships with specific members of the staff. The following, drawn primarily from sections titled "Statement of Facts" and "Finding and Action of Committee," is just an illustrative sample of the disciplinary and annual progress reports:

FAILURE TO COMPLY WITH COUNT PROCEDURE

Approximately 9:10 P.M., December 23, 1981, while making Master Count, on Q-Wing, Inmate FORD . . . failed to stand at his cell door or give his DC number. As I got to cell Q3W4 and called "Ford" he replied with "yes." Col. G. J. Kuck then instructed Inmate Ford to stand at his cell door and give his number. Ford just kept lying on his bed. I then filed this report.

Inmate Ford appeared before the Disciplinary team and pled no plea. The team found the subject guilty as charged based upon the statement of Officer . . . The Team recommends 15 days Disciplinary Confinement with no loss of gain time. Subject's response to the court was "I wasn't on door, I was asleep, and probably said yes."

DISOBEYING A VERBAL ORDER

At approximately 12:21 P.M. on 16 July, 1982, while myself and Counselor Harrington were on S-Wing on 1 North for haircuts, inmate FORD, Alvin B/M #044414 who is housed in cell S-1-N-17 was told that he needed to get a haircut. Inmate FORD stated that he did not need a haircut and that he was not going to get one. I then ordered inmate FORD to get a haircut and he stated that he was not going to get a haircut. I then filed this report. Counselor Harrington witnessed this incident.

Inmate Ford refused to appear before the disciplinary team and was therefore tried in absentereo. The Team found the subject guilty based upon the fact that Inmate Ford clearly refused to shave as ordered and that he was unable or unwilling to offer any defense in his behalf. The Team recommends 30 days disciplinary confinement with no loss of gain time.

POSSESSION OF A WEAPON

Approximately 10:00 P.M., on July 17, 1982, while searching S-1-N-17, Housing Inmate Ford . . . I found a homemade ice pick type weapon fashioned from two (2) ball point pens. This weapon was turned into the control room in support of this disciplinary.

Inmate Ford refused to appear before the disciplinary team . . . 60 days disciplinary confinement.

VERBAL THREATS

Approximately 10:15 A.M., August 2, 1982, while making routine rounds on S-Wing, First floor northside, Sgt. Combs and I noticed water all over the floor in front of cell 17, which is housed by inmate FORD . . . Sgt. Combs and I asked Inmate

Ford why and how the water got there and he started holler-
ing at us and stated that he was going to get another death
penalty by killing an officer. He also stated that we better stay
away from his cell.

. . . 30 days disciplinary confinement.

When the staff acknowledged Ford's bizarre behavior, they attributed it to malingering:

PROGRESS REVIEW 9/15/82

Complains of stomach and chest problems and has been
seen by medical and psychologist staff.

He has been on Disciplinary Confinement recently. He
made bizarre statements to staff, giving the surface impression of being mentally ill, when he was actually diagnosed as
malingering.

VERBAL THREATS

Approximately 3:15 P.M., October 18, 1982, Inmate FORD . . .
was standing on the second floor quarterdeck and yelled to
2-south to take care of his sister, "I'm going to kill some of
these crackers while I'm out here."

. . . 30 days D.C. . . .

DESTRUCTION OF STATE PROPERTY [same date as above]

Approximately 3:08 P.M., October 18, 1982, while assigned
to R-Wing, Sgt. Ansley, Officers . . . and I heard a loud crash-
ing sound come from the second floor, southside of the
wing. . . . found the television in the cell assigned to Inmate
FORD, Alvin B/M #044414 smashed lying in the floor,
SN#2456177, property of state #5143E. The Hall Sgt. was
notified and this report was filed. The television set remains
were given to Sgt. Gladish for evidence to support this report.

The Team found the subject guilty as charged based upon
the fact that Ford was the only one in the cell at the time and
Officers heard the crash, and when the Officers arrived at the
cell the TV set was on the floor and was destroyed.

. . . 90 days D.C. . . . recommended that Ford pay restitution in the amount of $79 for the TV . . .

DISORDERLY CONDUCT

Approximately 8:40 P.M. October 27, 1982, while escorting the Medical Technician on Q-Wing, I observed Inmate Ford . . . flooding the cell. The water was turned off and I filed this report.

Inmate Ford refused to make any statement . . . declined witnesses, staff assistance and further comment. . . . 30 days D.C. . . . Inmate Ford was unwilling to make any statement on his own behalf.

POSSESSION OF A WEAPON

At approximately 9:05 A.M., November 20, 1982, while working as D-2 Supervisor, was asked by Lt. C.D. Roberts to come with him to Q-Wing. Lt. Roberts said that Inmate FORD . . . was causing trouble and had a weapon. Lt. Roberts and I stopped by his office and he handed me a can of Mace. We went to Q-Wing, cell 2-Q-E-2. Inmate Ford was standing approximately 2 feet back from the gate door with what appeared to be a homemade knife in his left hand. I asked Inmate FORD to hand me the knife. He refused saying that he wasn't coming out. I again asked Inmate FORD for the knife and again he refused. I then obtained permission from Lt. Roberts to use the Mace. I shot Inmate FORD with a burst of Mace and closed the door. After approximately 30 seconds, I opened the door and asked Inmate FORD for the knife. He refused and I shot him again with the Mace. He then handed me the homemade knife and backed up to the cell door and Sgt. R.E. Thompson placed handcuffs on Inmate FORD. He was then escorted to the clinic by Sgt. Thompson, Col. Bridges, Lt. Roberts, and myself. I turned the homemade knife into the Control Room.

. . . Inmate FORD was advised of the charge placed against him and asked for any statement he would like to make . . . Inmate FORD stated "I have nothing to say. Close my door."

. . . guilty as charged based upon the fact that the weapon was observed in Ford's hand . . . 90 days D.C. . . .

[A second D.R., growing out of this same incident, involved a charge of verbal assault. "I'll kill you motherfucker—I ain't moving from this cell." During this response Inmate FORD was wrapping the handle of a homemade knife with portions of a torn sheet.]

At one point, Ford made a written request for the return of his personal property that had been removed from his cell. The official response said, in part, "you have since incurred numerous amounts of disciplinary time. Inmates on disciplinary confinement are limited in possession of their personal property. It is noted that as of 3-16-83 you have incurred a total of 315 days as disciplinary confinement time to serve; therefore your property will be retained in the property room until said time is served."

DISOBEYING A VERBAL ORDER

Approximately 5:20 P.M., May 23, 1983, Inmate FORD . . . was placed in the shower and ordered to shave. At approximately 5:25 P.M., on returning to the shower, Inmate Ford had not shaved.

"Give me a Disciplinary Report." "Give me my yellow copy and put one in my file."

. . . 30 days D.C. . . .

ASSAULT OR ATTEMPTED ASSAULT

At approximately 11:05 A.M., July 13, 1983, while assigned to Q-Wing, I was escorting the runner on Q-2-W-West while feeding the noon meal. As the runner put the tray on the door of Inmate FORD . . . inmate FORD picked up the tray, throwing it at me stating "Get this mother-fucking thing out of my cell."

[Ford refused to participate in the investigative interview, exclaiming "Get that shit away from here. Write me another one. Close my mother-fucking door."]

. . . 60 days D.C. . . .

ARMED ASSAULT

At approximately 4:20 P.M., July 28, 1983, while serving food trays on Q-2-West, Inmate FORD . . . threw his food tray at me, hitting me in the left side, also spattering food on Officer Sommerville. Inmate FORD's door was then closed and locked.

... 90 days D.C. ....

VERBAL THREATS

Approximately 6:25 P.M., August 24, 1983, while escorting Inmate FORD ... from the shower to his cell, Inmate Ford stated to me "Henderson, I haven't liked your face for a year so I am going to kill you. I am just going to walk right in and kill you."

... 30 days D.C. ....

The Department of Corrections annual progress review, September 1983, summed the situation this way:

Inmate Ford's institutional adjustment continues to be unsatisfactory as a result of D.R.'s. He has not received visits, nor has he been able to use the exercise yard, as a result of his D.C. status. Subject indicates that he spends most of his cell time sleeping and reading. Inmate Ford continues to make irrational statements indicating that he may be mentally ill, however, the professional staff feels that he is malingering in this area.

While the prison staff took the position that Ford was malingering, his family, friends, fellow prisoners, defense team, and several disinterested experts were thoroughly convinced by their observations and the dramatic changes in Ford's behavior that the evidence of madness was irrefutable. Because he was so irrational and impaired, however, communication with Ford was impossible.

The Governor's Commission

In 1983 the Florida statutes specified that when the governor is informed that a person under sentence of death may be insane, a commission of three psychiatrists is to be appointed to examine the convicted person to determine "whether he understands the nature and effect of the death penalty and why it is to be imposed upon him." Upon receiving the commission's report, the governor determines whether the inmate meets the statutory requirements (too much power for one politician, Ford's attorneys later argued). If he is found incompetent for execution, the inmate is transferred to a treatment center until restored to sanity. At the present time the inmate is sent to a Department of Corrections Mental Health facility, located on the grounds of the state mental hospital at Chattahoochee, 150 miles west of Starke.

In December 1983, following receipt of Dr. Kaufman's report, Richard Burr invoked this procedure, and a commission was appointed by the governor. The commission consisted of Drs. Peter Ivory, Umesh Mhatre, and Walter Afield. Their job, consistent with Florida Statute 922.07, was to examine Ford and "to determine whether he understands the nature and effect of the death penalty and why it is to be imposed upon him." That is the only definition the state gives for identifying inmates incompetent for execution.

On December 19, 1983, the commission (as a whole) met with Ford. The members' evaluation took only 25 minutes. In addition to the commission members, a number of others were present, including attorneys for Ford and the state, and two representatives of the Florida Clearinghouse on Criminal Justice. Following the meeting, prison guards were interviewed and a visit was made to Ford's cell. Because the reports stemming from this meeting soon became central in several years of litigation, they merit quoting in some detail.

Dr. Afield's report to the Governor consisted of one substantive paragraph (for which he billed the state $3,200):

> It is my medical opinion that Mr. Ford does indeed suffer from serious emotional problems. He is presenting himself in a very disorganized manner with a bizarre picture which does not fit any classical description of a psychiatric illness. The nature of his disorganization is somewhat "put on," but the profoundness of it forces me to put a "psychotic" label on the inmate. Again, this is not a classical psychiatric diagnosis, but the man is clearly quite emotionally ill. Much of this had to do with the sentence which he is currently facing and his situation within the prison setting. On the basis of all the data and in light of the Florida Statute 922.07, it is my opinion that although this man is severely disturbed, he does understand the nature of the death penalty that he is facing and is aware that he is on death row and may be electrocuted. The bottom line, in

summary is, although sick, he does know fully what can happen to him. If there is anything further you wish please let me know.[13]

The report from Dr. Mhatre was more detailed:

Dear Mr. Governor:

As per your order I examined Mr. Alvin Ford, on December 19, 1983 at Florida State Prison, along with my distinguished colleagues, Dr's. Peter Ivory and Walter Afield. Following is a summary of my evaluation with my conclusions:

Mr. Ford was evaluated at 11:00 A.M., in the courtroom of Florida State Prison. He was appropriately dressed, and exhibited good eye contact with all the people in the room, he did not exhibit any stranger anxiety or fears. He settled down in a chair, accompanied by his lawyers, and his friends through the Florida Clearinghouse on Criminal Justice. As per prior arrangement, Dr. Afield began to ask him questions. Mr. Ford did not initially respond but did so after his lawyers encouraged him. Most of his responses to the questions were bizarre. He continued to respond by gibberish talk such as "break one," "God one," "heaven one." However, throughout these bizarre responses, Mr. Ford kept good eye contact with the examiners. After awhile, his responses to questions became a little more appropriate indicating that he did understand the meaning of the questions asked of him, even though his responses remained somewhat bizarre. Throughout the interview which lasted about thirty minutes, there was no evidence of any hallucinations and Mr. Ford exhibited good ability to concentrate. He was relaxed and did not exhibit any physical aggression. In response to Dr. Afield's question, "What will happen when you die?", Mr. Ford responded "heaven one, hell one," indicating that he did understand the meaning of the question.

His mood appeared to be normal and affect was blunted. He did however smile and exhibited a good range of affect with his friends from his lawyer's office. His orientation and memory were not formally tested, but he did appear to be oriented to people and place. He did not exhibit any suicidal or homicidal thoughts.

The conversation with the guards at Florida State Prison who have been working with Mr. Ford, furnished the following information. His gibberish talk and bizarre behavior started after all his legal attempts failed. He was then noted to throw all his legal papers up in the air and was depressed for several days after that. He especially became more depressed after another inmate, Mr. Sullivan, was put to death and his behavior has rapidly deteriorated since then. In spite of this Mr. Ford continues to relate to other inmates and with the guards regarding his personal needs. He has also borrowed books from the library and has been reading them on a daily basis. A visit to his cell indicated that it was neat, clean and tidy and well organized.

The review of the extensive material provided by his lawyers including reports by Dr. Kaufman and Dr. Amin, and his correspondence with Gail Rowland of Florida Clearinghouse on Criminal Justice indicate that Mr. Ford has been gradually decompensating since July and has worsened since the death of Mr. Sullivan.

It is my medical opinion that Mr. Ford has been suffering from psychosis with paranoia, possibly as a result of the stress of being incarcerated and possible execution in the near future. In spite of psychosis, he has shown ability to carry on day to day activities, and relate to his fellow inmates and guards, and appears to understand what is happening around him. It is my medical opinion that though Mr. Ford is suffering from psychosis at the present time, he has enough cognitive functioning to understand the nature and the effects of the death penalty, and why it is to be imposed upon him.

I may further add that considering his present state of mind, Mr. Ford is in need of appropriate anti-psychotic medication, without such treatment he is likely to deteriorate further and may soon reach a point where he may not be competent for execution. I have discussed this with the psychiatrist of the Florida State Prison and hopefully, by the time you receive this report, Mr. Ford will be on appropriate treatment regiment [sic].

Thank you for giving me the opportunity to be of some help to you. If I can be of any further assistance in the future, please do not hesitate to call upon me.[14]

Hence, the first two physicians believed that Ford was psychotic. The third member of the commission was Dr. Peter Ivory, a psychiatrist at the Florida State Hospital in Chattahoochee (the place where Ford would have gone had he been found incompetent for execution). In marked contrast to his colleagues, Dr. Ivory concluded that Ford was malingering:

Pursuant to Executive Order Number 83-197, accompanied by Doctors Afield and Mhatre, I examined inmate Alvin Bernard Ford from 10:50 a.m. to 11:25 a.m. at Florida State Prison on December 19, 1983. We later talked to prison officers, viewed the inmate's cell, and talked to a prison psychiatrist.

The interview was conducted with great difficulty, from a verbal point of view, since the inmate responds to questions in a stylized, manneristic doggerel. Thus, an answer to a question might be "beckon one, cane one, Alvin one, Q one, king one."

It soon became apparent that our opinions would have to be based largely on inferential deduction from physical behavioral observation, and only to a limited extent from his verbalizations.

From a behavioral point of view then, the inmate entered the examination room in a quiet, cooperative, and appropriate manner. By helpful and responsive body movements, he helped the officer adjust the handcuffs. In an alert fashion he seemed interested and concerned about meeting the group of us, who also included attorneys and legal interns. When questioned, he answered promptly and then awaited the next question quietly and alertly. During his doggerel, and nonsensical, answers, if one of the examiners asked a question before he was finished, the inmate would raise his voice so as to dominate the situation and thus maintain control.

I formed the opinion that the inmate knows exactly what is going on and is able to respond promptly to external stimuli. In other words, in spite of the verbal appearance of severe incapacity, from his consistent and appropriate general behavior, he showed that he is in touch with reality.

Later exchanges seem to bear this out, if one "reads between the lines":

Q: "Are you aware that they can electrocute you?"
A: "Nine one, C one, hot one, die one."
    "Die one, gone one."
Q: "Are your attorneys trying to prevent your death?"
A: "Assassinate one, Bob Graham liable one, Jim Smith liable one, Senate one."
Q: "What happens if you die?"
A: "Hell one, heaven one."
Q: "Which?"
A: "Hopefully it will be heaven, but if I listen it will be hell."
    And later:
A: "If I die—no more fat cats
    —no more homicide
    —no more racism
    —in heaven with God."
Q: "Are you crazy?"
A: "Are *you* crazy?" (Said in such a tone as to indicate that he was no more crazy than I was).

At a time when we had been trying to establish if he read the Bible, he commented: "blood on the door posts, you know" (said with a knowing smile that indicated that he would be spared by the Angel of Death, Exodus 12:7).

By this time, I had formed the opinion that the inmate did comprehend the nature and effect of the death penalty and why it was imposed on him.

However, because of the severe adaptational disorder that had been developed by the inmate, by which he is trying to "hold at bay" an intolerable future that he cannot otherwise deal with, I decided to validate my ideas by examining his cell and talking to staff members. The rationale for this course of action was dictated by the reasoning that if the inmate was truly as disorganized as he would have one believe, there would be ample signs of it in his environment. The results were as follows:

   1) the cell was spotlessly clean and in order
   2) his toilet articles were neatly arranged around the sink
   3) his personal papers were all stacked neatly in the cell bars, arranged by category
   4) his writings were extensive, and the choice of vocabulary showed a good intelligence
   5) the arrangements were all logical, and there was nothing in the cell that seemed bizarre, as if he was out of contact with the real world
   6) the officers stated that the inmate behaves normally in that he feeds himself, clothes himself and keeps himself clean. He utilizes the available resources to his maximum advantage.
   7) he talks normally to the guards, but during the last week they have heard him practicing the strange speech from lists of words he had written in nonsensical order.

To comment briefly, a natural insanity is not selective, but is pervasive. This inmate's disorder, although severe, seems contrived and recently learned. My final opinion, based on observation of Alvin Bernard Ford, on examination of his environment, and on the spontaneous comment of groups of prison staff, is that the inmate does comprehend his total situation including being sentenced to death, and all of the implications of that penalty.

From a humanitarian point of view, this inmate is obviously having enormous problems dealing with his possible destiny. It is suggested that a medical review to look into the feasibility of psychotropic medication might be helpful, to allow the inmate to better assist his attorneys, and to set his affairs in order.

Please let me know if I can provide further information or be of other assistance.[15]

The defense attorneys had made available to the members of the examining commission a set of detailed records on Ford. These records included, among other things, psychiatric and medical reports that had accumulated over the years, copies of letters written by Ford (some of which were quoted earlier in this chapter), and related materials that documented the course of Ford's mental status. Dr. Ivory declined to accept these materials until he was leaving the prison subsequent to the interview with Ford, and there was no reference to them in his report to the governor. Since Dr. Ivory's report was submitted the day after the interview, it is probable that his opinion on Ford's mental status was formed without consideration of Ford's medical history or the observations (including medical evaluations) of others—which would explain his finding that Ford's disorder was "recently learned."

Although the three reports reflected differing views of Ford's mental status, they all agreed that Ford had "the mental capacity to understand the nature of the death penalty and the reasons why it was imposed upon him," and thus was competent to be executed. The governor accepted this finding.

But in the eyes of other observers, there was a plethora of unanswered questions. A number of these were identified in an affidavit submitted in May 1984, by Dr. George Barnard, Professor of Psychiatry at the University of Florida, who was asked to comment on the reports written by Drs. Amin, Kaufman, and the three commission psychiatrists. He wrote, in part, as follows:

> Dr. Ivory indicated that by his ability to "read between the lines" of verbal responses which Ford did give that Dr. Ivory was of the opinion that Ford knew exactly what was going on but if one relies on the transcript of the interchange between the psychiatrist and Ford then there is great doubt, at least to this observer, that there was a rational interchange between Ford and the psychiatrist, because Ford gave irrelevant responses to questions put to him although the words he used had some association with the questions asked. . . . Dr. Ivory expressed the belief that because Ford had a

clean and organized cell that this indicated to him that Ford could not have a disorganized mind or thought system in that insanity was not selective but pervasive. To this reviewer, it appears that Dr. Ivory is of the opinion that there is a significant correlation between disorganization of internal thoughts and the way that one keeps a room. From my understanding of the literature it is apparent that one can be highly disorganized internally and yet keep a clean room as well as one can be highly disorganized in the way he keeps his room and yet be very organized and productive in his thought processes. . . . Dr. Afield stated that his examination consisted of a complete mental status examination yet he did not document what his examination consisted of. In his report Dr. Mhatre had said that orientation and memory of Ford were not tested, so it is not readily apparent exactly what Dr. Afield considers to be necessary in a "complete" mental status examination.[16]

Dr. Barnard went on to point out that all three of the psychiatrists on the governor's commission failed to comment on Ford's long-standing delusional system. Dr. Barnard summarized the major problem as follows: "In my opinion the three examiners gave conclusionary opinions without documenting in a satisfactory manner their evidence or facts upon which their inferences are based . . . so that the factfinder must rely upon the credentials of the psychiatrists rather than their data."

Dr. Seymour Halleck of the University of North Carolina, another nationally known psychiatrist, was also retained by the defense to review the psychiatric reports. He filed an affidavit containing criticisms that were similar to Dr. Barnard's, arguing that the 30-minute interview with Ford in the company of eight other people was unreliable and not up to minimum standards for forensic evaluations.

In sum, over a period of several months Ford was seen by five different psychiatrists. Their impressions can be summarized as follows:

Dr. Kaufman: schizophrenia, undifferentiated type, acute and chronic; "no reasonable possibility that Mr. Ford was dissembling, malingering or otherwise putting on a performance to induce me to believe him to be psychotic or incompetent to be executed."

"He sincerely believes that he is not going to be executed because he owns the prisons, could send mind waves to the Governor and control him, President Reagan's interference in the execution process, etc."

Dr. Afield: "psychotic"; serious emotional problems which do not fit any classical description of a psychiatric illness

Dr. Mhatre: psychotic with paranoia

Dr. Amin: severe, uncontrollable, mental disease which closely resembles "Paranoid schizophrenia with suicidal potential"

Dr. Ivory: severe adaptational disorder which is contrived and recently learned; in touch with reality and knows exactly what is going on

The two psychiatrists who had worked with Ford over time, Drs. Kaufman and Amin, found him to be severely psychotic and not competent to be executed. Two of the three commission members, who had met with Ford for only 25 minutes, agreed that Ford was psychotic, but all three concluded that he was competent for execution.

The Second Warrant

On April 30, 1984, some 3 months after receiving the last of the reports from the commission members, Governor Bob Graham signed Ford's second death warrant. Execution was set for May 31.

Connie Ford was devastated. Stress, tension, fear, guilt, overwhelming powerlessness, disbelief, confusion, and grief fall on families of the condemned, and the combination of emotions takes its toll. Shortly before the signing of the second death warrant, Mrs. Ford had what she believes to be a number of religious experiences, including hearing voices speaking to her during the night. She felt a strong call to do evangelical work, and so her already strong commitment to Christianity was intensified. She began to speak in churches. In retrospect she interprets this as a strengthening in preparation for the demands of the death warrant. Church work continues to be a significant feature of her life today: Her car is covered with religious slogans, permitting her to "witness to the Lord every time I leave the driveway," and

DEATH WARRANT
STATE OF FLORIDA

WHEREAS, ALVIN BERNARD FORD, did on the 21st day of July, 1974, murder Dimitri Walter Ilyankoff; and

WHEREAS, ALVIN BERNARD FORD was found guilty of murder in the first degree and was sentenced to death on the 6th day of January, 1975, and

WHEREAS, on the 18th day of July, 1979, the Florida Supreme Court upheld the sentence of death imposed upon ALVIN BERNARD FORD and Certiorari to the United States Supreme Court was denied on the 14th day of April, 1980; and

WHEREAS, it has been determined that Executive Clemency, as authorized by Article IV, Section 8(a), Florida Constitution, is not appropriate; and

WHEREAS, attached hereto is a copy of the record pursuant to Section 922.09, Florida Statutes;

NOW, THEREFORE, I, BOB GRAHAM, as Governor of the State of Florida, and pursuant to the authority and responsibility vested by the Constitution and Laws of Florida, do hereby issue this warrant directing the Superintendent of the Florida State Prison to cause the sentence of death to be executed upon ALVIN BERNARD FORD on some day of the week beginning noon, Friday, the 25th day of May, 1984, and ending noon, Friday, the 1st day of June, 1984, in accord with the provisions of the laws of the State of Florida.

IN TESTIMONY WHEREOF, I have hereunto set my hand and caused the Great Seal of the State of Florida to be affixed at Tallahassee, the Capitol, this _30th_ day of April, 1984.

GOVERNOR

ATTEST:

SECRETARY OF STATE

82

in her front yard stand two giant signs mounted on posts, on which are written religious messages.

In an interview with a *Washington Post* reporter in 1985, in which she reflected on the preceding decade, Mrs. Ford said that she was horrified by the crime and "when this thing happened [with Alvin] I wanted to be dead myself. I was suicidal." But through her religion she came to terms with her son's fate. "Alvin is already in a spirit world. He is not really here. However the Lord sees fit to do things, I accept. God's will is my will. When the time comes I plan to do the eulogy. The Lord has prepared me."[17]

A death warrant also brings reactions from other than family members, and in the weeks prior to the execution date, there were a number of actions on Ford's behalf. The Florida Clearinghouse made relentless efforts to attract national media attention to the case and to secure the support of various mental health groups and African-American leaders. Such a task would be even more difficult today, but in 1984 the public was at least somewhat receptive to the question of whether it really wanted to execute a crazy prisoner.

While every execution in Florida meets with some protest, the issues raised in Ford's case made this protest especially vigorous. A group called "Florida Citizens Against the Death Penalty" announced a schedule of activities, including a candlelight vigil at the governor's mansion, a vigil at Florida State Prison at 6:30 a.m. (30 minutes before the scheduled execution), a protest gathering at the State Capitol Building later in the day, and a community assembly for conscience at the Bethel A.M.E. Church in Tallahassee. Rev. Joseph Lowery, president of the Southern Christian Leadership Conference, met with Governor Graham to express concern about racial bias in capital sentencing in Florida. Governor Graham insisted that the state was "color-blind"; cynics felt that the selection of whites for the first four Florida executions under the new statute was not a chance occurrence, but a matter of paving the way for easy executions of African-Americans later on.

John Conyers, chairman of the U.S. House of Representatives' Judiciary Subcommittee on Criminal Justice, on behalf of the Congressional Black Caucus, wrote a strong letter to Governor Graham. The letter focused on Ford's competency for execution and the role of race in Florida's application of the death penalty.

Representative Conyers stated that Florida had never executed anyone for killing a black person. (He was incorrect, although all such cases were prior to *Furman* in 1972, and never in Florida's history has there been an execution of a *white* for a crime against a black.) The letter called for a full and fair hearing on the issue of competency for execution, and a moratorium on executions until a blue ribbon commission could study and report on the role of race in capital punishment in Florida.[18]

During the period of the warrant, Ford's condition continued to deteriorate; in fact, during the last 2 weeks of the warrant, he stopped eating. On May 10, a fellow prisoner on death watch, James Adams, was executed. The precise effect of this execution on Alvin is unknown, however, because during the warrant he refused to see visitors. (Information about Ford's condition was given to his attorneys by Jack O'Callaghan, whose death warrant coincided with Ford's and who therefore lived in an adjoining cell.) Dr. Harold Kaufman, upon interviewing him (with three defense attorneys) on May 24, 1984, made these observations:

> He appeared to have lost at least twenty (20) pounds since I had last examined him on November 5, 1983. He was neatly dressed and was wearing rubber shower sandals. He did not greet the four of us when we entered and sat down. He sat with his body immobile and his cuffed hands in a prayerful position in front of his mouth. Occasionally he moved his hands, still in the praying mode, to each of us for no apparent reason. His lips were pursed intermittently, but his head moved very little. His eyes were closed or fluttering most of the time, although he occasionally glanced at one or more of us. His hands and fingers appeared to be trembling. We took turns asking him questions, and little or no response was forthcoming. He began muttering to himself after about five minutes. These utterances were largely unintelligible. This is the overall picture of what took place for two hours.[19]

Dr. Kaufman concluded: "Mr. Ford's condition, severe paranoid schizophrenia, has seriously worsened, so that he now has at best only minimal contact with the events of the external world."

Mrs. Ford, as her son's "next friend," was the one who authorized the filing of papers that requested a stay of execution. On May 25, the request for a stay was denied by the Florida Supreme

Court; likewise on May 29, Judge Roettger in Federal District Court denied a request for a hearing on Ford's competency.

On May 30, the day before the execution was scheduled to occur, 20 reporters attended a press conference with Ford at Florida State Prison. During most of the hour-long meeting, Ford sat mumbling unintelligibly with his eyes shut and eyelids flutter-ing. "I look forward to dying anytime. God told me to act crazy because you all been acting crazy to me. So I act crazy."[20] At one point he said that God had forgiven him for killing the officer and that he was ready to go to his death "because it'll make me see God."[21] At another point during the interview he expressed some contradictory feelings: "I'm going to fight tomorrow. They can't kill me . . . I'm gonna keep my eyes closed cause I don't want to see it." Evening newscasts throughout the state carried footage of the press conference; the clips were widely seen as *prima facie* evidence of psychosis.

Finally, the stay came. The Eleventh Circuit Court of Appeals blocked the execution by a 2-1 vote. As with the first warrant, the stay came only 14 hours before the scheduled execution.

The judges found that two of the grounds asserted by Ford merited relief. First:

> Ford asserts that he is entitled to a procedural due process hearing to determine whether he is currently insane. If so, this should delay his execution because such could be cruel and unusual punishment and thus proscribed by the Eighth Amendment. Ford has raised a substantial question and we stay his execution so that a panel of this court may answer it. Credible evidence presented by the petitioner indicates that Ford is insane. Two psychiatrists appointed by Florida's Governor found him psychotic.[22]

The court rejected the state's argument that Ford should have raised the issue in December 1981, pointing out that the incom-petency issue was not available to him at that time.

Ford's second successful ground for relief was "his argument that Florida administers the death penalty arbitrarily and discrim-inatorily on the basis of the race of the victim, the race of the defendant, and other impermissible factors, in violation of the Eighth and Fourteenth Amendments."[23] The full court was at that

time reconsidering a decision it had recently made on this issue
in another case arising in Georgia.[24]

Continued Mental and Behavioral Problems

The stay had no obvious effect upon Ford's emotional and
mental status. On the morning after the stay of execution, prison
guards asked Gail Rowland to try to make him eat, and she ended
up helping him break his fast by spoon-feeding him. Ford's lack
of control and psychotic thinking were readily apparent. In an
August visit, he made a number of sexual comments (references
to Rowland not wearing any underwear, God telling him not to
look at her breasts, an accusation that Rowland's vagina was
"talking to him," and so on). He accused one of his attorneys,
Larry Wollan, of having signed death warrants, and expressed the
belief that the Soviet Union had sent impostors to the prison
representing his family. He closed the interview by reading the
Twenty-Third Psalm.

The prison records also reflect his worsening condition throughout 1984, including more hostile interactions with the staff, and a
loss of concern with personal hygiene. In September 1984 his
Annual Progress Report read:

> During the past several years, inmate Ford has been the recipient of
> many disciplinary reports for offenses ranging from Failure to Com-
> ply with Count Procedures to Attempted Assault to Disobeying
> Verbal Orders, etc. Subject has been examined by professional staff,
> and has been diagnosed as "malingering." His behavior is totally
> irrational, he has made statements to staff and medical indicating
> that his family was "being held hostage here at FSP, in the back of
> one of the confinement wings." Subject will not communicate with
> staff and when he speaks it is in a bizarre fashion, as he counts from
> one to ten forwards and then backwards and reiterates numbers and
> does not appear to be able or willing to respond to questions posed
> to him. During this past reporting period, Inmate Ford has received
> 51 processed D.R.'s (total of 660 days D.C.). Subject does not appear
> to be in any physical difficulty in terms of his health, but he is unable
> or unwilling to discuss the issue with any staff member. Inmate Ford
> received his last visit from his mother and his sister on June 9, 1984.

He has not had a visit since that time. Subject does not use the exercise yard as a result of his disciplinary confinement status. ... Inmate Ford's prison adjustment is totally unsatisfactory as a result of numerous disciplinary reports that he incurs.

A year later, he received his 1985 Progress Report:

Inmate Ford's adjustment continues to be totally unsatisfactory, as he is the recipient of many disciplinary reports, unwilling to communicate or cooperate with staff, spends most of the time during interview sessions babbling or counting from one to ten repeatedly, and only on rare occasions does he even respond logically to a question put to him. At the time of this interview inmate Ford was not eligible for the outside exercise yard, and when asked what he did to occupy his mind while he was in his cell he stated "I think about my past." He had no further comments to offer. . . . Inmate Ford has been seen by the professional medical and psychiatric/psychological staff members at this facility and has been declared to be sane. His behavior however would indicate some form of mental illness but the professional staff advised classification that this inmate is malingering and acting out most of the time. Inmate Ford's overall prison adjustment continues to be completely unsatisfactory.

Then, strangely, more than a year went by without any Disciplinary Reports being recorded in his folder. Perhaps the prison staff simply gave up; perhaps the files were purged. The next entry was dated June 17, 1986:

[W]hile passing out linen on R-1-North, I noticed that Inmate Ford . . . had given me a torn pillow case. I then asked Inmate FORD why he tore the pillow case. He then mumbled some words that I could not understand. I then asked him the same question and he again mumbled something. . . . 30 days D.C. . . . It is further recommended that subject reimburse the State in the amount of $1.35 for pillow case.

The Progress Report dated September 1986, was devoid of comments, almost as if interaction between Ford and staff had ceased.

We have reviewed only a small sample of the Disciplinary Reports that Ford received. But this sample, in the context of the entire record, leads to the following conclusions:

1. The guards recorded a number of incidents and behaviors indicating severe mental illness (head banging, irrational statements, unintelligible comments, delusions).

2. At least some of the guards believed that Ford was mentally ill, even though they knew the professional staff's opinion that he was malingering.

3. Ford's behavior progressed from active, belligerent interplay with the staff and others to passivity and increased autism.

Ford's mental health problems and their effect on his legal status created controversy and problems not only for the prison and the criminal justice system, but for mental health professionals as well. The appeals resulting from the 1984 stay of execution eventually reached the U.S. Supreme Court. Before examining how the courts reacted, however, we first turn our attention to the dilemmas the death penalty in general, and the *Ford* case in particular, created for physicians and mental health care providers.

Notes

1. *Ft. Lauderdale News,* December 8, 1981, p. B3.

2. From the files of the Capital Collateral Representative, Tallahassee.

3. From the files of the Capital Collateral Representative, Tallahassee.

4. *Ford v. Strickland,* 676 F.2d 434 (1982).

5. Report of Jamal Amin, M.D., to Richard Burr, June 9, 1983.

6. Report of Jamal Amin, M.D., to Richard Burr, June 9, 1983.

7. *Panama City News Herald,* June 12, 1984, p. 1.

8. Letter from Richard Burr to Alvin Ford, December 28, 1982 (in the files of the Capital Collateral Representative, Tallahassee).

9. Governor's files, State Capitol, Tallahassee.

10. *Ft. Lauderdale News/Sun-Sentinel,* April 30, 1983, p. 1.

11. *Ft. Lauderdale News,* April 30, 1983, p. 1A.

12. Report of Harold Kaufman, M.D., December 14, 1983.

13. Report of Walter E. Afield, M.D., to Governor Bob Graham, January 19, 1984.

14. Report of Umesh Mhatre, M.D., to Governor Bob Graham, December 28, 1983.

15. Report of Peter B. C. Ivory, M.D., to Governor Bob Graham, December 20, 1983.

16. Affidavit of George W. Barnard, M.D., May 21, 1984.

17. *Washington Post,* November 11, 1985, p. A6.

18. News release from the Congressional Black Caucus, U.S. Congress, May 25, 1984.

19. Report to Richard Burr from Harold Kaufman, M.D., May 24, 1984.

20. *Florida Flambeau,* May 31, 1984, p. 1A.

21. *Florida Times Union* (Jacksonville), May 31, 1984, p. 1B.

22. *Ford v. Strickland,* 734 F.2d 538 (1984), p. 539.

23. *Ford v. Strickland,* 734 F.2d 538 (1984), p. 540.

24. *Spencer v. Zant,* 715 F.2d 1562 (1983). This issue was ultimately resolved by the Supreme Court in *McCleskey v. Kemp,* 481 U.S. 279 (1987).

6

Physicians, Mental Health Professionals, and the Death Penalty

Prior to the murder of Officer Ilyankoff in Ft. Lauderdale, Alvin Ford had experienced only one contact with a mental health professional. In 1974, when Ford was failing in his jobs and battling his depression, a Gainesville vocational rehabilitation counselor had referred him to a psychiatrist for treatment for depression. At trial, no questions were raised about his sanity at the time of the crime or his competence to stand trial. During the sentencing hearing, the defense did bring in a psychiatrist to present a "psychiatric profile" of Ford, with the hope that it might have a mitigating effect. Dr. David Taubel testified that he had found evidence of minimal brain damage and dyslexia, but not much was made of this by the defense, and the testimony had no discernible effect upon the jury or the judge.[1]

But eventually the mental health professions played a pivotal role in determining Ford's fate. In the past two decades, these professions have done likewise in countless other capital cases throughout the nation. Between 1981 and 1988 Ford was seen by almost two dozen psychiatrists and psychologists, many of whom interviewed him on several occasions. His case became a battle par excellence of and between mental health professionals, and also became a springboard for national debates about the involvement of psychiatrists in the evaluations of competence for execution. In this chapter we discuss some of the issues involved in these debates, as well as other ways in which health professionals have become involved in various aspects of capital punishment.

How have psychiatry and psychology come to play such significant roles in capital cases? Part of the reason is that the Supreme Court has essentially required their participation. In 1976, in a series of decisions that approved some death penalty statutes that had been passed in the wake of its 1972 *Furman* decision, the Court rejected capital statutes that made death sentences mandatory upon conviction for certain offenses and upheld only those statutes that allowed individualized sentencing (usually through the consideration of aggravating and mitigating circumstances). Justice Stewart, speaking for a plurality of the Court, said: "[I]n capital cases the fundamental respect for humanity underlying the Eighth Amendment . . . requires the consideration of the character and record of the individual offender and the circumstances of the particular offense as a constitutionally indispensable part of the process of inflicting the penalty of death."[2]

Two years later the Court further commented upon the need for individualization in sentencing decisions. It ruled that the jury (or sentencer) must be permitted to consider "as a mitigating factor, any aspect of a defendant's character or record and any of the circumstances of the offense that the defendant proffers as a basis for a sentence less than death. . . . The need for treating each defendant in a capital case with that degree of respect due the uniqueness of the individual is far more important than in noncapital cases."[3] In short, the Court said that procedures in capital sentencing must take into account not only what the offender did, but also who he is and why he did it. By insisting upon individualization, the mental health professionals were brought into action in at least two ways: testifying to mitigating and aggravating circumstances, and predicting future dangerousness. It was a natural evolution. Over the past two decades mental health professionals have been increasingly involved in court decision making and in the evaluation and control of troubled and troublesome people.[4]

Mental health issues are important at virtually every stage of a capital case. Involved are such questions as whether the defendant was insane at the time of the offense, whether he intended and premeditated the death in a cold and calculated manner, whether he was so intoxicated or drugged that he lacked the ability to intend to cause the death of another, and whether he perceived a threat to his own or others' physical safety (even if such a perception was the result of distorted or psychotic thinking). Determinations of factors related to mental health can often mean that a person who is guilty of homicide is innocent of capital murder. Further, a mental health examination can speak to the issues of the defendant's ability to knowingly and intelligently waive his right to counsel before making statements to law enforcement agents; the reliability and accuracy of any statements made, including statements made to fellow prisoners while in jail; the defendant's ability to aid and assist his attorneys as they prepare and present a defense and to have a rational and factual understanding of the legal proceedings surrounding his case; mitigating factors that weigh on the side of a prison sentence rather than death; the unique considerations that are relevant to clemency; finally, competence for execution.

In the years since the Supreme Court temporarily abolished the death penalty with the *Furman* decision in 1972, medical and other professional health care associations have filed *amicus curiae* ("friend of the court") briefs in several capital cases before the Supreme Court and have taken a variety of official stands on the subject. The concern of the medical profession with the death penalty in the United States is as old as the country itself,[5] but it was renewed soon after the *Furman* decision with apprehension about a new method of execution: lethal injection.[6]

Death on the Gurney

In 1977 the world's first lethal injection statute was signed into law. The bill was not the result of long debate and research—Oklahoma's electric chair needed $60,000 in repairs, and someone suggested that the use of lethal injection would save taxpayers' money. A state senator conferred with the then-chief of anesthesiology at the University of Oklahoma Health Sciences Center, Dr. Stanley Deutsch, who confirmed that the idea would work and would be "extremely humane" in comparison to either electrocution or the gas chamber.[7] Two months later, the bill was enacted. The next day, Texas did the same.

Today, 23 states authorize lethal injection as their method of execution (12 states use electric chairs).[8] Supporters argue that lethal injection is the cheapest and most "humane" means of execution, an argument used a century ago to support the replacement of the gallows with the electric chair.[9] Those opposed to the use of lethal injection argue the method simply makes executions more palatable to capital jurors—making them less reluctant to impose a death sentence—by creating the false impression that the prisoner does not suffer, and making it easier for society to deny the brutality of taking a life.[10] Extreme retributivists, of course, point to the argument that prisoners suffer less with lethal injection as a reason to stick with older, more painful methods.[11]

In contrast to other methods of execution, some medical expertise is needed to perform lethal injections: Someone with medical knowledge has to order the drugs, insert the catheter, and connect the monitoring equipment. Thus there was (and is) apprehension about the various ways in which physicians might be involved, such as determining fitness for execution and preparing and administering the deadly drugs.[12] As with other methods of execution, someone with medical knowledge must also examine the prisoner in the execution chamber to determine whether death has occurred or whether another jolt or shot is needed. Because of this latter requirement, even before lethal injections were proposed in the United States, some physicians urged the medical profession to totally boycott executions.[13]

Some prison officials also balk at lethal injection. At McAlester Prison in Oklahoma in January 1980, Warden Norman B. Hess resigned from his position rather than participate in lethal injections. "Taking a life is not part of me," he said, "and I can't stomach it. Who can say that the person may not strain or struggle against the straps?"[14]

Should physicians be involved in the deliberate cessation of human life? Some physicians saw some disturbing parallels between this request for medical expertise and the complicity of physicians in Nazi atrocities.[15] Recognizing the potential for huge problems, physicians in England were instrumental in securing Parliament's rejection of lethal injection some 40 years ago.[16] But unlike their British counterparts, organized medicine in Oklahoma and Texas was never invited to contribute to the discussion, and thus had little input in their own states' lethal injection debates.

When lethal injections were initially proposed, none of the states explicitly required that a physician personally inject the drugs. But none precluded their involvement. Allied health personnel, such as physicians' assistants, could do the actual killing. Nonetheless, an influential article in the *New England Journal of Medicine* by attorney William Curran and physician Ward Casscells denounced the new procedure and called upon the entire medical community to do likewise.[17]

> It is our contention that the ethical principles of the medical profession worldwide should be interpreted to unconditionally condemn medical participation in this new form of capital punishment. . . . We believe that it presents the most serious and intimate challenge in modern American history to active medical participation in state-ordered killing of human beings.[18]

Further, the authors denounced the use of nurses, medical technicians, and allied health personnel in executions on the same grounds: "The physician should not escape moral responsibility by ordering a subordinate to do what he or she may not properly do directly."[19] Now a decade old, the article still stands as the best statement of the ethical problems encountered by health care professionals when their knowledge is required to perform executions.

The rebirth of capital punishment in general and the advent of lethal injection in particular soon elicited reactions from a number of health care and professional organizations, including the American Medical Association, the American Psychiatric Association, the American Psychological Association, and the American Public Health Association.[20] Largely in response to the Curran and Casscells article, in late 1980 the American Medical Association formally took the position that "A physician, as a member of a profession dedicated to preserving life when there is hope of doing so, should not be a participant in a legally authorized execution."[21] Several state medical organizations, notably in Texas and Oklahoma, likewise declared physician participation in lethal injections to be unacceptable. The American Psychiatric Association (APA) went even further: "The physician's serving the state as executioner, either directly or indirectly, is a perversion of medical ethics and of his or her role as healer and comforter. APA therefore strongly opposes any participation by psychiatrists in capital punishment."[22] In 1986 the American Public Health Association passed a resolution that health personnel "should not be required nor expected to assist in legally authorized executions."[23] The following year they called for health care workers to lobby for total abolition of capital punishment.[24]

Not all physicians agreed with the positions of their professional associations. An extreme view has been taken by Dr. Jack Kevorkian, a Michigan pathologist who was to gain notoriety in the early 1990s for his invention and use of a "suicide machine." (In 1992, Dr. Kevorkian was briefly under indictment for first-degree murder for helping two women commit suicide with his machine.)[25] For more than 30 years, Dr. Kevorkian has been arguing that physicians have an ethical obligation to actively participate in lethal injections, and that while doing so they should conduct medical experiments and transplant the prisoner's organs for use by law-abiding citizens.[26] Thus far, his views have not prevailed.

But lethal injection did. Its first use took place on December 7, 1982, when Charlie Brooks died on the gurney in Huntsville, Texas. A physician, the then-medical director of the Texas prison system, Dr. Ralph Gray, supplied the drugs and examined the prisoner before the execution to make sure that his veins were large enough to accept the catheter. Although Dr. Gray did not actually insert the catheter or administer the drugs, his employees did, and he was there to observe the "procedure" and pronounce death.[27] Some medical professionals did not approve of where Dr. Gray drew the line, contending that his actions facilitated the execution, thus violating the AMA guidelines.[28] In fact, William Curran, co-author of the seminal article in *New England Journal of Medicine*, was so incensed by the Brooks execution that he "urged the Texas Medical Association to seek the revocation of the medical license of any doctor directly or indirectly involved in the execution."[29] Indirect involvement could include participation by those whom physicians teach and supervise, such as medical technicians and physician assistants.

The issue of physician involvement in lethal injection remains controversial up to the present day. In Illinois in 1991, Governor Jim Edgar signed a bill that continued the practice of involving physicians in lethal injections by requiring the presence of two physicians as witnesses at all Illinois executions.[30] In addition, the legislation mandated that the names of the physicians who are present or involved in executions be kept secret, making it impossible for their colleagues to monitor their participation or issue any reprimands.

The controversy that inspired the bill Edgar signed began on September 12, 1990, when Charles Walker, after dropping his appeals, became the first inmate to be executed in Illinois since 1962. After being guaranteed anonymity, three physicians installed intravenous lines in Walker's arm. In April 1991 the Illinois State Medical Society not only protested the anonymity required in the new Illinois legislation, but also adopted a resolution that discouraged all physician involvement in executions, including the pronouncement of death. The organization was joined in its protests against the 1991 legislation by, among others, the American College of Physicians, the American Public Health Association, and the American Association of the Advancement of Science. Thus far the secrecy provision has not been adopted by any other state, but the American College of Physicians issued a statement that expressed concern about the precedent.[31]

Meanwhile, in December 1990, the American Medical Association's House of Delegates both reaffirmed the group's opposition to physician participation in executions and expanded the definition of "participation." The resolution opposed participation "except to certify the cause of death," hence going a step further than the AMA's 1980 position. The wording indicates that physicians should not even *pronounce* death, because to do so would necessitate taking the responsibility for alerting other participants that the execution has been unsuccessful and saying, in effect, "This man needs another jolt." Physicians can get involved only *after* the prisoner's death has been confirmed. At their annual meeting in June 1991, the AMA's House of Delegates adopted a further resolution that urged state medical associations to work against any state legislation or statutes that invited physicians to violate the ban.[32] Similarly, in 1990, the British Medical Association established a "Working Party" to examine the participation of physicians in human rights abuses, including executions. That Working Party concluded that physicians should never attend executions, and that "the medical profession should work toward the objective of ending medical participation in those parts of the judicial process leading to execution."[33]

The Right to Access Mental Health Experts

Another issue involving physicians and health care personnel in capital punishment concerns testimony at trial about the mental status of the defendant. In the 1985 case of *Ake v. Oklahoma*, the Supreme Court recognized the importance of psychological and psychiatric testimony by ruling that the state must provide an indigent criminal defendant in capital cases with free and competent psychiatric assistance in preparing an insanity defense if the defendant's sanity at the time of the crime is seriously in question.[34]

The case involved an indigent defendant named Glen Burton Ake, who, after his arrest on two counts of murder, was diagnosed as having paranoid schizophrenia and found incompetent to stand trial. Six weeks later, after Ake received daily doses of Thorazine, the examining psychiatrist informed the court that Ake's competence to stand trial was returning. Ake's court-appointed attorney then told the judge that he would like to prepare an insanity defense, but the trial judge refused the request to appoint and fund a psychiatrist for an examination of the defendant. As a result, at trial Ake could present no testimony on his sanity at the time of the crime. He was convicted and sentenced to death, and the conviction and sentence were affirmed by the Oklahoma Court of Criminal Appeals. Soon thereafter, the Supreme Court granted *certiorari*.

The American Psychiatric Association and the American Psychological Association were among those organizations that submitted *amicus curiae* briefs urging reversal of Ake's conviction. On February 25, 1985, their arguments prevailed. The Court held that the state must provide a psychiatrist not only to examine the defendant, but also to "assist in evaluation, preparation, and presentation of the defense."[35] Justice Marshall, writing for the 8-1 majority, summed up the ruling in these words:

> We hold that when a defendant has made a preliminary showing that his sanity at the time of the offense is likely to be a significant factor at trial, the Constitution requires that a State provide access to a psychiatrist's assistance on this issue, if the defendant cannot otherwise afford one.[36]

Only now-Chief Justice Rehnquist dissented. The ruling was the first case in years that significantly expanded the rights of capital defendants: Not only do indigent defendants have the right to have an attorney appointed to represent them, but that attorney must also have access to minimal resources to mount a reasonable defense.

The ruling also redefined the role of the expert in capital cases, making the role less consistent with "objective reporter of facts" and more in line with the role of consultant and advocate—an expert who would even "assist in preparing the cross-examination of a State's psychiatric witnesses."[37] At first, some forensic psychiatrists and psychologists, trained to be objective and impartial, feared the *Ake* case required a level of involvement that they were unprepared to offer. A detailed examination of the issues by psychiatrist Paul Appelbaum identified several ways in which psychiatrists could become too involved in supporting one side in capital cases, but concluded that consulting on a case in the ways specified by *Ake* did not necessarily require one-sided blind advocacy.[38] For example, Appelbaum concluded that *Ake* did not oblige expert witnesses, in their role as consultants, "to present data or conclusions [on the witness stand] that are biased in favor of the defendant's position."[39] Nor did he feel the decision required psychiatrists to act as advocates in the sense of "a single-minded pursuit of a particular outcome." In sum, Appelbaum concluded "the fear that *Ake* will transform psychiatrists who testify at criminal trials into advocates for the defense is over-blown."[40]

The *Ake* decision means not only that indigent defendants on trial for their lives be provided with free mental health experts when there is a need, but also that the mental health experts must be competent. Unfortunately, many mental health evaluations in capital cases are inadequate and unreliable and "do not meet existing standards in the mental health profession governing the adequacy of a forensic mental state examination."[41] A competent and reliable mental health evaluation should include at least five elements:

1. An accurate medical and social history must be obtained.
2. Historical data must be obtained not only from the patient, but from sources independent from the patient.
3. A thorough physical examination (including neurological examination) must be conducted.
4. Appropriate diagnostic studies must be undertaken in light of the history and physical examination.
5. The standard mental status examination cannot be relied upon in isolation as a diagnostic tool in assessing the presence or absence of organic impairment.[42]

The most common deficits in forensic examinations, at least according to one experienced death penalty defense attorney, are that they are too often based on inadequate histories of the patient, and they too often include inadequate testing for neurological dysfunction.[43]

Mental health examinations are important not only for questions involving sanity and competency to stand trial, but also to document aggravating and mitigating circumstances during the sentencing phase of capital trials. In Florida, for example, statutorily defined mitigating circumstances include (a) "The capital felony was committed while the defendant was under the influence of extreme mental or emotional disturbance"; (b) "The defendant acted under extreme duress or under the substantial domination of another person"; and (c) "The capacity of the defendant to appreciate the criminality of his conduct or to conform his conduct to the requirements of the law was substantially impaired."

The defense is also permitted to present mitigating factors related
to sentencing that are not listed in the statute, such as evidence
of maltreatment, abuse, poverty, and other kinds of trauma during
childhood, developmental years, and adulthood.[44] For example,
a large number (perhaps the majority) of those who commit
aggravated homicides are survivors of chronic and severe child
maltreatment of one form or another. Considered as stemming
from diverse "frailties of humankind,"[45] these life experiences
and their effect on subsequent behavior do not excuse the crime
or argue against imprisonment, but must be considered by juries
and judges before deciding who lives and who dies. Attorneys are
trained in law, not child development, and may not even recognize signs that their clients were severely abused as children.
Without assistance from mental health professionals, evidence of
such childhood victimization may not be discovered and brought
to the attention of judges and jurors.

Physicians and mental health professionals can also be asked by
prosecutors to counter any mitigating testimony offered by the
defense. For example, in a highly contested California case the
prosecution hired Dr. Thomas Szasz, well known for his view that
mental illness is a "myth." Dismissing the defense's argument that
the defendant's background of abuse and psychological problems
were important mitigating factors, Dr. Szasz told the jury that
criminality was a "product of evil" and that the defendant should
be executed because "people choose to be bad."[46] This met with
agreement from a psychologist on President Ronald Reagan's
crime commission, Dr. Stanton Samenow, who told the jury that
criminals are "born evil." Neither he nor Dr. Szasz had ever
examined the defendant, David Carpenter, who in early 1993 was
still on death row at San Quentin.

Predicting Future Dangerousness

While in most states jurors in capital cases are asked to examine
both aggravating and mitigating circumstances in making their
sentencing decision, in Texas things are done differently. After
convicting the defendant of capital murder, jurors are asked a

maximum of three questions. If their answers to all are affirmative, the defendant is automatically sentenced to death.

Two of the questions are virtually always answered with a "yes"; in fact, in most cases the answer to the second question is so obvious that the jurors are rarely asked to consider it. The questions are:

> 1. Whether the conduct of the defendant . . . was committed deliberately and with the reasonable expectation that the death . . . would result;
> 2. Whether the conduct of the defendant in killing the deceased was unreasonable in response to the provocation, if any, by the deceased.

Since the defendant has already been convicted of capital murder before these questions are asked, it is difficult to imagine juries answering the questions negatively.[47] Yes, the killing was done deliberately. Yes, the victim was not asking for it.

So, the real question in Texas death penalty cases is the third one:

> 3. Whether there is a probability that the defendant would commit criminal acts of violence that would constitute a continuing threat to society.

Ambiguities aside (e.g., what is a "probability"? What is "society" when the defendant will be in prison for life?), the statute asks for predictions of future dangerousness. The central problem with this criterion is that psychiatrists and other mental health professionals have no crystal balls that allow them to predict future dangerousness with any distinctive accuracy.[48]

Nonetheless, this has not stopped a small group of Texas physicians from claiming expertise in predicting dangerousness. One, Dallas psychiatrist James Grigson, has achieved special notoriety. By 1992 he had testified in 144 capital cases in Texas. In 5 cases the defense hired him so he would not work for the prosecution, but in 139 cases he testified for the prosecution, and in 131 of these, the juries returned with verdicts of death (including the case of Randall Dale Adams, later shown to be innocent).[49] Dr. Grigson usually testifies, with "medical" or "psychiatric" certainty, that he is positive that the defendant will kill again.[50] Texas juries tend to believe the man, who *The New York Times* described as looking "a bit like Marcus Welby in cowboy boots."[51]

The behavior of Dr. Grigson and his few counterparts in Texas has met with widespread condemnation from the profession.[52] This reaction was fueled by a critical article in *Hospital and Community Psychiatry* by Dr. Paul Appelbaum.[53] Even before Appelbaum's 1981 article was published, on July 22, 1980, the Board of Trustees of the American Psychiatric Association formally reprimanded Grigson because he had told defendants that he was examining them to determine their competence to stand trial, but later used the information from the interview in sentencing-phase testimony about the defendants' future dangerousness. One case in which such testimony was used went to the U.S. Supreme Court in 1981, and the American Psychiatric Association submitted an *amicus curiae* brief, arguing "that psychiatric prediction of dangerousness, whatever its basis, is of such low reliability as to confound the fact-finding process and to warrant exclusion of such predictions as a matter of law."[54] But the Court did not reach the issue of the validity of predictions of dangerousness in its 1981 decision—it simply held that psychiatrists in general, and Dr. Grigson in particular, must advise defendants before interviewing them that their statements might be used against them at trial.[55] Defendants who did not want to take this risk were under no obligation to consent to a psychiatric interview.

On November 1, 1982, Dr. Grigson was again reprimanded, this time for claiming 100% accuracy in predictions of dangerousness and because he regularly testified at trials without examining the defendants. As one defense attorney remembers it, Dr. Grigson dismissed the reprimands, saying that the American Psychiatric Association was composed of, "a bunch of liberals who think queers (*sic*) are normal."[56]

Not surprisingly, given the right to refuse examination by the above Supreme Court decision, most capital defendants in Texas did just that. Dr. Grigson and others reacted by escalating the use of a tactic they had begun to employ a few years previously: While sitting on the witness stand, they render opinions on "hypothetical" case scenarios given to them by attorneys. Prosecutors pose long questions (in one case it took 40 minutes), asking about the future dangerousness of a "hypothetical" defendant who coincidentally resembles the defendant about to be sentenced. Since the cases are supposedly hypothetical, no examinations are made, yet the psychiatrist or mental health expert makes definitive statements about the future dangerousness of a person remarkably similar to the defendant.[57]

Again these issues went to the Supreme Court; again the American Psychiatric Association, among others, filed an *amicus curiae* brief, arguing that the Supreme Court should ban all such testimony because of its unreliability (the APA brief took the position that two-thirds of such predictions were erroneous).[58] The case challenged the use of both predictions of future dangerousness and the use of hypotheticals in death penalty cases. The case involved Thomas Barefoot, a Texas death row inmate whose sentencing hearing had included Dr. Grigson's response to hypothetical questions. Dr. Grigson and a second psychiatrist who testified for the prosecution had never examined Barefoot, but both were convinced of the defendant's dangerousness. (Grigson said there was a "one hundred percent and absolute" chance of future dangerousness.)

But in a 6-3 vote, the Justices rejected the APA stand, holding that jurors were capable of listening to experts with opposing points of view and deciding which expert to believe.[59] On October 30, 1984, Thomas Barefoot was executed by lethal injection in Huntsville.

In another Grigson case, in 1988 the Court threw out a death sentence because Dr. Grigson's testimony in it was based on a psychiatric examination of the defendant that had taken place without the knowledge of the defendant's lawyer.[60] But today Dr. Grigson continues to testify in death penalty cases. Perhaps not coincidentally, by the end of 1992, Texas had not only the largest death row in the United States (367 inmates), but also led the country in the number of post-*Furman* executions, with 54.

Competence for Execution

It was against this backdrop that the case of Alvin Ford arrived on the doorsteps of the Supreme Court. Several articles in scholarly journals have now addressed the issues that were presented.[61] The issue in *Ford* was whether the most severely mentally ill inmates on America's death rows had a constitutional right to be exempted from execution. If so, further issues were procedural: who should draw the line, where it should be drawn, and how it should be done. The questions of why mentally ill death row inmates should not be executed, and indeed why anyone at all *should be* executed, were never far from the surface.

Vague Criteria

One of the biggest challenges generated by the necessity to exempt the mentally ill from execution, whether it be done by executive clemency or by constitutional dictates, is the difficulty of defining and evaluating "incompetency." It is a legal concept, not synonymous with diseases and syndromes that physicians are trained to diagnose, such as depression or schizophrenia. In addition, there are many forms of "competency" defined by the law, such as competence to stand trial,[62] competence to make out a will, competence to refuse treatment—indeed, there are more than 30 legal actions that can involve determinations of competency.[63] The criteria for competency differ markedly, so a person may be competent for one type of action (e.g., making a will) but not for another (e.g., adopting a child). Even for one type of competency, such as competency to consent to treatment, there are different definitions and tests.[64]

The American Bar Association's Criminal Justice Mental Health Standards defines competence for execution in this way:

> A convict is incompetent to be executed if, as a result of mental illness or mental retardation, the convict cannot understand the nature of the pending proceedings, what he or she was tried for, the reason for the punishment, or the nature of the punishment. A convict is also incompetent if, as a result of mental illness or mental retardation, the convict lacks sufficient capacity to recognize or understand any fact which might exist which would make the punishment unjust or unlawful, or lacks the ability to convey such information to counsel or the court.[65]

Florida's definition of competence for execution is less detailed. The prisoner must understand the nature and effect of the death penalty and why it is to be imposed upon him.[66] While at first this definition may sound simple, close reflection on the wording reveals it is far from clear. The evaluating psychiatrist is therefore charged with the responsibility of determining what she or he *thinks* the statute means, introducing much room for subjectivity and variability.

A first question arises over what it means to "understand." In the case of Arthur Frederick Goode, executed in Florida in 1984 despite both a documented lifelong history of mental illness and profound questions of competency, a psychiatrist who examined the prisoner distinguished "cognitive understanding" from "affective understanding." Goode, who was both mentally retarded and mentally ill, discussed his anticipated death as a young child would: He was factually correct but lacked any emotional response. One of his biggest concerns in the days before his death was a lack of toilet paper with which to blow his nose. The involuntary use of denial as a defense mechanism may also prevent some inmates from understanding the nature of the death penalty.

At various times, several observers were convinced that Alvin Ford did not "understand" his predicament. At other points he seemed to have enough understanding to render him competent for execution under Florida's extremely narrow criterion. At one point Ford told a psychiatrist, "I know that there is some sort of death penalty, but I'm free to go whenever I want because it would be illegal and the executioner would be executed."[67] When asked if he would be executed, Ford replied, "I can't be executed because of the landmark case. I won. *Ford v. State* will prevent executions all over."[68] Often Ford doubted that he had killed anybody. At various times he held that the officer died of a heart attack or that the gun he used in the Red Lobster robbery contained blanks.

Second, what is the "nature" of the death penalty that prisoners are asked to understand? To be sure, American citizens hold a wide variety of viewpoints on the "nature of the death penalty." In one sense, the "nature" is not fixed; it is affected by morality and politics, and reasonable people can differ when discussing it. If the nature of the death penalty were to be defined minimally as the government's right to inflict death as a punishment in response to a specific act or deed, some people with delusions, hallucinations, and other signs of thought disorder would be unable to understand it. Such people might be unable to reflect upon and recognize their past deeds as crimes they actually committed, or understand the cause/effect relationship between their deed and their execution.

Third, the inmate must understand "the effect" of the death penalty. The level of understanding required is not specified; it could be very concrete ("I will die"), or it could be abstract (understanding how the death will affect friends, family, and future political campaigns). These outcomes are uncertain, and thus difficult or impossible to predict. Again, delusions of invincibility and hallucinations cause confused, disoriented thinking.

Fourth, death row prisoners are required to understand "why the death is to be imposed upon [them]." Some might argue this requires feelings of guilt and remorse; to understand the imposition of the death penalty in any given case could also necessitate an understanding of the effects of race, competence of counsel, the role of bad luck, and, indeed, the skills of any mental health professionals who worked on his case at trial. At a more basic level, a defendant simply must recognize that he was convicted of a capital crime.

A fifth ambiguity in the statute is that a prisoner may waver in and out of the "state of competence" between the time of the examination and the time of the execution. Some prediction of the prisoner's mental prognosis therefore appears to be necessary. Evidence in *Ford* indicated that, as with many mentally ill people, Alvin Ford's psychosis waxed and waned in intensity, and his attorneys could have legitimately demanded that another commission of psychiatrists be appointed to examine him if a third warrant had been signed.

Finally, the statute gives no definition of the standard or level of proof that is necessary for a finding of incompetence. How certain must psychiatrists be before arriving at their conclusion? Should it require a "preponderance of the evidence," "clear and convincing evidence," or "beyond a reasonable doubt"? It could be argued that since the outcome of a finding of competence for execution is death, any doubt whatsoever about the prisoner's competence, not just "reasonable" doubt, should require a finding of incompetence. The American Bar Association's Criminal Justice Mental Health Standards recommends that the standard should be "preponderance of the evidence."[69]

The vagueness of the criteria makes the personal values of the examining experts extremely important in the type of evaluation performed. As psychologist Stanley Brodsky puts it,

> A rule of thumb may be applied here: The vaguer the goals and criteria are for any given task, the more likely the clinician is to utilize her or his own values. Similarly, the more unstructured and vague the assessment methods are, the more likely it is that values will impose.[70]

Hence, the question of who it is that determines competence becomes crucial.

Who Evaluates? Who Decides?
The Problems of Selection, Selective Boycotts, and Political Influence

Definitional and evaluative problems aside, a more fundamental problem facing physicians and mental health professionals involved in determinations of competence for execution is that, unlike their testimony in competency to stand trial hearings or in insanity determinations, under the circumstances presented in *Ford* their opinions about competency could not be challenged in an adversarial judicial hearing. In other words, there was no mechanism for the attorneys of the condemned inmates to challenge the accuracy and reliability of the psychiatrists' conclusions. Until *Ford*, the exemption of the mentally ill from execution was an issue of executive grace or clemency (with only the minimum level of incompetence specified by statute or common law), not of a constitutional right.

This created three problems. First, the final decision regarding competence for execution was not made by a neutral fact finder: It was made by a governor, who is an elected politician. Community pressures for execution may be great, creating the possibility that the mental health professional's involvement would only legitimate what in the end was a purely political decision. Second, the decision was made by the governor privately and secretly, and no explanation or judicial review of this decision was permitted. Third, there was no opportunity to challenge the commission's findings by presenting the opinions of other mental health professionals. Hence, the lack of due process presented a formidable barrier to the participation of conscientious physicians, psychologists, and other health professionals.

This third point is particularly salient because of the high probability that the psychiatrists who are invited and agree to do competency evaluations are not a representative sample of the profession. In theory it is possible for the governor to find three psychiatrists who will rubber-stamp all condemned prisoners as competent to be executed after a perfunctory examination, and some might argue that this is exactly what happened in Alvin Ford's case.

At the very least, the opinions on Ford's competency for execution formed by various observers and the clinicians who evaluated him were directly related to where these people worked and which side asked them to become involved. Most of the staff at the prison saw Ford as a malingerer. This is not surprising; few prison employees oppose executions, and they are socialized to distrust virtually everything that prisoners say or claim. Further, the one psychiatrist on the original commission who found Ford to be malingering, Dr. Peter Ivory, was an employee of the State of Florida, and thus an employee of the governor who had ordered the execution to proceed. This created the potential for conflict of interest. Similarly, mental health professionals brought in by the defense who were free of ties to government agencies consistently found Ford to be seriously disturbed.

The issues presented in *Ford* ignited a long and continuing debate about whether physicians and other mental health professionals should participate in evaluations of competency for execution, and if they do participate, how they should do it.[71] Some choose not to participate,[72] and the evidence indicates that this selective boycott makes the situation even worse. A survey of 222 forensic psychiatrists and psychologists in Florida in 1988 found that 36% of the respondents were unwilling to participate in such evaluations.[73] The members of this group were also found to differ significantly from their pro-participation counterparts. Those un-willing to participate in the evaluations were more likely to oppose capital punishment, lack "prosecution-oriented" experience, have strong ethical concerns against participating, and attribute criminal responsibility to the environment rather than the individual.[74] This suggests that the mental health professionals who are willing to do competency evaluations come from a select pool that tends to be prosecution-oriented. Ironically, this provides a strong argument that the less prosecution-oriented professionals should not boycott the process, as their involvement is needed to attain more balance.

Professional Reactions to the *Ford* Issues

After Ford's execution was stayed in 1984 and the issues raised in his case were studied and debated by mental health professionals, a number of professional organizations took formal stands on various aspects of the case. For example, in 1984 the Florida Mental Health Association adopted a policy that not only opposed the execution of any person lacking the mental capacity to be executed, but also opposed the use of government-employed psychiatrists in the process and the involuntary restoration of mental capacity to those who have been judged incompetent. The policy statement also urged all mental health professionals to boycott assessments of competence to be executed.[75]

Psychologists were not far behind. The Board of Social and Ethical Responsibility of the American Psychological Association passed a resolution in 1983, stating that conducting examinations for competency for execution was inconsistent with the promotion of human welfare, and asking the parent American Psychological Association to deem it inappropriate for psychologists to involve themselves in such evaluations. The Board of Professional Affairs, another unit of the American Psychological Association, opposed the resolution on the grounds that "any blanket restriction on participation by psychologists in the judicial process relating to the death penalty would constitute an invasion of the individual psychologist's prerogatives." Because of the conflicting positions of the two boards, the directors took no further action. The issue resurfaced in 1989 when members of the Board of Ethical and Social Responsibility again introduced a resolution opposing the use of psychologists in routine certification for competency for execution.[76] The proposal would have limited justification for participation in such evaluations to the bringing of new information that might change the verdict and sentence. This was paired with another resolution, which called for the American Psychological Association to oppose the death penalty. Both proposals were withdrawn, in part because such an adversarial stance was seen as clouding the objective role of clinicians.

After the Supreme Court agreed to hear *Ford*, the American Psychological Association, joined by the Florida Psychological Association, submitted an *amicus curiae* brief to the Supreme Court that, for the most part, supported the positions of the defense. The brief argued that condemned prisoners should have the right to have their sanity determined through a reliable fact-finding proceeding, specifically one that was adversarial and one that required evaluators to specify what factors they relied upon to make their competency evaluations.

The American Psychiatric Association also submitted an *amicus* brief. The brief charged that the Florida procedures recognized, in principle, a right for the mentally incompetent not to be executed, but "denigrate[d] its significance by subjecting it to the most cursory form of procedural review."[77] It criticized three aspects of the Florida procedure: (a) the toleration of quick, group evaluations by state-appointed psychiatrists; (b) the failure to consider psychiatric evaluations prepared for the defense; and (c) the absence of the possibility for cross-examination. The summary argument was that "the Florida procedures for determining competence to be executed are constitutionally flawed because they do not provide for professionally adequate psychiatric evaluations and proper procedures for assuring reliable decisions."

Nonetheless, the question of whether psychiatrists should participate in evaluations of competency for execution was not resolved with *Ford*. The American Psychiatric Association's Council on Psychiatry and Law continued to debate the problem—without consensus—in 1987, as did its Commission on Judicial Action and the Ethics Committee.[78]

But there were also other issues raised in Alvin Ford's appeals, and we next turn our attention to them.

Notes

1. Trial transcript, *Ford v. State*, July 1974, p. 1330.
2. *Woodson v. North Carolina*, 428 U.S. 280 (1976), p. 304.
3. *Lockett v. Ohio*, 438 U.S. 586 (1978), p. 604-605.
4. Miller, 1980.
5. In fact, one of the first Americans to present a systematic argument for the total abolition of capital punishment was Dr. Benjamin Rush, a signatory of the Declaration of Independence and today known as the "Father of Psychiatry" (Mackey, 1976, pp. 1-13).

An excellent book, from earlier this century, on capital punishment was written by Dr. Amos Squire (1938), an ardent foe of the death penalty who nonetheless participated in 138 executions in New York.

Dr. Louis Jolyon West's essay (1976), written just before Oklahoma and Texas changed their means of execution to lethal injection, is another powerful statement of a medical perspective on the death penalty. Among other things, West argues that it is unethical for physicians even to certify the fact and time of death for executed inmates (see also West, 1970, and the discussion of West's contributions in Bedau, 1992).

Dr. Karl Menninger, who died in 1990, was also active in the anti-death penalty movement. In his words, "Eliminating one offender who happens to get caught *weakens* public security by creating a false sense of diminished danger through definite remedial measure. Actually, it does not remedy anything, and it bypasses completely the real and unsolved problem of *how to identify, detect, and detain potentially dangerous citizens*" (Menninger, 1968, p. 108, emphasis in original).

6. A French physician once had a new method of execution named after him. In a humanitarian gesture, in 1789 Dr. Joseph-Ignace Guillotin denounced hanging as cruel and unjustifiable, and proposed that France adopt a decapitation machine that would be swift and sure. The device, the guillotine, was adopted in 1791 and bears his name. It was not "invented" by him. See Scott, 1950, pp. 186-188; Soubiran, 1964; Weiner, 1972.

7. Colburn, 1990.

8. NAACP Legal Defense and Education Fund, "Death Row, U.S.A." (Winter 1992). In August 1992, California passed legislation that allows death row inmates to choose between lethal injection and the gas chamber. *Los Angeles Times*, August 29, 1992, p. 17A. In the November 1992 elections, voters in Arizona changed its method of execution from the gas chamber to injection.

9. Jones, 1990.

10. Henry Schwarzschild's comments on lethal injection (1982) have come to be known as "Schwarzschild's Paradox" (Bedau, 1991). "Lethal injection represents a paradox for death-penalty abolitionists: Some methods of execution are worse than others (for example, drawing-and-quartering is worse than the gas chamber), but no method of execution is better than any other (lethal injection is no improvement over electrocution)."

11. For example, in a letter to the editor of the *Arizona Republic* on February 15, 1992, State Representative John C. Keegan defended his vote (and that of a colleague) against changing Arizona's method of execution to lethal injection with the argument that "this method of execution is an act of kindness that should not be awarded to these criminals." Rep. Keegan said that he and his colleague expected "these criminals to pay their debt to society in a way that is not only distasteful to them, but will also serve as a catharsis to society."

12. For an overview, see Haines, 1989.

13. Bedau, 1992; West, 1970, 1976.

14. Jendrzejczyk, 1982. Indeed, through 1992 there have been nine executions by lethal injection that have been "botched," primarily because technicians took more than 30 minutes to find a vein in which to insert the catheter. Haines, 1992; *San Francisco Examiner*, April 22, 1992, p. 14.

In 1991 Louisiana became the 21st state to adopt lethal injection as its means of execution. Two prisoners were ordered to construct the new gurney, and when they refused, they were placed in a lock-down cell. The next day, the remaining 37 prisoners who worked at the Metal Fabrication Plant at Louisiana's Angola Prison also refused. They, too, were locked up. Soon, more than 300 supportive prisoners who worked in the prison's farms went on strike. They joined their comrades in the lock-down cells. As the protest spread and the prison authorities prepared for a full-scale riot, the warden finally announced that prisoners would not have to construct the gurney (Wikberg & Rideau, 1991, pp. 21-22).

15. For information on the Nazi doctors see Lifton, 1986.

16. Zimring and Hawkins, 1986, p. 110.

17. Curran and Casscells, 1980. See also their follow-up paper (Casscells & Curran, 1982).

18. Curran and Casscells, 1980, pp. 227, 230.

19. Curran and Casscells, 1980, p. 229.

20. The discussion also involved nurses; see Annas, 1980. In this book we will treat the ethics of mental health professionals as a homogeneous category and not attempt to differentiate, for example, psychiatric ethics and psychological ethics.

21. Bayer, 1984, p. 13.

22. American Psychiatric Association, 1980; Bayer, 1984, p. 13; Casscells and Curran, 1982, p. 1532.

23. American Public Health Association, 1986.

24. American Public Health Association, 1987.

25. Through March 1993, Dr. Kevorkian had assisted in fifteen suicides. *Newsweek*, March 27, 1993, pp. 46-47; *The New York Times*, September 27, 1992, p. 32.

26. Kevorkian, 1960, 1985. In 1991 Georgia death row inmate Ronald K. Spivey, apparently after being convinced by Dr. Kevorkian, requested that he be executed by having a surgeon remove his vital organs for donation to those in need of transplants. *National Law Journal*, December 2, 1991, p. 6.

27. Cohen, 1983; Colburn, 1990. Interestingly, Brooks's arm was swabbed with alcohol before the injection was given, although it obviously was not done to prevent infection.

28. Haines, 1989, pp. 449-450.

29. *Chicago Tribune*, December 12, 1982, p. 1.

30. In 1982 Illinois Governor James Thompson had vetoed legislation that would have changed the means of execution in Illinois from the electric chair to lethal injection.

Thompson believed that lethal infection was too humane, and that the electric chair would act as more of a deterrent (*Chicago Tribune,* December 12, 1982, p. 1).

31. *American Medical News,* September 23-30, 1991.

32. Resolution 163, AMA House of Delegates, Chicago, June 23-27, 1991.

33. British Medical Association, 1992, p. 118.

34. *Ake v. Oklahoma,* 470 U.S. 68 (1985).

35. *Ake v. Oklahoma,* 470 U.S. 68 (1985), p. 83.

36. *Ake v. Oklahoma,* 470 U.S. 68 (1985), p. 74.

37. *Ake v. Oklahoma,* 470 U.S. 68 (1985), p. 82.

38. Appelbaum, 1987; see also Showalter and Fitch, 1987.

39. Appelbaum, 1987, p. 19.

40. Appelbaum, 1987, p. 20.

41. Blume, 1990, p. 42.

42. Blume, 1990, pp. 43-44.

43. That attorney is John Blume; see Blume, 1990. For the importance of neurological examinations, see Lewis et al., 1986.

44. Curran, 1982. In Virginia, the Forensic Psychiatry Clinic of the Institute of Law, Psychiatry, and Public Policy at the University of Virginia evaluated 39 defendants charged with capital murder between 1978 and 1989. For accounts of their experiences, see Showalter, 1990; Showalter and Bonnie, 1984.

45. *Woodson v. North Carolina,* 428 U.S. 280 (1976), p. 304.

46. White, 1991, p. 85.

47. For a detailed discussion of the peculiarities of the Texas statute, see Black, 1981, pp. 65-72.

48. See, for example, Dix, 1977a, 1977b, 1978; Monahan, 1981.

49. Adams, Hoffer, and Hoffer, 1991; *Dallas Morning News,* February 16, 1992, p. 1.

50. Rosenbaum, 1990.

51. *The New York Times,* June 7, 1988.

52. See Appelbaum, 1983; Ewing, 1983.

53. Appelbaum, 1981.

54. Appelbaum, 1981, p. 762.

55. *Estelle v. Smith,* 451 U.S. 454 (1981).

56. Rosenbaum, 1990, p. 147.

57. For more discussion of the use of hypotheticals in death sentencing, see Appelbaum, 1984.

58. Curran, 1984.

59. *Barefoot v. Estelle,* 463 U.S. 880 (1983).

60. *Satterwhite v. Texas,* 108 S.Ct. 1792 (1988).

61. We note here only a sample of this literature: American Psychological Association Symposium, 1986; Appelbaum, 1986, 1990; Bonnie, 1990a; Brodsky, 1990; Heilbrun, 1987; Heilbrun and McClaren, 1988; Heilbrun, Radelet, and Dvoskin, 1992; Podgers, 1980; Salguero, 1986; Schopp, 1991; Small and Otto, 1991; Ward, 1986; White, 1982.

62. The standard used to determine whether a defendant is competent to stand trial is "whether he has sufficient present ability to consult with his lawyer with a reasonable degree of rational understanding—and whether he has a rational as well as factual understanding of the proceeding against him" (*Dusky v. U.S.,* 362 U.S. 402 (1960), p. 402).

63. Mezer and Rheingold, 1962.

64. Roth, Meisel, and Lidz, 1977.

65. American Bar Association, 1989, p. 290.

66. When Ford's case went to the Supreme Court, Florida's Statute 922.07 read as follows:

Proceedings when a person under sentence of death appears to be insane.

1. When the Governor is informed that a person under a sentence of death may be insane, he shall stay execution of the sentence and appoint a commission of three psychiatrists to examine the convicted person. The Governor shall notify the psychiatrists in writing that they are to examine the convicted person to determine whether he understands the nature and effect of the death penalty and why it is to be imposed upon him. The examination of the convicted person shall take place with all three psychiatrists present at the same time. Counsel for the convicted person and the state attorney may be present at the examination. If the convicted person does not have counsel, the court that imposed the sentence shall appoint counsel to represent him.

2. After receiving the report of the commission, if the Governor decides that the convicted person has the mental capacity to understand the nature of the death penalty and the reasons why it was imposed upon him, he shall issue a warrant to the warden directing him to execute the sentence at a time designated in the warrant.

3. If the Governor decides that the convicted person does not have the mental capacity to understand the nature of the death penalty and why it was imposed on him, he shall have him committed to the state hospital for the insane.

4. When a person under sentence of death has been committed to the state hospital for the insane, he shall be kept there until the proper official of the hospital determines that he has been restored to sanity. The hospital official shall notify the Governor of his determination, and the Governor shall appoint another commission to proceed as provided in subsection (1).

5. The Governor shall allow reasonable fees to psychiatrists appointed under the provisions of this section which shall be paid by the state.

67. Cited in Ford v. Wainwright, 477 U.S. 399, p. 403.

68. Ford v. Wainwright, 477 U.S. 399, p. 403.

69. American Bar Association, 1989, p. 294.

70. Brodsky, 1990, p. 92.

71. See, for example, Appelbaum, 1986, 1990; Bonnie, 1990a, 1990b; Brodsky, 1990; Heilbrun, 1987; Heilbrun and McClaren, 1988; Heilbrun et al., 1992; Radelet and Barnard, 1986.

72. Dr. Paul Appelbaum, for example, once favored this position, but does no longer (Appelbaum, 1990, Note 4; Appelbaum, Bonnie, Dietz, and Thorup, 1987, p. 25).

73. Deitchman, Kennedy, and Beckham, 1991.

74. Deitchman et al., 1991.

75. Policy Position Regarding Mental Capacity to be Executed, Adopted by the Board of Directors of the Mental Health Association of Florida, July 21, 1984.

76. Board of Social and Ethical Responsibility in Psychology. (1989). Agenda: Meeting of May 5-7, 1989. Washington, DC: American Psychological Association.

77. American Psychiatric Association, Amicus Brief in Ford v. Wainwright, p. 6.

78. Roth, 1987, p. 412.

Officer Dimitri Walter Ilyankoff.
*Photo courtesy of David Exterkamp, Photo Lab,
Ft. Lauderdale Police Department.*

Alvin Ford, age 12 (seventh grade).
Photo courtesy of Connie Ford.

Alvin Ford, age 16,
with his cow "Joe."
Starting when Joe was
a calf, Alvin raised her
through his involvement
in Future Farmers of
America.

Photo courtesy of Connie Ford.

Alvin Ford in High School, circa 1970.
Photo courtesy of Connie Ford.

Alvin Ford upon admission
to Florida's death row,
January 1975.

*Photo courtesy of Capital
Collateral Representative.*

Alvin Ford at a prison press
conference, May 30, 1984. At
the time of the press conference,
he was scheduled for execution
the following morning.

*Photo by Joe Burbank,
courtesy of the
Independent Florida Alligator
(University of Florida).*

Prosecutor Michael Satz (1992).
Photo by Elliot J. Schecter, courtesy of the Sun-Sentinel *(Ft. Lauderdale).*

Defense Attorney Richard H. Burr (1993).
Photo courtesy of Susan Cary.

Mrs. Connie Ford (1991).
Photo by Michael L. Radelet.

7

Alvin Ford and the Courts:
Additional Issues

When Alvin Ford was sentenced to death in 1975, it was not yet certain that the U.S. Supreme Court would approve the new death penalty statutes that had been passed in the wake of the 1972 *Furman* decision. Ford was already on death row when the Supreme Court approved Florida's revised capital statute in 1976.[1] Hence, he was party to a large part of the extensive litigation regarding the constitutionality of capital punishment as it is presently practiced. While Alvin Ford's case centers on the issue of competence for execution, its story would be incomplete without a brief look at some of the major death penalty issues of the 1980s and 1990s that were raised, albeit some only briefly, in his appeals. In this chapter we review a few of the nonmental health issues raised at one time or another by Ford's attorneys—issues that have continuing relevance for scores of death row inmates today.

Courts have been less than consistent in dealing with death penalty cases over the past two decades. This is especially true of the Supreme Court, in considering which cases it will and will not hear, and in the increasingly narrow manner in which it rules (i.e., its decisions tend to affect only a small number of death row inmates, not whole groups). Over the past 20 years, the Court has moved from finding the death penalty to be a cruel and unusual punishment (as applied), to a period of rationalizing and routinizing the punishment, and finally, to a third phase, in which "the Court proclaimed the end of its doubts and correspondingly signalled its intention to turn away from any continuing scrutiny of the enterprise."[2] The shift away has not been total, as the Court continues to hear arguments in 10 or so capital cases every year, and still spends a considerable amount of time reviewing and rejecting appeals. The subject remains very time-consuming and occasionally divisive. But most of this is a matter of nibbling at the edges, not dealing with fundamental questions or challenges to the constitutionality of any widespread aspect of death penalty procedure.

While recognizing the primacy of the interest of the state in carrying out its laws, the Supreme Court has held that "death is different," and that the review process must be careful and thorough. Because of this, appellate courts have been receptive to a wider range of challenges than in other areas of law and frequently have been compelled to grant last-minute stays because of insufficient time to review appeals. Indeed, in about half the cases in which a trial court has imposed a death sentence since 1972, appellate courts have been receptive to the claims made by the defense, and the death row inmate has won some form of relief.[3]

During the 1970s and 1980s the Supreme Court was sharply divided on capital punishment, with numerous 5-4 decisions. Some decisions had as many as eight or nine different written opinions, with agreement on some points and strong differences on others.[4] The 1990 replacement of Justice William Brennan (a firm death penalty opponent) with Justice David Souter (no friend to death row inmates) made it increasingly difficult for condemned inmates to win relief, and the 5-4 votes of earlier years evolved into 6-3 or even larger victories for the pro-capital punishment majority. The resignation of the last remaining death penalty abolitionist on the Court, Thurgood Marshall, which took effect on October 1, 1991, spelled even worse news for death row inmates. His successor, Clarence Thomas, has no reservations about the death penalty, and during his first year on the Court voted with the conservative wing in every death penalty case that was considered. The October 18, 1991, execution of Michael McDougal in North Carolina was the first post-*Furman* execution in America to proceed without at least one voice of dissent from the Supreme Court. As we write, the effects on the Supreme Court of the election of President Bill Clinton in 1992 and 1993 resignation of Justice Byron White remain to be seen.

The differences of opinion on the Court are further reflected in the fact that the justices' receptivity to a given legal challenge can change within a relatively short period of time. There are a number of examples of cases in which an appellate issue was rejected and, after the prisoner was executed, the same issue was accepted for review in another case. Ford's case gives a good example. In 1984 the Supreme Court turned down Arthur Goode's challenge of the Florida procedures for determining competency to be executed; on April 5, 1984, he went to the electric chair. Less than 2 years later, the same Court granted a hearing to Ford on the same issue. Decisions can also be completely revoked. In 1987 the Court ruled that testimony from the family of the victim on the "victim impact" of the homicide could not be admitted at the penalty phase of capital trials.[5] Four years later, with a 6-3 vote, the decision was reversed,[6] and today the families of homicide victims are again permitted to testify in states that allow it.

Over the years, Ford's attorneys raised many of the major questions that have occupied the appellate courts since the 1972 *Furman* decision. On some of these, his case was strong. But there were also issues raised in his appeals (including issues discussed in this chapter) that were more developed and compelling in other death penalty cases. Today's death penalty litigation involves new issues, but some of these are variants on themes raised more globally in the 1970s and 1980s. Was the jury fairly selected and unbiased? Was the defense attorney competent? Was the sentence proportional, considering the crimes and punishments received by others who committed comparable crimes? Was race a factor in sentencing? Was there an opportunity to present all of the evidence that might have had a mitigating effect? A close inspection of these questions reveals a plethora of rules that must be followed before a prisoner can be executed. The examination also develops a theme introduced in Chapter 1: Once a society decides that some of its citizens will be executed, hairs must be split to determine who these people are and how they should be selected. All parties agree that the task is neither easy nor inexpensive; some argue the task is simply not possible to do in an impartial and consistent manner.

Jury Composition

After Ford's conviction was affirmed by the Florida Supreme Court in 1979 and the U.S. Supreme Court declined to review the decision, the next step was for the defense team to return to trial court to request "post-conviction relief." They did this during Ford's initial death warrant in 1981. One of the challenges the defense team presented concerned jury composition.[7] The trial court and appellate courts refused to consider it, ruling that it should have been brought up by attorney Robert Adams in Ford's initial appeal.[8] It was not, and so the issue was lost by default.

Potential jurors who stand firmly opposed to the death penalty are not permitted to participate in death penalty cases, either in determining guilt or in advising or rendering sentence. One of the first questions asked of prospective jurors in a capital case is whether they support the death penalty; those who stand firmly opposed are thanked and sent home. Juries culled of death penalty opponents are referred to as "death-qualified." For the past 25 years, the courts have struggled over the question of precisely how "death penalty opposition" should be defined and how firm the opposition must be before the citizen can be automatically excluded from jury service.

In a 1968 case, the Supreme Court ruled that a person could not be excluded from the jury "for cause" unless it was unmistakably clear that the person would automatically vote against a verdict of death or could not be impartial on the issue of guilt or innocence.[9] The most recent statement of when citizens can be excluded from juries because of opposition to the death penalty was handed down in 1985.[10] In that case, which made it easier for prosecutors to exclude anti-death penalty jurors,[11] the Court said the proper standard for exclusion was whether the juror's stand on the death penalty would "prevent or substantially impair the performance of his duties as a juror in accordance with his instructions and oath."

The problem is an important one because there is strong evidence indicating that a death-qualified jury is not only more likely to favor a death sentence, but also more "conviction prone" than are juries that are representative of the general population.[12] Death-qualified juries also disproportionally exclude women, African-Americans, and other minorities, reflecting the higher levels of opposition to the death penalty among these groups.[13]

During the selection of the jury for Ford's trial, 12 of the first 29 potential jurors (plus 3 more later) said that they could not return any verdict which might result in a death sentence. This is an unusually high number of death penalty opponents, but they were dismissed with little questioning.

The composition of the jury might not have had any effect upon the phase of the trial in which Ford's guilt was determined, although because of Ford's relatively diminished premeditation, another jury could easily have returned a conviction for second-degree murder instead of capital murder. But in light of the initial 6-6 straw vote on penalty (life vs. death), even a modest change in the composition of the jury would have altered the recommendation. In Florida a defendant can still be sentenced to death even though his jury votes for life imprisonment (one of four such states), but on appeal such cases stand a good chance of being reduced to life imprisonment.[14]

The Crisis in Securing Competent and Effective Counsel

Also in the 1981 appeal for post-conviction relief, Ford's attorneys claimed that at trial Ford had been denied effective assistance of counsel. This challenge cannot be brought up on the initial, or "direct" appeal, so there was no way the courts could dismiss it as lost by default, as they had done with Ford's complaint about jury selection. The appeal attorneys argued, among other things, that trial attorney Adams had failed to move for a change of venue, to support adequately a motion to sequester the jury, to conduct an appropriate jury selection, to see that the jury was instructed properly on the role of aggravating and mitigating circumstances, to argue that aggravating factors were required to be proven beyond a reasonable doubt, to overcome Ford's uncommunicativeness due to his view that Adams was the father of a police officer, and some 18 other deficiencies. Both the trial court and the Florida Supreme Court dismissed these allegations, setting the stage for a hearing on the issue in federal district court in 1981. Claims for post-conviction relief are presented to federal courts in the form of a petition for writ of habeas corpus, a request for the federal court to review the constitutionality of the legal proceedings that led to the conviction and sentence.

At Ford's 1981 hearing in federal court, conducted after his first death warrant had been signed, there were some testy and heated exchanges between Ford's trial attorney, Robert Adams, and his new attorneys, Larry Wollan and Richard Burr. Three criminal defense attorneys testified as expert witnesses, arguing that crucial errors made by Adams rendered his representation of Ford at trial ineffective.

Informed observers can disagree about whether Adams's defense of Ford was competent, by legal or other professional standards, and we do not know for certain whether a more talented trial counsel, or one with more resources, would have avoided the death sentence. But it is likely. One definite possibility is that a defense attorney with more rapport with his or her client would have been able to convince Ford to accept the plea bargain offered by the state, thereby altogether avoiding the necessity of a trial. Not debatable is the fact that capital litigation is highly complex, subject to rapid change, and not possible to carry out effectively without abundant resources and assistance. Millard Farmer, one of the best death penalty attorneys in the nation, puts it this way: "It's not that the lawyer gets into a trial and offers less skill than he is capable of giving. But it would be just like appointing me to play for the Chicago Bulls—it's beyond my capability."[15] Vivian Berger, Vice-Dean of Columbia University Law School, describes the problem of poor defense in capital cases as similar to chiropractors doing brain surgery.[16]

The courts uniformly denied Ford's claim of ineffective assistance of counsel. But the problem of competent and effective representation continues to have crucial significance for death row inmates—in many cases the level of assistance falls far below what was given to Ford. Stories about drunken attorneys who fail to make even the most rudimentary motions are not hard to find.[17] Consider three brief examples: In the 1982 capital trial of Jerry White in Florida, the judge made the prosecutor smell the defense attorney's breath each morning before trial to see if there were signs of alcohol. There were not, although the attorney's investigator later stated that he saw the man shoot up cocaine during trial recesses. White is still on death row.[18]

In the 1981 California trial of Richard William Garrison, the California Supreme Court noted that the court-appointed defense attorney "drank in the morning, during court recesses and throughout the evening." In fact, it is undisputed that one day during the trial the defense attorney was arrested for drunk driving on the way to the court house—and was found to have a blood alcohol level of .27. Garrison was convicted and sentenced to death, with the trial judge telling the defendant, "I personally can assure you that you probably have one of the finest defense counsel in this country." The California Supreme Court affirmed the conviction on appeal.[19]

The Alabama trial of Judy Haney was delayed for one day when the trial judge ordered her drunken attorney to spend a night in jail. Haney, too, was sentenced to death.[20]

The problem of ineffective assistance of counsel in death penalty cases is not confined to intoxicated attorneys. It is a problem generally acknowledged by both supporters and opponents of the death penalty. An American Bar Association Task Force report sums it up this way:

> The principal failings of the capital punishment review process today are the inadequacy and inadequate compensation of counsel at trial and the unavailability of counsel in state post-conviction proceedings . . . the lack and inadequacy of counsel in state capital proceedings forces state and federal post-conviction judges to: adjudicate cases on the basis of incomplete and often incomprehensible records; resolve manifold colorable claims of ineffective assistance of counsel; dispose of myriad procedural questions . . . and grant constitutionally mandated relief and costly retrials in numerous cases.[21]

Still, the legal profession has been slow to recognize any ethical obligation of the profession to improve the quality of representation in death penalty trials and appeals.

As a general rule, as a capital case passes through successive levels of review, more competent, experienced, and specialized attorneys (with their own drawbacks of overwork and underfunding) are likely to be involved. But this is not always the case. For example, in 1989 the Supreme Court heard arguments about the death sentence of a mentally retarded Texas death row inmate, Johnny Penry. Harvard Law Professor Alan Dershowitz was in the audience. He later described the defense attorney's presentation as a disaster, involving an inability to understand the questions posed by the Justices, giving the wrong answers when he did, unable to find needed references, and so on. With 3 minutes left of the time allotted for his argument, Justice Sandra Day O'Connor had to remind the attorney that he had not addressed the main issue in the case. Dershowitz expressed compassion for the lawyer who was so clearly out of his league, but insisted that something had to be done to assure the competence of the attorneys defending death row inmates:

> While lawyers help the rich get richer through leveraged buyouts and other fancy financial footwork, those most in need of excellent legal representation—the mentally retarded, the poor, the homeless, the stateless—have to rely on well-motivated volunteers, retired lawyers, and underpaid public defenders. There is something drastically wrong with this system[22]

The involvement of high-quality attorneys in death penalty cases often comes for short periods of time when the execution is imminent and no other attorney can be found.[23] Often, by that time it is too late to appeal crucial issues in the case. Consider the case of Roger Keith Coleman. His appellate attorneys did an outstanding job of investigating and documenting serious questions about Coleman's guilt. They brought the case to the attention of the country with skillful use of the media—the case even attracted a cover story in *Time* magazine.[24] But because earlier attorneys on the case filed his notice of appeal with the Virginia Supreme Court one day past the deadline, the U.S. Supreme Court ruled that he had forfeited his right to federal review of his claims.[25] On May 20, 1992, Coleman was executed, without the question of his possible innocence fully being addressed.

Despite the problems of securing competent and effective counsel in death penalty cases, it is almost impossible to win a challenge of a capital conviction and sentence in state courts on the grounds of ineffective assistance of counsel.[26] The criteria for judging ineffectiveness require not only that the counsel's performance be deficient, but the defense must also show that but for the trial attorney's errors, the jury or judge would have arrived at a different decision.[27] It is a prejudice that few death row inmates can prove, as Alvin Ford learned. In fact, in the first 5 years after the above criteria were announced, relief was won on the grounds of ineffective assistance of counsel a combined total of only 14 times in the state courts of Alabama, Florida, Georgia, Louisiana, Mississippi, and Texas.[28]

Recent efforts to improve the quality of representation have been helpful in a few cases, but overall have fallen short because of extremely limited resources. Mississippi and Louisiana still pay court-assigned attorneys in death penalty cases a maximum of $1,000 to investigate and try a capital case for indigent defendants; often that averages less than $5 per hour.[29] Volunteer attorneys (like Larry Wollan) have done what must be considered heroic work in many death penalty cases, but it is becoming more and more difficult, if not impossible, to find replacements for these volunteers as they become overwhelmed or burned out and find it necessary to retreat to more conventional modes of law practice.

Racial Bias

Under his 1984 death warrant, among the grounds on which Ford pleaded for a stay was that studies had by then shown that Florida administered the death penalty arbitrarily and discriminatorily on the basis of race of victim, race of defendant, and other impermissible factors in violation of the Eighth and Fourteenth Amendments.[30] The stay eventually granted by the Eleventh Circuit was based both on Ford's competence for execution and on the basis of this race-discrimination claim.

The state immediately appealed the stay order to the U.S. Supreme Court. Three justices (Berger, Rehnquist, and O'Connor) voted to lift the stay. Justices Brennan and Marshall, as usual, voted not to vacate the stay. Three other justices (Powell, White, and Blackmun) voted to deny the state's effort to lift the stay, but explicitly said their vote was only because of the issue of competence for execution; they would not support the stay on the discrimination claim. The ninth justice, Stevens, did not explicitly reject the discrimination claim, but said that because he accepted the competence issue, he would not bother to judge the discrimination claim. The three justices who denied the state's effort to lift the stay solely on the competence issue said that Ford had defaulted on the discrimination issue because he had not raised it sooner.[31] In effect, that vote ended Ford's legal claim of discrimination.

It did not end his moral and empirical claim. Ford's argument was almost identical to that raised by Warren McCleskey, an African-American convicted of killing an off-duty white police officer in Atlanta in 1978. Those who might think that a death sentence is a sure bet for defendants convicted of killing police officers (like McCleskey or Ford) will find the actual probability surprising. "Of the 17 defendants, including McCleskey, who were arrested and charged with homicide of a police officer in Fulton County [Atlanta] during the 1973-1979 period, McCleskey, alone, was sentenced to death."[32] Evidence was presented to the Supreme Court that in Georgia, all other factors being equal, the odds of a death sentence for killers with white victims were four times higher than were the odds of a death sentence for those with black victims.[33] The statistical evidence was based on the most sophisticated study of sentencing ever conducted. Justice Brennan described it as "far and away the most refined data ever assembled on any system of punishment." Additional evidence of racial disparity in death sentencing, consistent with the Georgia results, was available for Florida.[34]

Even some federal agencies concede that the victim's race is strongly associated with death sentencing. In 1990 the U.S. General Accounting Office, an investigative organization of the federal government, systematically reviewed all of the existing research on the issue and concluded that, other things being equal, those who murdered whites were more likely to be sentenced to death than those who murdered blacks. The finding held across data sets, states, various methods of data collection, and analytic techniques, and it appeared at all stages of the criminal justice system. More than half of the studies reviewed found that race of the defendant also influenced the likelihood of being charged with a capital crime or receiving the death penalty.[35] Of some 16,000 documented executions in American history, there have been only 31 cases in which whites were executed for crimes against blacks, and nearly all were treated as economic crimes—or involved defendants who were hated, had low status, or posed a threat or challenge to the white power structure.[36]

In April 1987, in a 5-4 vote, the Court rejected McCleskey's challenge. Justice Lewis Powell, Jr., author of the majority opinion, acknowledged the statistical discrepancy, but upheld the Georgia death statute because McCleskey had presented no clear evidence that he was an *intentional* victim of racial discrimination. Powell claimed that disparities in sentencing were an inevitable part of the criminal justice system, and that existing safeguards made trials "as fair as possible."[37] The Court, he stated, "would demand exceptionally clear proof before we would infer that the discretion has been abused."[38] Powell and the majority justices demanded explicit proof of discrimination, such as a prosecutor saying on the record that the death sentence was based on the victim's or the defendant's race.

At the end of the majority decision, the justices suggested that "McCleskey's arguments are best presented to legislative bodies." This was reminiscent of Kenneth Culp Davis's distinction between "adjudicative facts" (facts concerning parties in dispute, their activities, and their properties) and "legislative facts" (facts sought by a tribunal to create law or determine policy).[39] Despite the suggestion from the justices in *McCleskey*, legislation designed to reduce racial bias in death sentencing—introduced in the U.S. Congress in 1990 and 1991—failed to gain passage.

The dissenting justices argued that *McCleskey* made it more difficult to prove racial bias in death sentencing than to prove discrimination in other areas of the law. Had McCleskey been asking for judicial intervention because of discrimination related to voting, housing, or a job, he would not have had to prove the discrimination was intentional, and he would have won relief. The dissenting judges also stressed that the evidence of racial bias was strong. Justice Brennan wrote, "Surely, we should not be willing to take a person's life if the chance that his death sentence was irrationally imposed is *more* likely than not."[40] Indeed, as University of Michigan Law Professor Samuel Gross points out, the relationship between victim's race and death sentencing is stronger than the relationship between smoking and heart disease.[41] In Florida, only the presence of felony circumstances is a better predictor of what types of murders end in death sentences; the race of the victim is a better predictor than such factors as the victim-defendant relationship and the number of victims.[42] On September 25, 1991, McCleskey was executed.[43]

Proportionality

Racial bias is only part of a much larger problem in death sentencing: It is not always the worst murderers who are condemned. There were upwards of 2,700 death row inmates in America at the end of 1992, all of whom had been convicted of murder. Still, less than 2% of all murders in America are avenged with a death sentence.[44] Some of those whose murders and prior records would not rank them among the worst 2% are sentenced to death, whether through racism, poor attorneys, or sheer arbitrariness (recall that Ford had once been in a position to exchange a guilty plea for a prison sentence). Some murderers who arguably are among the worst are sentenced to life or less, again because of race, good attorneys, or good luck (e.g., their case comes at the same time as other complicated cases, and the prosecutor does not have the resources to seek a death sentence). One of the reasons for an automatic review of every American death sentence by the state's highest criminal court is concern over procedural propriety and proportionality—making sure that similar cases receive similar punishment.

Proportionality in sentencing requires evenhandedness in application of aggravating and mitigating circumstances. Among the
aggravators used by Judge Lee to justify Ford's sentence was his
finding that the crime was especially "heinous, atrocious, or
cruel." That factor is among the nine statutorily defined aggravating circumstances that can be used to justify a death sentence in
Florida—and, with some minor language differences, in many
other states as well. Inconsistencies in its application can be used
to illustrate the larger problem of proportionality.

In 1981 Ford's attorneys argued that the Florida Supreme Court
failed to employ consistent standards in its review of aggravating
and mitigating circumstances in general, and this factor in particular.[45] To support the trial court's use of this aggravating circumstance in capital cases, the state supreme court has generally held
that the victim has to suffer substantially between the infliction
of the wounds and death, experience a great fear for life as a result
of taunting, or be compelled to plead for life. Ford's attorneys
argued that the wording of the phrase "heinous, atrocious or
cruel" was ambiguous, and that his case did not fit that description as it had been applied to other capital cases in Florida. They
cited Florida cases in which the "heinous, atrocious or cruel"
aggravator was *not* found, but where the circumstances of the
murder included:

- the victim had raised his hands in the air in surrender
- the victim was bound and gagged before being shot
- the victim was shot in the chest and, as he tried to flee, was shot in
  the back several times
- a bludgeoning which did not produce immediate death
- a murder involving numerous stab wounds as well as shooting

In contrast, the evidence in Ford's case was that Officer Ilyankoff
was unconscious within "a minute or two" of being shot.

Nonetheless, the Florida Supreme Court rejected the argument,
ruling that the fact that Officer Ilyankoff was shot three times
justified the finding.[46] The federal circuit court agreed.[47] A later
study of the application of the "heinous, atrocious or cruel"
standard in Florida concluded it was a "catch-all provision for

murders that do not fall neatly within any of the other statutory aggravating circumstances," and that it failed in its ability to channel the sentencing decisions of judges and jurors.[48] Perhaps because of the momentous difficulties in assuring uniformity in the application of aggravating circumstances, the U.S. Supreme Court eventually ruled that proportionality review of capital cases is simply not required.[49]

Jury Responsibility and the Right to Present Potentially Mitigating Evidence

As the years passed after Ford's death sentence was imposed, there were many changes in the procedural rules that must be followed when a trial court hands down a death sentence. Problems that in one case had been ignored or tolerated were examined at length in another case, and if the appeal in the latter case was successful, the former case might also have grounds for relief. So, in 1988, after most of the original issues in Ford's appeal had been lost (although not the competency issue), Ford's attorneys once again went before the Florida Supreme Court seeking relief. This time they presented two issues, each of which had been successful in other cases.

One complaint related to the denigration of the sentencing procedure. At Ford's trial, the judge had told the jury that its function was "advisory only." The concern was that under this understanding, a juror might be inclined to vote for a death sentence with the feeling that his or her decision was not crucial, since the ultimate decision would be made by the judge. To say "advisory" understated the importance of the juror's vote. Ford's attorneys argued that this was not acceptable because it undermined the role of the jury "as the conscience of the community." But the Florida Supreme Court rejected this argument on the grounds that it should have been raised earlier, and that the claim could not be sustained on its merits because in Florida, the judge is indeed the ultimate sentencing authority.[50]

Ford's second claim was that he was entitled to relief because his jury had been under the misunderstanding that they were able to find only mitigating circumstances that were specified in Florida's death penalty statute. The jury erroneously believed that nonstatutory mitigating circumstances could not be used. A recent U.S. Supreme Court ruling in another Florida case had found reversible error because the jury was instructed to consider only the seven statutorily enumerated mitigating circumstances, and the trial judge refused to consider nonstatutory factors that could have justified a life sentence.[51] Ford's attorneys pointed to a number of nonstatutory factors that were not considered by the jury: his potential for rehabilitation, the fact that he was personally troubled and had considered suicide, his responsible work history and care for his family, and the absence of a history of violence.

On February 18, 1988, in a 5-2 vote, the Florida Supreme Court ruled that the trial court's error in instructing the jury on its function and on not allowing the jury to consider nonstatutory mitigators was "harmless." The justices in the majority wrote that they were "convinced beyond a reasonable doubt that the judge would have sentenced Ford to death regardless of whether the jury had made a life recommendation." The two justices who dissented were not convinced that the errors were harmless, and argued that the case should be returned to trial court for a new sentencing hearing.

In Chapter 1 we introduced the problems of "drawing the lines." Debates about the morality of the death penalty aside, the case of Alvin Ford clearly shows that once society decides to employ executioners, it is not an easy task to separate those who should be executed from those who should not. The definition of what is "fair" and what is not varies over time, and often the decision on whether to grant relief is highly dependent on such factors as whether the attorney objects to the troubling procedure at trial, the timing of when the issue is raised on appeal, and the willingness of appellate courts to grant relief in other cases with similar issues. In the end, the heinousness of the offense alone does not do much to explain who is sentenced to prison and who ends up seated in the electric chair.

Notes

1. *Proffitt v. Florida,* 428 U.S. 242 (1976).
2. Burt, 1987, p. 1741; see also Weisberg, 1983.
3. Greenberg, 1982; Tabak and Lane, 1989, note 169.
4. Stewart and Nelson, 1988.
5. *Booth v. Maryland,* 482 U.S. 496 (1987).
6. *Payne v. Tennessee,* 111 S.Ct. 2597 (1991).
7. Motion for Post-Conviction Relief (Rule 3.850, Florida Rules of Criminal Procedure) filed in the Circuit Court of the seventeenth Judicial Circuit (Broward County), November 13, 1981.
8. *Ford v. State,* 407 So.2d 907 (1981).
9. *Witherspoon v. Illinois,* 391 U.S. 510 (1968).
10. *Wainwright v. Witt,* 469 U.S. 412 (1985).
11. Brown, 1986; Callans, 1985; Neises and Dillehay, 1987.
12. See Haney, 1984a, 1984b, 1984c, and the collection of papers in the issue of *Law and Human Behavior* in which these papers are contained. The Supreme Court ruled in 1986 that the "conviction proneness" of death penalty juries was not a large enough problem to stop death qualification, even for the guilt phase (*Lockhart v. McCree,* 476 U.S. 162 (1986)).
13. Jacoby and Paternoster, 1982.
14. Mello and Robson, 1985; Radelet, 1985.
15. Coyle, Strasser, and Lavelle, 1990, p. 31.
16. Berger, 1990-1991.
17. See, for example, Coyle et al., 1990.
18. See Coyle et al., 1990, p. 30.
19. *People v. Garrison,* 47 Cal.3rd 746 (1989); *San Francisco Examiner,* February 17, 1991.
20. Coyle et al., 1990, p. 36.
21. See American Bar Association, 1990, p. 7; Goldstein, 1990; Mello, 1988.
22. Dershowitz, 1989.
23. Mello, 1988.
24. *Time,* May 19, 1992.
25. *Coleman v. Thompson,* 111 S.Ct. 2546 (1991).
26. See Bright, 1990.
27. *Strickland v. Washington,* 466 U.S. 668 (1984).
28. Coyle et al., 1990, p. 42.
29. Coyle et al., 1990.
30. *Ford v. Wainwright,* 734 F.2d 538 (1984).
31. *Wainwright v. Ford,* 467 U.S. 1220 (1984).
32. *McCleskey v. Kemp,* 481 U.S. 279 (1987), p. 334.
33. This claim was based on extensive research by University of Iowa Law Professor David Baldus and his colleagues; see Baldus et al., 1990.
34. Gross and Mauro, 1989; Radelet, 1981; Radelet and Pierce, 1985, 1991; Zeisel, 1981.
35. General Accounting Office, 1990.

36. Thirty of these cases are described in Radelet, 1989. The most recent execution of this type was of Pee Wee Gaskins in South Carolina in 1991.

37. *McCleskey v. Kemp,* 481 U.S. 279 (1987), p. 313.

38. *McCleskey v. Kemp,* 481 U.S. 279 (1987), p. 313.

39. Davis, 1951, p. 153.

40. *McCleskey v. Kemp,* 481 U.S. 279 (1987), p. 328.

41. Gross, 1985.

42. Radelet and Pierce, 1991, p. 28.

43. *Atlanta Constitution,* September 26, 1991, p. D3.

44. Pierce and Radelet, 1990-1991.

45. Mello, 1984.

46. *Ford v. State,* 374 So.2d 496 (1979), p. 503.

47. *Ford v. Strickland,* 656 F.2d 804 (1983), p. 819.

48. Mello, 1984, p. 524.

49. *Pulley v. Harris,* 465 U.S. 37 (1984).

50. *Ford v. State,* 522 So. 2d 345 (1988).

51. *Hitchcock v. Dugger,* 481 U.S. 393 (1987).

8

Competence for Execution:
The Supreme Court Speaks

On May 30, 1984, Alvin Ford's attorneys succeeded in obtaining a stay of execution from the U.S. Court of Appeals, Eleventh Circuit. The stay came just 14 hours before Ford's scheduled execution. It was granted on two grounds: on the question of whether the state could execute a person who appears to be mentally incompetent without first using procedures that might reliably determine his competency; and on questions pending in a similar case, then under review, that alleged racial discrimination in capital punishment.[1]

The state quickly appealed the stay order to the Supreme Court; on May 31 the Court refused to vacate the stay.[2] Three justices (Burger, Rehnquist, and O'Connor) voted to let the execution proceed immediately. In a short opinion, Justice Powell (joined by White, Blackmun, and Stevens) noted that the Court had never spoken to the issue of whether the Constitution allows the execution of the insane. However, since the issue of race discrimination had been decided in earlier cases by the Court, they felt the Eleventh Circuit abused its discretion in granting a stay based on the discrimination claim. The opinion, however, made it clear that the Court was interested in the competency issue. When the death warrant expired, the case was in the Eleventh Circuit in Atlanta.

It took the three-judge panel of the Eleventh Circuit 7 months to consider the arguments and render its decision. The victory was awarded to the state. On January 17, 1985, the three judges ruled, in a split vote, that the Florida procedures for determining competency to be executed were acceptable, thus upholding Judge Roettger's denial of Ford's appeal. The panel found that previous cases decided by the Supreme Court had made it clear that the exemption of the mentally ill from the death penalty was a function of the executive branch—not an Eighth Amendment right protected by due process standards. They said that if this precedent were not to be followed, "it must be done by the Supreme Court or at least by this court sitting "en banc" [as a whole]."[3]

In a six-page dissent, Judge Thomas Clark asserted that, in his view, there was indeed an Eighth Amendment right not to be executed while insane. What makes execution of mentally ill prisoners "cruel and unusual punishment," prohibited by the Eighth Amendment? He wrote that the execution of the insane "violates both contemporary standards of decency and the basic dignity of man," which are the criteria on which Eighth Amendment violations are judged.[4] And, said Judge Clark, in large part because Florida's provision gives the governor sole responsibility for determining who is or is not competent for execution, there is insufficient due process in protecting this right. "The Florida procedure is totally lacking in due process protections. There is no room for advocacy, no written findings, and no judicial review."[5]

Ford's attorneys, now acting not only for Ford but also for his mother Connie (since Ford was in their judgment mentally incompetent to consent to an appeal), took the case to the Supreme Court. They were cautiously optimistic about the chances of the Court voting to hear the case, in part because of the interest shown in the issue by several justices in their denial of the state's request to overturn the Eleventh Circuit's stay during the 1984 warrant.[6] The defense team presented the following question: Do the Eighth and Fourteenth Amendments permit the states to execute a person who appears to be mentally incompetent without having first determined his competency through a reliable and accurate fact-finding procedure? The question of whether a mentally ill death row inmate had any due process rights to a judicial determination of his sanity had not been considered by the Court since 1950,[7] when the Eighth Amendment had not yet been applied to the states.

The Court liked the question; on October 3, 1985, *certiorari* was granted.[8] The case was called *Ford v. Wainwright*. It was named after Louie Wainwright, who since 1962 had served as the controversial head of Florida's Department of Corrections. The first case using his name that gained national attention, *Gideon v. Wainwright*, was a 1963 ruling requiring states to provide attorneys to indigent defendants charged with felonies.[9]

Oral arguments were held in Washington on April 22, 1986. Representing Alvin and Connie Ford was Dick Burr; for the state was Joy Shearer. *Amicus* briefs urging reversal of the Eleventh Circuit's decision were filed by the American Psychiatric Association, the American Psychological Association, and the Capital Collateral Representative of Florida.

There was a variety of responses to the Supreme Court's acceptance of the case. Wrote John Harwood, the Washington correspondent for the *St. Petersburg Times*: "I must confess to some reservations about the idea that it is especially cruel to execute the insane. Perhaps I'm savage and inhumane, but it seems to me to be, if anything, somewhat *less* cruel than electrocuting a sane man who can grasp the horror of his fate."[10] Rev. Joe Ingle, the then-director of the Southern Coalition on Jails and Prisons who had befriended Ford in 1978, held a press conference and released a press kit that outlined the case against executing Ford. The charge was made that Governor Graham was using this and related death cases to improve his chances of being elected to the U.S. Senate. Ernest van den Haag, a strong supporter of capital punishment, at the time from Fordham University Law School, said that Ford did not have much of a chance with the Court on the question of constitutional protections for proving incompetence: "You can find psychiatrists to certify almost anything. An impending execution is certainly an anxiety-arousing event. It is not supposed to help you be comfortable." Van den Haag went on to offer the opinion that the Court should not have accepted the case and that it did so only to placate opponents of capital punishment.[11] George Smith of the conservative Washington Legal Foundation added that if Ford's appeal was successful, "it would provide a tremendous incentive" for other death row inmates to feign madness and escape the death penalty.[12] He was not alone in debating the issue of whether Ford was feigning his symptoms, although in reality the most crucial issues assumed madness; that is, the real questions dealt with how to identify and what to do with the category of mentally ill death row inmates, and whether their executions posed Eighth Amendment issues, without getting bogged down too much in the argument of whether Ford actually belonged in that category.

Vernon Bradford, the public relations secretary of the Florida Department of Corrections, added his thoughts. He emphasized that Ford had received more than 150 disciplinary reports while in prison. Bradford told the press that he felt that Ford was completely sane until the press started to show interest in his case. "I would talk to him and he would be just fine. Completely rational."[13] This statement only added fuel to the arguments by Ford's defenders that evaluations of Ford's mental status by prison or state employees were completely unreliable.

The Supreme Court Ruling

On June 26, 1986, the Supreme Court held that the Eighth Amendment prohibits the state from inflicting the death penalty upon a prisoner who is insane, and that Florida's statutory procedures for determining sanity failed to provide adequate protection for this right.[14] Because there had been no fact-finding procedures that could be described as a full and fair hearing, the Court ordered the case be remanded for a full evidentiary hearing in Federal District Court.

It was not a simple decision. Justice Marshall wrote for the majority, joined by Justices Brennan, Blackmun, Powell, and Stevens. To that extent, it was a 5-4 decision, although seven of the justices gave at least a partial victory to Ford. Four of the majority justices—

excluding Justice Powell—also thought that Florida's procedures for determining a condemned prisoner's sanity were insufficient. Justice Powell, writing only for himself on this point, agreed that the Florida procedures were insufficient, but tried to specify what would constitute adequate procedures for determining who on death row was insane. Justices O'Connor and White concurred in the result of the majority's opinion, but also dissented in part. They held that the Eighth Amendment did not prohibit the execution of the insane, but that "Florida . . . law has created a protected liberty interest in avoiding execution while incompetent."[15] Because Florida does not provide minimal due process to protect this liberty, the two justices would have returned the case to the Florida courts for further proceedings. Justice Rehnquist and Chief Justice Burger dissented, not because they believed that insane death row inmates should or could be executed, but because they felt that existing bans on the execution of the insane were sufficient to prevent it without enacting a constitutional ban.

The majority opinion began by declaring that the Eighth Amendment prohibits the execution of insane prisoners. This section essentially accepted the rationale of Judge Clark's dissent from the Eleventh Circuit's decision. The rationale for the exclusion is to prevent inmates from suffering without understanding why, and to protect the dignity of society from "the barbarity of exacting mindless vengeance."[16] In interpreting the Eighth Amendment's ban against cruel and unusual punishment, we are not bound "by the sparing humanitarian concessions of our forebears," but instead by "evolving standards of decency that mark the progress of a maturing society."[17] No more precise statement about exactly what was cruel and unusual about executing mentally ill prisoners was given.

The Court then said that there must be careful procedures that safeguard this constitutional right:

> [T]he ascertainment of a prisoner's sanity as a predicate to lawful execution calls for no less stringent standards than those demanded in any other aspect of a capital proceeding. Indeed, a particularly acute need for guarding against error inheres in a determination that "in the present state of the mental sciences is at best a hazardous guess however conscientious."[18]

It found that the procedures employed by the State of Florida in the *Ford* case did not live up to these requirements.

The Court called particular attention to the failure of the Florida process to include the prisoner in the truth-seeking. In his order establishing the examining commission, Governor Graham specifically directed that the attorneys should not participate in the examination in any adversarial manner. This was in keeping with his "publicly announced policy of excluding from the process all advocacy on the part of the condemned from the process of determining whether a person under a sentence of death is insane."[19]

Reference was also made to *Ake v. Oklahoma*,[20] the 1985 Supreme Court decision that underscored the importance of considering "differing psychiatric opinions when resolving contested issues of mental state."[21] Quoting *Ake*, the Court recognized that "because 'psychiatrists disagree widely and frequently on what constitutes mental illness [and] on the appropriate diagnosis to be attached to given behavior and symptoms,' the factfinder must resolve differences in opinion within the psychiatric profession 'on the basis of the evidence offered by each party' when a defendant's sanity is at issue in a criminal trial."[22] The absence of this process with Ford was of particular significance, given the fact that the psychiatric opinions that Ford's attorneys had attempted to submit on his behalf were based on a much more extensive evaluation than that carried out by the state-appointed commission.

The Court also found that "a related flaw in the Florida procedure was the denial of any opportunity to challenge or impeach the state-appointed psychiatrists' opinions,"[23] and thus to question the basis for the conclusions, the possibility of personal bias, the meaning of ambiguous words, and the like. In a footnote the Court called particular attention to the single group interview employed by the commission psychiatrists appointed by the governor in this case, finding that the "inconsistency and vagueness of the conclusions reached by the three examining psychiatrists in this case attest to the dubious value of such an examination."[24]

The majority found the placement of the decision wholly within the executive branch as "perhaps the most striking defect" of Florida's procedures for ensuring the insane would not be executed.

The governor, who may have already gone on record as believing the execution should proceed, appoints the commission to do the evaluation and then makes the final decision himself. Those responsible for every aspect of the case, from arrest through prosecution, also must answer to the governor, hence creating the possibility—even the likelihood—for conflict of interest. This is a situation not conducive to the kind of neutrality necessary for reliable fact-finding.

In returning the case to federal district court for a hearing, the Court declined to spell out the details of standards it would find acceptable to identify incompetent prisoners. The justices left that up to the states. This vagueness that leaves the issue open for further litigation. The opinion did require that an acceptable procedure (a) must provide redress for those with substantial claims[25] and must encourage accuracy in fact-finding, and (b) must permit unrestricted adversary presentation, and the selection and use of experts must be conducive to producing neutral, sound professional judgments. The Court did not speak directly to the American Psychological Association's request that a comprehensive psychological evaluation be included in all competency evaluations, but the Court did stress the need for more comprehensive evaluative techniques than were used with Ford.

Justice Powell disagreed with the extent of required due process guarantees that the majority opinion seemed to demand. His concurring opinion attempted to specify what kinds of procedures the states would need to implement before he would find them acceptable. He did not require a full "sanity trial," but only a hearing before an impartial officer or board in which various arguments and pieces of psychiatric evidence would be presented. Justice Powell also tried to define the insanity that would trigger an Eighth Amendment prohibition, a point the majority did not address. He took the position that the Eighth Amendment would forbid execution "only of those who are unaware of the punishment they are about to suffer and why they are to suffer it."[26]

In their opinion, Justices O'Connor and White concurred with some aspects of the majority's decision, including the judgment, but disagreed with other parts of it. They did not find an Eighth Amendment ban to the execution of the insane; they instead found the prohibition grounded in Florida law. However, one aspect of the Florida procedures for determining competency troubled them: It provided insufficient opportunity for the prisoner and his representatives to be heard. While not calling for an adversarial hearing or even cross-examination, they would want the decision maker to at least *consider* the prisoner's input.

Justice Rehnquist and Chief Justice Burger were not persuaded by these arguments. They pointed out that since no state permitted the execution of the insane, and no state was asking for the right to do so, the real issues in *Ford* related to the procedures used in determining competency. Neither Rehnquist nor Burger was bothered by vesting the decision in the executive branch of government. Instead, they were bothered by the prospect that "creating a constitutional right to a judicial determination of sanity . . . needlessly complicates and postpones" executions.[27]

The *Ford* decision was greeted with a negative reaction by many Florida politicians. The unhappiness of Florida Attorney General Jim Smith, a gubernatorial candidate at the time, was typical. When he had earlier announced his candidacy for governor, he urged his opponents to drop the "me too" rhetoric on the death penalty, characterizing it as a distracting and pointless debate. But as the campaign got under way, the lure of political gain led him to set aside this advice and he released television advertisements denouncing his major opponent as weak on capital punishment.

The *Ford* decision gave Smith an opportunity to try to score some points. A few days after the court decision he called a press conference and made a plea for Governor Graham to call a special session of the legislature to deal with the problem. Smith said that if the governor did not call such a session, "soon after my inauguration in January, they'll all be up here in a cold January dealing with some of these problems."[28] He went on to say that the state was in a crisis because executions could be halted by a flood of death row inmates claiming mental incapacity. Skeptics noted that the legislature was scheduled to meet within 4 months and that it was unlikely that the state would be trying to execute any insane inmates during the interim. In fact, in the 6½ years since the *Ford* decision, the legislature still has not revised the Florida statute that deals with competency to be executed.

The passage of time has shown that Smith's prophecy about a flood of incompetency claims has not come to fruition. There is no real incentive to raise frivolous claims, since the inmate will quickly have another warrant signed after the evaluation, and the filing of frivolous claims would simply make it more difficult to find receptive ears when a meritorious case arises. In the first 6 years after the *Ford* opinion, the question of competency to be executed was raised only twice in Florida, and in both instances the prisoner was executed.[29] Occasionally, other death row inmates are sent to mental institutions for treatment,[30] but they are moved after the prison uses its discretion, not because of any formal finding of incompetence.

Notes

1. That issue was ultimately resolved in *McCleskey v. Kemp,* 481 U.S. 279 (1987).

2. *Wainwright v. Ford,* 467 U.S. 1220 (1984).

3. *Ford v. Wainwright,* 752 F.2d 526 (1985). By "en banc" is meant the full court sitting with all its active judges, not in three-member panels.

4. *Ford v. Wainwright,* 752 F.2d 526 (1985), p. 531.

5. *Ford v. Wainwright,* 752 F.2d 526 (1985), p. 533.

6. *Wainwright v. Ford,* 467 U.S. 1220 (1984).

7. *Solesbee v. Balkcom,* 339 U.S. 9 (1950).

8. To "grant *certiorari*" means that the Supreme Court agreed to hear the case. Technically, it is an order from a higher court to a lower court, ordering the latter to certify and send the record of the case to the former. At least four votes are needed for the Supreme Court to "grant *cert*."

9. In subsequent years, Wainwright had survived charges of nepotism, brutality toward inmates, misappropriation of funds, and revelations that whole pages of his 1978 Master's thesis at Nova University had been plagiarized. *Tallahassee Democrat,* February 24, 1981, p. 1; United Press International, December 1, 1986.

10. *St. Petersburg Times,* April 20, 1986, p. 4D.

11. *Tampa Tribune,* April 20, 1986, p. 6A.

12. *Tampa Tribune,* April 20, 1986, p. 6A.

13. *Tampa Tribune,* April 20, 1986, p. 6A.

14. *Ford v. Wainwright,* 477 U.S. 399 (1986). A number of notes in law reviews commented on the decision; see Dick, 1987; Moore, 1987; Note, 1986; Small, 1988.

15. *Ford v. Wainwright,* 477 U.S. 399 (1986), p. 427.

16. *Ford v. Wainwright,* 477 U.S. 399 (1986), p. 410.

17. *Ford v. Wainwright,* 477 U.S. 399 (1986), p. 406.

18. *Ford v. Wainwright,* 477 U.S. 399 (1986), p. 411-412.

19. *Ford v. Wainwright,* 477 U.S. 399 (1986), p. 412-413, quoting *Goode v. Wainwright,* 448 So.2d 999 (1984), p. 1001.

20. *Ake v. Oklahoma,* 470 U.S. 68 (1985).

21. *Ford v. Wainwright,* 477 U.S. 399 (1986), p. 414.

22. *Ford v. Wainwright,* 477 U.S. 399 (1986), p. 414.

23. *Ford v. Wainwright,* 477 U.S. 399 (1986), p. 415.

24. *Ford v. Wainwright,* 477 U.S. 399 (1986), p. 415.

25. In at least two post-*Ford* cases, hearings on competence for execution were denied because the prisoner failed to make a substantial threshold showing of incompetency. *Lowenfield v. Butler,* 843 F.2d 183, *cert. denied,* 109 S.Ct. 546 (1988); *Johnson v. Cabana,* 818 F.2d 333, *cert. denied,* 481 U.S. 1061 (1987).

26. *Ford v. Wainwright,* 477 U.S. 399 (1986), p. 422.

27. *Ford v. Wainwright,* 477 U.S. 399 (1986), p. 435.

28. *Tallahassee Democrat,* July 3, 1986, p. 6B.

29. The cases involved Nollie Lee Martin (evaluated November 13, 1986) and Aubrey Dennis Adams (evaluated March 1, 1986). Adams was executed on May 4, 1989, and Martin was executed on May 12, 1992. Between June 1986 (when the *Ford* decision was issued) and December 31, 1992, there were 278 death warrants signed by three governors in Florida.

30. Examples include William Cruse, who was sent from death row to a mental institution on February 20, 1990 (*Gainesville Sun,* April 29, 1990, p. 3B), and Carlos Bello, who was among the mental patients in Cuba sent to Florida during the Mariel boat lift. Bello was sentenced to death in 1987. In 1988 he was moved from death row to a psychiatric hospital. *St. Petersburg Times,* March 24, 1990, p. 3B. Charles Pridgen was sentenced to death for a 1984 murder, despite another man's confessing to it. The Florida Supreme Court ruled that Pridgen should have been found incompetent for sentencing, so that court vacated the death sentence (*Pridgen v. State,* 531 So.2d 951 (1988)). While confined to a mental hospital awaiting resentencing, Pridgen committed suicide.

9

Back to Federal Court:
The 1988 Hearing and Beyond

Acting on the U.S. Supreme Court mandate in *Ford*, on November 13, 1986, the Florida Supreme Court adopted emergency rules for dealing with death row inmates thought to be mentally incompetent.[1] At the request of the state supreme court, amendments to the Florida Rules of Criminal Procedures were proposed by the Florida Bar Criminal Rules Committee. On May 1, 1987, the Florida Supreme Court invited comment on these proposed amendments;[2] on December 31, 1987, the rules were made permanent.[3] These rule changes made action by the Florida legislature unnecessary, so the Florida statute dealing with mentally incompetent death row prisoners was never changed in the wake of the *Ford* decision.

Like the Florida legislature, mental health experts were not involved in the procedural revisions necessitated by the *Ford* decision. No input from those professions was sought. Hence, issues such as how to define and evaluate competency for execution (and, indeed, how not to) were not debated, and no professional standards were developed. The assumption was that psychiatrists and other mental health practitioners could be found who would do exactly what the courts and lawyers wanted them to do.

The new rules slightly modified Florida's definition of incompetency, but the definition remains extremely narrow: The prisoner must lack "the mental capacity to understand the fact of the impending execution and the reason for it." As was true before the *Ford* decision, the governor is required to evaluate claims. Only if the governor rejects a claim *and* signs a death warrant can the prisoner litigate. The rules specify that a prisoner's objections to a governor's decision on competency are to be heard in the circuit where the prisoner is to be executed, or by another judge assigned by the Chief Justice of the Florida Supreme Court. Both the defendant and the state can submit to the court any materials that they believe are relevant. The judge then has the discretion to decide whether an evidentiary hearing on the claim should be held. If the judge's decision is unfavorable, the defendant has the right to appeal to higher courts.

The Supreme Court's ruling in *Ford* occurred in June 1986; it concluded that Ford was "entitled to an evidentiary hearing in the District Court."[4] The mandated rehearing took place in federal district court in Ft. Lauderdale on June 20 and July 5, 1988. This was 14 years after the murder, 4 years after Ford's first formal competency evaluation, and 2 years after the *Ford* decision. Throughout the 2-day hearing, Ford sat silently at the defense table, not showing any reaction to the detailed discussions of his mental status and behavior.

Ford was once again in the courtroom of U.S. District Judge Norman Roettger, who was not especially enthusiastic about hearing anew from the mental health professionals. As he said from the bench to one expert witness:

[A] day-and-a-half of testimony of a psychiatrist or psychologist has a—no offense, sir—anesthetic effect and I kind of need to wake up and get alert again every so often. I can remember days on the farm bucking bales of hay or shoveling wheat were easier days than trying to stay alert with eight or nine hours of psychiatric testimony or psychological testing.[5]

At another point he expressed a preference for hearing from psychologists rather than from psychiatrists. Upon learning that a proposed expert witness was a psychologist, he brightened up and said:

That's promising. They don't take so long. More objective on less—You know, I have just found that over the years, don't get all that many of them, but I notice that it's true again today, and trouble with psychiatrists, there is no such thing as less than a day of testimony.[6]

Before the hearing, Judge Roettger had appointed a commission of three mental health experts to evaluate Ford's competency for execution. The trio had independently examined Ford within a 10-day period in April. Both the defense and the state had been asked to suggest names of experts who could serve. The commission was composed of David Rothenberg, Ph.D., a clinical psychologist (board certified in forensic psychology), and two psychiatrists, Dennis F. Koson and James A. Jordan.

The position of the defense was that Ford suffered from schizophrenia, a disorder that frequently (and in Ford's case) moved in and out of remission. With proper medication or at unpredictable times, the symptoms were less severe. Hence, they contended, whether Ford was competent for execution varied with time and treatment.

Dr. Rothenberg found clear signs of psychosis, including a loosening of associations (an inability to stick to one topic) and "word salad" (incoherent speech). During his interview Ford began working at assigned tasks, but gradually drifted off and become absorbed in internal thought processes. For example, Ford began the "Sentence Completion Test" with appropriate responses, but by the end of the test he was simply making random marks on the paper. "There was no question in my mind that he was reflecting an underlying psychotic process."[7] More specifically, Dr. Rothenberg concluded that Ford was suffering from paranoid schizophrenia, with symptoms that varied through time in intensity. On the day he visited the prison, Dr. Rothenberg found that Ford was doing well and, under the state's conservative criteria, was technically competent to be executed. But he hastened to add that the course of the illness was unpredictable: "Sometimes he does well and most of the time he does very poorly."[8] So, he believed that on most days Ford would be incompetent for execution.

Dr. Koson was the next to testify. The following exchange between Dr. Koson and Ford's attorney tells us a little about some of Ford's symptoms:

Q: Did you ask him questions related to the competency inquiry that Judge Roettger asked you to?

A: Yes, I did.

Q: How did he respond to those questions?

A: Usually unintelligibly and irrationally.

Q: By unintelligibly, what do you mean?

A: I couldn't even discern often what he was saying. He was using some kind of idiosyncratic code or speech. Sometimes I didn't even understand it, and I couldn't get it clarified. Other times his answer would be irrational or tangential.

If I asked about the circumstances surrounding his commitment to prison, trial, the death sentence, he would speak in metaphors or riddles and give answers that were illogical and not related to what I asked.

Q: Was there any time during your interview when you asked Mr. Ford a question and he responded with what you thought was an appropriate answer?

A: Well, there were bits and pieces here and there. If I asked about previous treatment by doctors or psychiatrists he would in a roundabout symbolic abstract way talk about people from his past who were doctors, but then go on to say that he too was a psychologist and be off and running in a sense. So there were kernels of responsiveness in some of his answers, but they were short-lived and not helpful.

If I asked about the trial, he remembered certain things, at least in a symbolic or metaphorical way. He was angry at the prosecutor, had a lot of anger and homicidal thoughts about participants in the trial who he still perceived to be on the other side appropriately. But I couldn't get him to say anything material about them and about the circumstances of the trial.

Q: What about very simple questions like did he remember your name, did he know the time of day, did he know what day it was, did you ask him questions like that?

A: I did, but it was in a period of time when I was getting back just unintelligible answers and illogical answers. He wouldn't even agree that he was Alvin Ford.

Q: Was not?

A: No. Asked him his name and he always spoke of Mr. Ford in the third person. So I couldn't possibly assess those areas of functioning for orientation because of the unreliability of his answers.

Q: From your clinical interview, was there any other relevant data that you gathered that we have not touched on?

A: I think in questioning him further about his death sentence and what it means, yes, he understood the death sentence. His speech and his answers were relevant from time to time, suggesting to me that he had an extensive delusional system or a system of fixed false beliefs that could change over time that centered around himself as a kind of either a victim or a kind of all-powerful conqueror. He used many metaphors, i.e., he electrocuted guards at the prison and he made the chair, he owned the chair, it was his, he would electrocute anybody who got in the way, including myself, should I testify against him. There were many metaphors like that through his speech that suggested he was extremely grandiose, like the kind of person who thinks they are Jesus Christ. He believed that he was all-powerful and had in essence turned the tables on the State.[9]

Dr. Koson also testified about medical records from the prison that showed that at least some of the medical staff agreed that Ford was seriously disturbed, if not psychotic. In fact, Ford's mental problems had necessitated his transfer to the prison's medical ward three times in 1987 and 1988, for a total of 6 months. Like Dr. Rothenberg, Dr. Koson concluded that Ford was schizophrenic. In addition, Dr. Koson also thought that on the day of his interview with Ford (the day before Dr. Rothenberg's interview), Ford was incompetent for execution.

The third member of the commission was Dr. James Jordan, who characterized his work in forensic psychiatry as a minor part of his practice. Unlike the other two experts, whose names had been suggested by the defense, Dr. Jordan had been selected by Judge Roettger from a list of names suggested by the state. He concluded that Ford was malingering.

Dr. Jordan testified that during the initial part of his interview, Ford was controlling and uncooperative, often referring the physician to "the record" to find answers to questions being posed. Ford said that he was a storehouse of information but that he would not give it to Dr. Jordan unless paid for it.

The disoriented, tangential quality of Ford's thinking during the interview is illustrated at a number of points in Dr. Jordan's testimony. The following extracts are typical:

He then went on to state that he was a black professor and he bets I never met a black professor before. And I asked him where he obtained his degree and [he] said "this planet." I asked him what special area he was in. He said he can teach anything. I asked him what he meant by "this planet" and he said that "I have been to college, every college."[10]

Then he moved away from this to go into sort of another rambling account, that he was going to Smith and Wesson, Colt and Remington weapons school, and he also said "I had to go to robbery schools," studied how to make guns and bullets. Said he was a manager at a department in Sears at one time, and then he mentioned Independent Life Insurance.[11]

At times he would be mumbling and it would be difficult to understand what he was saying. He would make other statements such as "But this time Alvin don't want to be on the planet. He don't want anybody to know he's on the planet."[12]

I asked him about the chains on his body. He said "I have been making these to sell to the Smith and Wesson." I asked him if he has any other names for any other planets. He replied "I just go from planet to planet. I'm a Jedi."[13]

He also said that the police officer had suffered a heart attack. I might add this came out without my questioning about this incident. He went on to add that some people "say I shot him." He says however that he shot the police officer with a "blank gun." He said that he used a blank gun "because I have to do indoor track and field." He stated that he ran all events.[14]

Thus, Dr. Jordan observed symptoms and behavior similar to those noted by the other examiners. Nonetheless, he came to a radically different conclusion: "I feel that Mr. Ford knows very well what he is doing. I feel that his symptoms are contrived, deliberate and conscious. I do feel that he has been malingering in this fashion so as to avoid his sentence of execution. I feel that he does understand that he is facing execution and I feel that he knows why he faces execution."[15]

Unlike the provisions under which Ford was first evaluated for competency in 1984, in the 1988 hearing the defense and state were permitted to bolster their positions with testimony from individuals who were not members of the appointed evaluating commission. Because the commission members did not disagree about the presence of behavior consistent with psychosis—their disagreement concerned whether Ford's behavior was a product of mental illness or malingering—Ford's attorneys recognized the need to solicit the opinions of authorities with expertise in the issue of malingering (Judge Roettger decided to allow each side to call only one noncommission expert, but he did not restrict the number of lay witnesses). For their expert, the defense retained J. Randall Price, Ph.D., a psychologist from Dallas and a specialist in the detection of malingering.

Dr. Price had interviewed Ford and administered some psychological tests to him. On this basis, like Drs. Rothenberg and Koson, Dr. Price concluded that Ford was not malingering.[16] He gave particular attention to the pattern of symptoms and the fact that they came and went, pointing out that people who are consciously attempting to fake their symptoms tend to persist in expanding the severity and frequency of symptoms. Dr. Price was not asked to address the question of competency for execution.[17]

The defense also presented testimony from Gail Rowland, the staff member from the Florida Clearinghouse on Criminal Justice who had first met Ford in 1981 while volunteering to assist with his defense. As a paralegal her job was to gather background information, carry papers to Ford, meet his family and keep them informed, and generally help the attorneys get a picture of Ford as a person. In this role she had spent more time with Ford than any other person outside the prison, developing a friendship which made Ford, in her words, "almost like he was a part of my family."

Rowland testified that in her first meetings with Ford he impressed her as being alert, articulate, and easy to talk with. In the first few weeks of his death warrant in November 1981, she saw no significant mental health problems. But that changed quickly. In a December 4 visit, she found Ford to be frantic and upset; that turned out to be the beginning of his decline into psychosis (or at least when outside observers began to notice it). After the 1981 death warrant was stayed, Ford's correspondence became more and more bizarre, incoherent, and delusional. For example, occasionally he sent letters of 20 to 30 pages that consisted of words and definitions copied from a dictionary, with certain words underlined in a nonsensical, code-like fashion. A year after the warrant he had fixed delusions that Rowland was being held in the pipe alley behind his cell, keeping him awake all night by playing the piano. He came to blame her for natural disasters occurring around the world and for tormenting his family. On one visit he asked to see Rowland's shoe, took it, and started talking into it as if he were making a radio transmission.

Rowland told the court that Ford had always kept an immaculate physical appearance. But when he came out of his cell for a visit in December 1983, she was shocked by his deterioration. He had lost a substantial amount of weight, his skin looked bad, he was disheveled, his hair was not combed, and his body odor was noticeable.[18] In a subsequent contact he made no sense at all, and mumbled and shouted incoherently.[19] Thus Rowland, who had more contact with Ford over a longer period of time than any of the other witnesses, was able to provide an historical overview of Ford's psychosis. She was convinced that he was not faking it.

The three witnesses the state called to support its position that Ford was malingering were employees of Florida State Prison—a "registered professional nurse specialist"; a correctional officer, who had not had contact with Ford in 4 years; and Robert Miller, a mental health specialist with a Master's degree in psychology. The nurse and the correctional officer told the court that they had heard Ford express fear of the electric chair, that he had been heard conversing normally with other inmates at times when he was not aware that he was being observed, and that they had found most of Ford's behavior to be normal.

Miller testified that Ford's behavior was inconsistent. Prison staff viewed Ford as malingering until 1987, but then changed their view and admitted him to the inpatient mental health ward at Florida State Prison three times within the 9 months preceding the Ft. Lauderdale hearing. Each time, Ford acted in a bizarre fashion upon admission, and then improved dramatically after medication. Ford had been housed in this ward for the 2 months preceding the Ft. Lauderdale hearing. Miller testified that he had once asked Ford "Why are you here?" Ford replied "I'm here because I killed somebody. They want to hurt me. They want to put me in the electric chair." Because this indicated that Ford understood that he was facing execution, Miller concluded that the prisoner was malingering.

Under cross-examination, Miller admitted that in the fall of 1987 two prison psychiatrists had diagnosed Ford as schizophrenic.[20] Ford's attorney attacked the "malingering" conclusion by trying to get Miller to admit that, in a deposition given 10 days previously, he had said he thought Ford was psychotic. At first Miller stated that as a Master's-level psychologist he did not have the authority to render a diagnosis, a position the state supported. But he conceded that indeed he had given Ford a diagnosis of schizophreniform disorder.[21]

With that, the hearing ended. The state's position was that Ford was malingering. Its back-up position was that even if Judge Roettger found Ford mentally ill to some degree, there was still sufficient evidence that he was competent to be executed, because he knew that he was on death row for the murder of a police officer. Psychosis, they stressed, is not the same as incompetence.

The defense's argument can be summarized in six points:

1. It was highly unlikely, if not impossible, for anyone to falsely present the consistent clinical picture seen in Ford, over a 7-year period, to such a wide range of audiences (prison staff, friends, family, lawyers, examining commissioners, privately engaged mental health professionals, and other inmates). The quality and consistency of Ford's symptoms argued for their authenticity.

2. The symptoms persisted in the presence of friends and family members, such as his mother, with whom he was close and who had stopped visiting because of Ford's unpredictable behavior and language. Mail, highly valued by most prisoners, was often refused.

3. Ford's condition did not vary in a predictable manner with changing external circumstances (e.g., a stay of execution did not result in a lessening of symptoms).

4. Ford's occasional departures from a consistent psychotic state—times when Ford was relatively rational and the disorder was apparently in remission (usually in response to medication)—were inconsistent with a judgment of malingering. Most malingerers

are not sophisticated enough to know that periods of remission are common.

5. Seven of the nine psychiatrists and psychologists from outside the prison who examined Ford between 1984 and 1988 found him to be psychotic or seriously disturbed. Only Dr. Jordan and one of the three psychiatrists who participated in the 25-minute 1984 evaluation had concluded that Ford was malingering.

6. The medical records from the prison showed that even the prison's mental health staff thought Ford was seriously disturbed.

The Ruling

On February 15, 1989, 7 months after the hearing, Judge Roettger issued his eight-page decision. He concluded that Ford was malingering and not mentally ill, and that he was competent for execution. Judge Roettger again made it clear that he believed Ford should be executed promptly. Further, he blamed the disagreements among those who had evaluated Ford on the "subtleties and nuances" of the mental health professions, not on any ambiguity in the definition of competency or in the standards for expert evaluations:

> The Court notes that upwards of a dozen doctors have examined [Ford] over the years since [his] symptoms first occurred. These opinions cover the spectrum, and illustrate that the question of the petitioner's sanity calls for a basically subjective judgment. The variety of opinions also demonstrates that the fields of psychiatry and psychology are disciplines fraught with subtleties and nuances.[22]

This conclusion exaggerates how much the opinions on Ford's competence "cover the spectrum," as the vast majority of experts had concluded that Ford was psychotic. Nevertheless, Judge Roettger also accepted the state's argument that even if Ford had in fact suffered from mental illness in the past, he no longer did so.

Ford was again miserable. On June 18, 1989, 4 months after Judge Roettger's ruling, he sent the following letter:

S-2-South

Governor Martinez:

Please sign my death warrant, I'm dropping all my appeals.
Thank you.

(Signed) Alvin B. Ford
P.S. Please contact my lawyer Larry Wollan FSU.

There are no indications that either the governor's office or the prosecutors handling the case took the letter seriously.

In December 1989 the defense formally appealed Judge Roettger's decision to the Eleventh Circuit Court of Appeals in Atlanta. Two questions were raised: (a) whether the District Court's finding that Ford had no mental illness and was "malingering" was clearly erroneous; and (b) whether a condemned person who suffered from schizophrenia and whose illness frequently, but intermittently, caused him to be incompetent was competent to be executed.[23]

It would not be easy for the defense to convince the appellate court to overturn Judge Roettger's rulings. The defense acknowledged that they had to move beyond showing that the evidence *could* have supported a finding of schizophrenia—appellate courts had previously ruled that where there are two permissible views of the evidence, the fact-finder's (district court judge's) choice cannot be overturned unless it is "clearly erroneous."[24] The question for the appellate court was not "is he" or "is he not" mentally ill. Judge Roettger's finding that Ford suffered from no mental illness and was malingering had to be shown to be *implausible* in light of the totality of the evidence.

The defense argued that Ford had exhibited the classic symptoms of schizophrenia over a long period of time. Like most other victims of schizophrenia, Ford experienced some periods when his illness was in remission, rendering him competent to be executed. The defense repeatedly stressed that three of the four experts who testified in Ft. Lauderdale agreed with the conclusion that Ford suffered from schizophrenia. Ford's symptoms improved when he was given even small doses of antipsychotic medication (Navane and Haldol); again, a pattern seen in many other schizophrenic patients. Psychological tests confirmed that he suffered from schizophrenia and that he was not malingering. Yet Judge Roettger had rejected all of this evidence on the basis of one expert's opinion. Ford's attorneys argued that when a person exhibits an intermittent psychosis, and the periods of competency cannot be predicted, he should be judged incompetent.[25]

In deciding that Ford was competent to be executed, Judge Roettger had stated that he found the testimony of Dr. Jordan to be the most credible. Consequently, Ford's brief alleged that Jordan's testimony contained several essential flaws. For example, Jordan and the other experts had testified that if Ford were malingering, the antipsychotic drugs would have had no effect on him. However, medical records from the prison clearly showed that Ford improved with drugs—no mention was made of this in Judge Roettger's decision. Jordan concluded that Ford could not be delusional because he was following his appeals—Ford had often mentioned the "landmark" case of *Ford v. State*. But when the defense pointed out that there had never been any such landmark case, Jordan admitted that this supported a finding of delusional thinking, not the contrary. Another reason why Jordan concluded that Ford's symptoms were inconsistent with the typical picture of schizophrenia was that Ford's thinking could be interrupted and redirected. To rebut this, Burr quoted other witnesses and authorities who took the position that such behavior was not inconsistent with a diagnosis of schizophrenia.

Thus, Burr argued that Dr. Jordan, and ultimately Judge Roettger, had derived patently inaccurate conclusions: "There is no single piece of data which suggests a deviation from the expected course and symptomatology of schizophrenia and there is no currently accepted psychiatric or psychological measure of schizophrenia which suggests any reason to doubt that Mr. Ford has schizophrenia."[26]

The state's brief took the position that Judge Roettger's findings were not implausible and that Ford was indeed malingering. Their brief went through several symptoms of psychosis listed in the defense brief (e.g., delusional thinking, blunted affect) and pointed to evidence that would cast doubt on the existence or intensity of the symptoms. It argued that Ford had repeatedly made comments that showed he was aware that he was on death row for the murder of a police officer, and that he was there because he was going to be executed.

The state made no attempt to respond systematically to the points raised by Ford's attorneys; at 22 pages, their brief was much shorter than the defense's 55-page product. The brief concluded with a blanket wrap-up statement: "In coursing through the abundant evidence before this Court, it is easy to pick out a statement here or a word there that may be challenged or questioned. That is not the test. Ford must demonstrate that Judge Roettger's conclusions were totally implausible."[27] It also reiterated the state's back-up position: "Even if this Court were to find that Ford is mentally ill to 'some degree,' there is still sufficient evidence he is competent to be executed."[28]

A three-judge panel of the Eleventh Circuit's U.S. Court of Appeals heard oral arguments on these issues on September 18, 1990. One judge asked the assistant attorney general what would happen if Ford continued to cycle in and out of a psychotic state. She replied that the defense could always ask for another commission to be appointed for a new evaluation, but she acknowledged that at some point the state would ask the court to decide when "enough is enough."

The panel asked several questions about the role of medication in maintaining Ford's competency. They made reference to a case, then before the U.S. Supreme Court, in which the main question was whether a prisoner could be executed if the only way to maintain his mental competence was through the involuntary administration of antipsychotic medication.[29]

Ford's Death

Before the Eleventh Circuit could rule on these questions, Alvin Ford was dead. On the morning of February 26, 1991, Ford's response was quite weak when the prison runner arrived at his cell with milk for the morning's breakfast. A few minutes later, when the runner appeared again with the full breakfast tray, Ford was totally unresponsive. The wing sergeant was called to the cell and spent the next several minutes yelling at Ford and otherwise trying to rouse him from outside the cell. About 10 minutes later, a medical technician arrived. Perhaps because the medical staff at the prison had labeled Ford as a malingerer for so many years, their reaction indicates they did not immediately see the problem as a medical emergency.

It took 30 minutes to obtain a stretcher and transport Ford to the prison's medical clinic, and an additional 90 minutes before an ambulance was called. The ambulance technicians quickly realized the seriousness of the symptoms (his blood sugar level was astronomical), and made arrangements to transport Ford to the University of Florida's Shands Teaching Hospital in Gainesville, some 40 miles away. The helicopter that usually made such calls was down for service, so ground transportation was used. En route, the ambulance stopped at the small Bradford County Hospital in Starke to pick up a second paramedic and to have a physician come to the ambulance and perform a quick examination.

Two days later, on February 28, Ford died at Shands Hospital, barely a mile from the spot where he had been taken into custody in 1974. The autopsy report listed "acute respiratory distress syndrome associated with fulminant acute pancreatitis" as the cause of death. What caused these problems remains unknown. To our knowledge, no in-depth studies of brain tissue were conducted, so it is unknown if any of Ford's behavior was caused by neurological impairment.

Ford's mother, Connie, was not informed of her son's hospitalization until she learned of his death. She was in her car, not far from her Palmetto home, when a police officer friend (one of her former Sunday School pupils) named Gary Lowe stopped her. He told her that the police department had been notified that Ford "passed today," and that a note had been left at the front door of her home.

Mrs. Ford called the chaplain at Florida State Prison to get the details. He addressed her as "Carol Brown," a source of some confusion for Mrs. Ford. But he was not able to offer an explanation for the failure to contact her earlier, or for the confusion regarding her name—he just said that "Carol Brown" was the name given to him by prison officials.

Before the murder of Officer Ilyankoff, Alvin Ford was a prison guard and had no record of violent criminality. The murder had not been especially heinous or premeditated—Ford had panicked during a botched robbery attempt. His years in prison were marked by misery and madness. Judge J. Cail Lee, who presided over Ford's 1974 trial, commented: "This man survived for 15 or 16 years, and he died of natural causes. That's wrong. He should have been executed a long, long, long time ago. He richly deserved it."[30]

Officer Ilyankoff's widow, Maryanne, refused to comment on Ford's death.[31] When invited to share her thoughts with us for this book in 1992, she politely declined through her attorney, who wrote, "[S]he remains firm in her position that the sentence for Mr. Ford should have been carried out as set forth by the Court."

A week after Ford's death, Susan Cary, one of the attorneys on Ford's defense team, delivered a box to Mrs. Ford containing all of Ford's possessions. There wasn't much: a pair of rubber thongs, a Bible, combs, two towels, a few letters and legal papers, a jar of peanut butter, and a jar of grape jelly.

On Saturday, March 9, an afternoon service was held in the Ford family's church, the Turner Chapel A.M.E. Church in Palmetto. Connie Ford participated by offering prayers and a tribute to her son, something for which she had been preparing herself for years. The church was crowded with mourners who continued to puzzle over how Alvin Ford's life had taken the course that it did. Dick Burr came from New York, Larry Wollan and Kent Miller drove down from Tallahassee, and Susan Cary came from Gainesville. Other friends came from as far away as Ohio. High school classmates served as pallbearers and flower attendants. Interment was at the Skyway Memorial Gardens in Palmetto.

It was at this point that the defense team learned, for the first time, that Ford had fathered a child, Carolyn, before entering prison. In fact, by that time Carolyn had borne a son and daughter, so Ford was a grandfather.

Because of Ford's death there will not be a ruling from the Eleventh Circuit Court of Appeals. Nonetheless, the story of the issues raised in Alvin Ford's case is not over yet.

Notes

1. *In re Emergency Amendment to Florida Rules of Criminal Procedure (Rule 3.811, Competency to be Executed),* 497 So.2d 643 (1986); see also *The Florida Bar News,* December 1, 1986.
2. *The Florida Bar News,* May 1, 1987, p. 2.
3. *In re Amendments to the Florida Rules of Criminal Procedure,* 518 So.2d 256 (1987). See also *Florida Rules of Court, 1991,* Rules 3.811 and 3.812.
4. *Ford v. Wainwright,* 477 U.S. 399 (1986), p. 418.
5. Transcript of hearing in *Ford v. Dugger,* U.S. District Court, Southern District of Florida, Case No. 84-6493-CIV-NCR (1988) (hereinafter 1988 Transcript), p. 336.
6. 1988 Transcript, pp. 244-245.
7. 1988 Transcript, p. 16.
8. 1988 Transcript, p. 23.
9. 1988 Transcript, pp. 54-56.
10. 1988 Transcript, p. 167.
11. 1988 Transcript, pp. 168-169.
12. 1988 Transcript, p. 173.
13. 1988 Transcript, pp. 176-177.
14. 1988 Transcript, p. 178.
15. 1988 Transcript, p. 199.
16. 1988 Transcript, p. 335.
17. 1988 Transcript, p. 335.
18. 1988 Transcript, p. 150.
19. 1988 Transcript, p. 152.
20. 1988 Transcript, p. 425.
21. A schizophreniform disorder is identical to schizophrenia, with the exception that its duration is less than 6 months. American Psychiatric Association, 1987, p. 207.
22. *Ford v. Dugger,* U.S. District Court, Southern District of Florida, No. 84-6493-CIV-Roettger (February 15, 1989), p. 6.
23. Brief for Petitioners-Appellants, *Ford v. Dugger,* U.S. Court of Appeals for the Eleventh Circuit, No. 89-5268 (December 15, 1989), p. 1.
24. Brief for Petitioner, 1989, p. 5.
25. *Bruce v. Estelle,* 536 F.2d 1051 (1976).
26. Brief for Petitioners, 1989, p. 49.
27. Brief for Appellee, *Ford v. Dugger,* U.S. Court of Appeals for the Eleventh Circuit, No. 89-5268 (dated February 16, 1990), p. 19.
28. Brief for Appellee, 1990, p. 20.
29. *Perry v. Louisiana,* 111 S.Ct. 449 (1990).
30. *Sarasota Herald-Tribune,* March 9, 1991, p. 10B. A contrasting view has been attributed to Winston Churchill: "The mood and temper of the public with regard to the treatment of crime and criminals is one of the most unfailing tests of the civilization of any country."
31. *Sarasota Herald-Tribune,* March 9, 1991, p. 10B.

10

The Cure That Kills

We now turn our attention to a critical question that never had a chance to be raised in the *Ford* case: What happens when a death row inmate is actually found mentally incompetent for execution? The answer is that the criminal justice system again requests assistance from medical and mental health professionals. Clinicians are asked by the state to develop and furnish a treatment aimed solely at allowing the prisoner to be killed.[1]

When mental health professionals get involved in treating mentally incompetent death row inmates, the ethical problems encountered in rendering evaluations of competency to be executed, discussed in Chapter 6, are further compounded. Effective health care results not in well-being, but in death. If Ford had been found incompetent to be executed, he would have been transferred to a treatment facility where the goal would have been to restore his mental competency. If that medical care had been successful, he would have been returned to prison and executed.

Gary Alvord: Treating the Incompetent[2]

Since the advent of the modern era of capital punishment in 1972, only one death row inmate in the United States (through 1992) has been formally found to be incompetent for execution and sent to a mental hospital so his competence for execution could be restored.[3] Coincidentally, like Alvin Ford, the prisoner came from Florida. His name is Gary Alvord, a man who escaped from a Michigan mental hospital in 1973, headed south, and—on June 17, 1973—strangled three Tampa women to death. The victims were a grandmother, her daughter, and her 18-year old granddaughter (whom Alvord had also raped). Alvord was found competent to stand trial and convicted. On April 9, 1974—just 3 months before Alvin Ford shot Officer Ilyankoff at the Red Lobster in Ft. Lauderdale—he was condemned to death.

A Jacksonville attorney, William Sheppard, volunteered to handle the defense. In 1984, after a series of appeals—during which Alvord struggled with mental illness and inadequate treatment in prison—his second death warrant was signed. The execution was scheduled for Thursday morning, November 29, 1984. It was just 6 months after Alvin Ford's execution had been stayed because of the competency questions.

As in the *Ford* case, Sheppard raised questions about Alvord's competency. The governor appointed a commission of three psychiatrists, who saw Alvord 48 hours before the scheduled execution. This time, however, in a report dictated in the prison's parking lot, the psychiatrists decided that Alvord was indeed incompetent for execution. The report was quite brief and offered only a conclusion; exactly how the psychiatrists arrived at their judgment was never explained. Nonetheless, within a matter of hours Governor Graham accepted the report and ordered Alvord's transfer to the Florida State Mental Hospital in Chattahoochee. These events demonstrated that it was the psychiatrists, not the governor, who (for all practical purposes) made the determinations of competency; the governor neither sought nor received any other input, and he accepted the physicians' judgment without question or hesitation.

Coincidentally, on the same day that the governor halted Alvord's execution, 26 of the top religious leaders in Florida released a "Letter to Christians," in which they denounced the death penalty as immoral and called for its abolition. Included among the signatories were the leaders of the Catholic, Lutheran, Presbyterian, Episcopal, and Methodist churches of Florida, as well as the leaders of several other denominations.[4]

The announcement that Alvord would be transferred to Florida State Hospital in Chattahoochee sparked immediate controversy among the hospital's staff. Treating a death row inmate presented no special problems; it was treating him so he could be executed that caused the strife. The hospital's Human Rights Advocacy Committee issued a statement saying that the presence of a patient under these conditions "would negatively impact upon the morale of both the patients and the staff of the unit." The committee expressed support for staff members who might refuse to participate in any treatment of Alvord aimed ultimately at his execution, not his well-being, and called for Florida law to be changed so that a commutation to life imprisonment would be required when death row inmates are found incompetent for execution (and before being sent for treatment). In spite of this outcry, Alvord arrived in Chattahoochee on December 10, 1984. Later interviews with staff members revealed that nobody was quite sure what to do.[5]

Alvord's presence at the hospital created what has been called "ethical chaos with only one solution."[6] That solution is to commute the death sentence to life imprisonment before beginning treatment. Maryland has adopted a statute that does just that,[7] although—in part because mental health professionals have not been vocal in demanding change—other states have not followed its lead. Unfortunately, in Florida and elsewhere, the question faced by individual therapists remains; death row inmates can still be delivered to mental hospitals with the demand that they be treated and made competent for execution.

What, then, were the health professionals at Chattahoochee to do? They were trained in the helping and healing professions, and they were employed in a state with widespread unmet demands for their skills. If nothing else, executing the product of successful treatment would seem to be a massive waste of professional skills. More practically, they would lose the trust of their other patients, who would perceive that their therapists were getting into the business of preparing fellow patients for the executioner. Broadly speaking, the professional staff had essentially three options:[8]

1. Treat, but only when the condemned prisoner wants to be treated.

2. Treat mental illness whenever possible, since psychosis is a painful state and the primary goal of treatment is to relieve suffering.

3. Do not get involved. The temporary relief of suffering through treatment is not justified because, if successful, the inmate will experience even greater suffering when he again faces the executioner. "Any therapy not grounded in the patient's welfare is inherently dishonest."[9]

The first option can be rejected, because in practice those prisoners who are found incompetent for execution would not be able to give an informed consent to treatment. As we have seen, the definition of incompetence for execution is so narrow that only the most seriously disturbed prisoners can meet it. Their interests would have to be pursued by a third party.[10] Further, it is doubtful that the governor's office would appreciate it if the clinicians looked to the prisoner's defense attorney for direction. Therefore, we are left with the treat/don't treat dilemma.

While there can be no blanket rules about what to do when mentally incompetent death row inmates arrive at hospitals for treatment, there is some middle ground between the polar positions. In part, this is because "treatment" can come in many forms, not all of which directly address the issue of competence for execution. A recent paper that grappled with these issues concluded the following: It is unethical to treat an unwilling inmate; treatment is permissible if the prisoner demands it; broadly defined "treatment" (e.g., stress management) is justifiable if it does not affect the symptoms most relevant to the legal question of competency for execution; and other individual circumstances should be considered (e.g., is there a possibility that the information gathered in treatment could be used in making an assessment of competency for execution?). The authors of that paper take the position that under no circumstances should any clinician make an assessment of competence for execution after first entering into a therapeutic relationship with the prisoner.[11]

As it turned out, the prediction by Florida State Hospital's Human Rights Advocacy Committee that staff morale would be affected by Alvord's presence was correct. In an attempt to evaluate the conflicts involved in treating someone who has been determined to be incompetent for execution, Radelet and Barnard interviewed 12 members of the professional staff at Florida State Hospital after Gary Alvord was sent there. The investigators found considerable conflict in the minds of the treatment staff, primarily because of the necessity of pleasing several constituencies (including the patient, his attorneys, and the state) in a situation in which all allegiances could not be honored.[12] Without warning, the staff found itself right in the middle of the politics of the death penalty in Florida.

Alvord was initially diagnosed by the hospital psychiatrists as having paranoid schizophrenia and an antisocial personality. The primary mode of treatment was with drugs (usually Thorazine); Alvord refused individual counseling. His ability to interact with staff and other patients was inconsistent, and he frequently expressed delusions.

In March 1987, after Alvord had been in residence at Chattahoochee for 31 months, a psychiatrist, a psychologist, and a hospital administrator prepared a 10-page, single-spaced clinical summary of Alvord's condition, summarizing his social and medical history (and changes therein) since his hospitalization. The writers noted that his delusional conversations had changed little since his admission, but that his ability to interact with others at the hospital had improved. The trio specifically refused to offer an opinion on competence for execution, but recommended that a panel of experts (from outside the hospital) be appointed to reassess Alvord's competency. On July 24, 1987, the governor appointed a panel of three psychiatrists to conduct that reassessment.

On August 4, the three members of the Chattahoochee staff signed a two-page addendum to the above report. This supplement, which was essentially an exit evaluation, concluded that Alvord was "stable on medications" and "in a substantial state of remission for a chronic schizophrenia major mental illness (*sic*)." Alvord "has received maximum benefit from his hospitalization at [Chattahoochee]." In a statement that seems to contradict their specific refusal in March to assess competence for execution, they added that "there is little doubt that he understands the nature of his true legal situation."

Alvord was transferred 150 miles east to Florida State Prison for his competency exam, which was held on September 29. However, defense attorney Sheppard instructed Alvord not to cooperate with the exam, based on the arguments that the proceedings were a direct violation of the Supreme Court's decision in *Ford*, and that if Alvord's death sentence were vacated because of other legal issues (unrelated to mental competency), the material uncovered in the exam might be used against him at resentencing. The transcript of the September 29 hearing reveals that Alvord had "no response" to 64 questions posed by the persistent psychiatrists (who did not warn the prisoner of any right to be silent). The three psychiatrists then wrote to the governor, on prison letterhead, saying that Alvord's refusal to be interviewed showed that "the patient" "responded appropriately to his attorney's order," but they could not "render an opinion within reasonable medical probability as to his competency to be executed."[13] Note that the physicians referred to Alvord as a "patient," although he certainly was not in such a role, and the three said they were trying to assess a legally defined state with "medical" probability.

While there was never a formal finding of competence, on October 15, 1987, Governor Bob Martinez (Governor Graham's successor) formally lifted the stay of execution that had been granted in 1984 when Alvord was originally found incompetent for execution. At the end of 1992, Alvord remained at Florida State Prison, with no end in sight to the litigation over his fate. Of the

2,700 inmates on America's death rows at that time, he was the one with the longest-standing death sentence.

Alvord was found incompetent for execution before the *Ford* decision. There has been only one post-*Ford* case that resulted in relief for a death row inmate in the United States because of incompetence for execution. It comes from South Carolina. In that case, the death sentence was immediately commuted to life imprisonment, and therefore avoided all of the ethical issues about treating an inmate to restore competence for execution. Using the standard for competence adopted by the Criminal Justice Mental Health Standards of the American Bar Association (instead of the narrower standards that Justice Lewis F. Powell had tried to develop in *Ford*), on May 8, 1991, a trial judge in New-berry County, South Carolina, commuted the death sentence of Fred Singleton.[14] Most of the mental health experts who had testified at an evidentiary hearing on the issue agreed that Singleton was psychotic, mentally retarded, incompetent for execution (under either the ABA standard or Justice Powell's standard), and—because of structural damage to the brain—unlikely ever to become competent again, with or without treatment. As of the end of 1992, the state's appeal of this order is still pending.

Michael Perry: Forcibly Medicating the Incompetent

The issue of competency in Alvord's case has never been examined by the courts; it has been handled solely by the executive branch. The first post-*Ford* case to reach the Supreme Court with issues related to competency for execution involved the Louisiana case of Michael Owen Perry, who, like Alvin Ford, was never found incompetent for execution. Instead, he was found semi-incompetent. The case merits close attention.[15]

Perry was charged with the 1983 murders of his parents, a nephew, and two cousins. He had a long history of severe mental illness and was sent to a facility for evaluation and treatment. Following a period of treatment, in 1984 he was found competent, convicted of five counts of murder, and sentenced to death. In 1986 the Louisiana Supreme Court, in affirming the sentence, suggested that prior to his execution the state might want to evaluate him to be sure that he met the criteria for competence.[16]

After four separate hearings in 1988, the trial court agreed that Perry had a psychotic disorder. For example, he had expressed the belief that he is God; that he had killed Adam and Eve; that he had been married since the age of 7; that robots, the President, and the CIA told him what to do; that if he were shot in the head it would not kill him; that shaving his eyebrows increased the flow of oxygen to his brain; and that his parents were still alive. Depending on the occasion, he both denied and admitted that he murdered his family. Nonetheless, when the trial court issued its findings in October 1988, it determined that Perry was competent for execution—but only if he was taking Haldol, a commonly prescribed antipsychotic medication. Although the trial court recognized that Perry had some right to refuse medication, these rights were determined to be overridden by Louisiana's interest in proceeding with the execution. The Louisiana Department of Corrections was ordered to keep Perry on Haldol, and, if necessary, to administer the medication forcibly. The Louisiana Supreme Court refused to review the decision.[17]

In *Perry v. Louisiana*, the central question for the U.S. Supreme Court was whether the state court order directing that petitioner be involuntarily medicated for the purpose of restoring his competence to be executed was consistent with the Due Process Clause of the Fourteenth Amendment.[18] Perry's attorneys argued that the state could not administer psychotropic drugs against an incompetent prisoner's will. In addition, they took the position that the state could not allow mentally ill inmates to languish in a permanent psychotic state without running afoul of the Constitution. They contended the sentence *must* be commuted to life. They argued that Perry had a significant interest in avoiding the unwanted administration of psychotropic medication, particularly when the medication was contrary to his medical interests and not necessary to treat a condition dangerous to others. The interest related to Perry's right to be free from the proposed invasion of his body and the right to safeguard his dignity and bodily integrity. Unable to administer the drug, the state would not be able to execute him. This would then put the state in the position of violating the constitutional right to needed medical treatment. The defense attorneys argued that the only appropriate solution would be to commute the sentence to life imprisonment and provide the treatment.

In its brief, the state argued that the "medication is actually good for Perry" and that the state was required to treat him, with or without his consent. They argued that "the medicine is in . . . Perry's . . . best interest," even though taking the drug would lead to his death. They contended that death row inmates do not have the right to refuse medication, and that even if they do have such a right, it is overridden by the state's interest in carrying out the execution.

The American Psychiatric Association and the American Medical Association submitted an *amicus curiae* brief agreeing with Perry's attorneys. The brief argued that several of their organizations' ethical principles, including the ban on physicians' participation in executions, were relevant to this case. The brief also contains an excellent statement of the ethical conflicts that mental health professionals face:

> It strains credulity to invoke the *parens patriae* power in this case. Louisiana's efforts are aimed not at benefiting Perry as a ward of the State, but rather at facilitating his death to serve separate state interests. Any benefit that Haldol might confer on Perry would be both fleeting and purchased at the cost of his life.[19]

As noted in our Chapter 9 discussion of the 1990 hearing in Alvin Ford's case before the Eleventh Circuit Court of Appeals, several judges participating in that hearing had expressed interest in learning if Ford's competence could have been assured through antipsychotic medication. Had events unfolded differently, Alvin Ford's and Michael Perry's fates could have been joined. The Perry and Ford situations were similar in several respects. Both men presented evidence of severe psychosis, but both were at least occasionally responsive to psychoactive drugs, thus presenting "moving targets" in terms of the variability of their condition and competence. Similar ethical dilemmas are presented in both cases. Under the circumstances of the *Perry* case, administering the medication could be seen as the first step in participating in the execution itself. This could be seen as a corruption of the treatment function of the psychiatrist. Two of the experts involved with Perry expressed ethical reservations about medicating a patient to create competency for execution.[20] It is as if the physician were becoming the executioner's assistant.

Meanwhile, in a February 1990 ruling in a noncapital case, *Washington v. Harper*, the Supreme Court held that a prison inmate possesses a "significant liberty interest in avoiding the unwanted administration of antipsychotic drugs under the Due Process Clause of the Fourteenth Amendment."[21] The ruling gave prisoners at least some rights to refuse psychotropic medication. The Court agreed to hear *Perry* a month after it decided *Washington v. Harper*. But the Court, absent the participation of newly appointed Justice David Souter, was apparently unable to decide. On November 13, 1990, the Court sent *Perry* back to the trial court for reconsideration in light of *Washington v. Harper*, which it could have done 8 months earlier instead of agreeing to hear the *Perry* case.[22]

Five months after the Supreme Court's action, a Baton Rouge trial judge issued another ruling in the case, again holding that the state can force psychotropic drugs on an insane death row inmate to make him competent for execution.[23] Then, finally, the Louisiana Supreme Court ended the litigation. In a 5-2 vote, that court ruled that forcible medication would violate Perry's right to privacy and his protection against cruel and unusual punishment. "Carrying out this punitive scheme would add severity and indignity to the prisoner's punishment beyond that required for the mere extinguishment of life."[24] Because the court based its decision on the Louisiana Constitution, undoubtedly a similar case from a different state will arise in the future.

As the courts continue to develop standards relating to informed consent and the right to refuse treatment, numerous questions arise, some of which are as old as the exemption of the mentally incompetent from execution itself, and others that are brand-new. Do mentally incompetent death row inmates have such rights?[25] Could they refuse to take the drugs that are the standard treatment for their psychosis? If not, should physicians force them to take the drugs? If the prisoners take the medications, by what standards does "chemically induced" competence equal "natural" competence? Do the drugs simply mask the symptoms of mental illness? In those cases where it was the stress of death row that led to the madness, could the inmates be expected to deteriorate upon their return to the prison? How many times should the bus run back and forth from prison to treatment center?

The facts in *Perry* are also seen, with slight variations, in other capital cases. One example involves Carlos Bello, who was in and out of mental hospitals in Cuba for a decade before coming to America in the Mariel boat lift. In 1981 he was arrested for the murder of a Tampa police detective. Severely catatonic, for the next 6 years he moved back and forth between mental hospitals and the county jail while his mental status improved with medication and regressed without it. Finally put on trial in 1987, he was condemned to death. But after the Florida Supreme Court ordered a new sentencing hearing in 1989 (because Bello had been shackled in front of the jury),[26] a judge found him incompetent for resentencing and ordered him transferred to a mental hospital.[27] As of the end of 1992, Bello had not yet been resentenced.

A second case with similarities to *Perry* is the Nevada case of David Riggins. After being arrested for the 1987 stabbing of a Las Vegas casino worker, Riggins began to talk aloud with Satan, babble about evil spirits, claim that John F. Kennedy and Marilyn Monroe were his abusive parents, and display other symptoms of psychosis. A psychiatrist prescribed Mellaril. Thereafter, the defense sought permission for Riggins to stop taking the drugs during the trial, reasoning that their argument for an insanity verdict would be bolstered by Riggins's unmedicated demeanor. The judge, however, ordered the trial to proceed with Riggins medicated, and in December 1988 he was sentenced to death. In May 1992 the U.S. Supreme Court, in a 7-2 decision, overturned the conviction. This time accepting the arguments put forward in an *amicus* brief filed by the American Psychiatric Association, the Court ruled that forced administration of antipsychotic medication during trial violates Sixth and Fourteenth Amendment rights, "absent a finding of overriding justification and a determination of medical appropriateness."[28]

Legal scholars have used the issue of competence for execution in general and the *Perry* case in particular to illustrate the need for "therapeutic jurisprudence": "the study of the role of law as a therapeutic agent."[29] This would involve more use of input from mental health disciplines when making decisions that affect mental health treatment.[30] In this book we have reviewed several examples of cases in which the Supreme Court's decisions rejected the positions put forth in *amicus* briefs submitted by various mental health professional organizations. In a focused application of this perspective to issues of competency to be executed and the *Perry* case, Bruce Winick writes, "Applying therapeutic jurisprudence to the *Perry* question allows the identification of a series of issues in addition to those traditionally considered. . . . What are the therapeutic implications of permitting the state to treat coercively a prisoner found incompetent to be executed?"[31]

Keith Nordyke, Michael Perry's volunteer defense attorney, has reached this conclusion: "As a society we ought not to tolerate it. Using the tools of medicine to accomplish the ends of the criminal justice system is one of the scariest things I can imagine—it's Orwellian."[32] Alice Miller, director of the capital punishment project for Amnesty International, U.S.A., added: "The use of medication in this way is a perversion of the therapeutic role of medicine." She uses the *Perry* case as a prime example of the "moral meltdown" that inevitably results when societies open the doors to deciding which of their citizens they will put to death.[33]

The Mentally Retarded

Yet another post-*Ford* issue concerns the constitutionality of executing mentally retarded death row inmates.[34] As with the mentally ill on death row, no one knows for sure what proportion of America's death row inmates are mentally retarded, but some experts have offered a guess of 10%.[35] The issue was addressed by the Supreme Court in 1989.[36] If it violates the Eighth Amendment to execute mentally ill prisoners such as Alvin Ford, would these same arguments prohibit the execution of the mentally retarded?

The case involved a Texan named Johnny Paul Penry, who was convicted of forcing his way into the home of Pamela Moseley

Carpenter,[37] raping her, and stabbing her to death with a pair of scissors. The crime occurred in 1979, when Penry was age 22. Although he could neither read nor write, after 11 hours of questioning Penry signed two confessions. Various tests over the years estimated his IQ to be somewhere between 50 and 63, about the functioning level of an average 7-year-old.[38] Nevertheless, he was sentenced to death.

In 1988 Penry's execution was temporarily postponed by the Supreme Court. The Court wanted to decide two issues: (a) Should Texas juries be permitted to consider mental retardation when they make sentencing decisions in capital cases, and (b) does the Eighth Amendment's ban on cruel and unusual punishment prohibit the execution of the mentally retarded? The American Association on Mental Retardation sided with Penry in its *amicus* brief,[39] arguing that capital defendants with mental retardation do not have the "level of blameworthiness" that would make them eligible for the death penalty, and that the execution of the mentally retarded would not serve any valid penological purpose.

The American Bar Association (ABA) also made known its view that the Supreme Court should rule in Penry's favor. On February 7, 1989, the ABA's House of Delegates passed a resolution urging "that no person with mental retardation . . . be sentenced to death or executed." Such executions, they contended, would violate contemporary standards of decency. They adopted the definition of mental retardation used by the American Association on Mental Retardation, which includes an IQ score of 70 or below and deficits in adaptive behavior.[40] The passage of this resolution by the House of Delegates made the resolution official ABA policy.[41]

Nonetheless, the argument lost in the Supreme Court. In two 5-4 decisions announced on June 26, 1989, the Court ruled that the execution of the mentally retarded is not categorically prohibited by the Eighth Amendment.[42] The justices felt there was no national consensus that would support such a ban, since at that time only one state (Georgia) prohibited executions of the mentally retarded. They agreed that "mental retardation is a factor that may well lessen a defendant's culpability for a capital offense," but felt that its importance could be evaluated on a case-by-case basis.[43]

On the other hand, Penry won a limited victory because the Court ruled that juries must be able to consider retardation and abused background in their sentencing decisions. As discussed in Chapter 6, the sentencing juries in Texas are asked only questions about whether the victim precipitated the murder, whether the killing was deliberate, and whether the defendant would be dangerous in the future. Hence, evidence of mental retardation was deemed not relevant—until the Supreme Court in *Penry* decided that evidence of retardation could indeed influence the jurors' answers to these questions, and that the jurors therefore should have been permitted to consider retardation as a mitigating factor. Since Texas law does not provide for a new sentencing hearing without a completely new trial, Penry was granted a new trial.

That retrial was held in Huntsville in July 1990. This time, volunteer attorneys from New York handled the defense. In addition to the evidence of Penry's history of extreme abuse as a child, test results presented by an expert for the defense put Penry's IQ in the mid-60s. A prosecution expert argued the IQ was in the low-70s, just over the conventional cut-off line of 70.[44] Another prosecution witness, Dr. Stanton Samenow (mentioned for his role in a California case in Chapter 6) testified that there was no link between child abuse and criminality. After 2½ hours of deliberation, the jurors returned with their findings, and, for the second time, Johnny Penry was sentenced to death.[45]

Penry's is not the only post-*Furman* case to raise the issue of the constitutionality—or wisdom, or morality—of executing the mentally retarded. Another case that brought international attention to this issue (in part through a national concert tour of stars, including U2 and Sting, sponsored by Amnesty International) was that of Jerome Bowden, an African-American convicted in Columbus, Georgia,[46] of beating a 55-year-old white woman to death. Although evidence pointed to a friend as the real killer and there was no direct evidence against Bowden, he signed a confession. Experts measured Bowden's IQ at 57.

Less than 24 hours before Bowden's date with the executioner, on June 17, 1987, the Georgia Board of Pardons and Paroles issued a 90-day stay so that Bowden's mental status could be further evaluated.

They hired Dr. Irwin Knopf, the chair of the Psychology Department at Emory University, to examine the defendant, which he
did on June 23. That afternoon, after receiving Knopf's report that
Bowden had a "full-scale IQ of 65,"[47] the Board of Pardons and
Paroles concluded that this was high enough for Bowden to know
the difference between right and wrong, and hence too high to
make him eligible for mercy. Within 18 hours, Bowden was dead.[48]

The Board of Pardons and Paroles received hundreds of letters
of protest from throughout the world. While some defended the
execution of the mentally retarded as justified under principles
of retribution,[49] the uproar over the pending Bowden execution
was so loud that a statewide opinion poll taken in January 1987
found some 66% of the respondents disapproved of the death
penalty for mentally retarded defendants. Finally, in 1988, the Georgia legislature became the first in the country to enact a bill that
prohibited the execution of mentally retarded defendants. Within 2
years, Maryland, Kentucky, Tennessee, and New Mexico did likewise,[50] although through 1992 no other states have followed suit.

Drawing the Line

Noted death penalty attorney David Bruck commented on the
Perry case with these words:

> The legislators who passed our current death penalty laws did not
> intend to force grotesque issues to the center stage of constitutional
> adjudication. The death penalty was supposed to be about getting
> even with Charles Manson and Ted Bundy, not executing teenagers
> and the retarded, or wrestling condemned schizophrenics to the
> gurney for forced doses of Haldol. But here we are.[51]

Yes, here we are. Debates about capital punishment need not
center on the question of whether Alvin Ford or Michael Perry or
any other single individual convicted of a capital crime deserves to
live or deserves to die. The question is whether our system of
criminal justice, with all its good aspects and all its frailties, is
capable of drawing the line between who should live and who
should die—in a consistent way, blessed with societal consensus, and

in a way not blemished by caprice or racism. Then we can ask whether the benefits of making those decisions are worth the costs.

Exempting the mentally ill and mentally retarded from execution creates more continua on which lines must be drawn to determine who will live and who will die. And the more lines that must be drawn, the more room there is for inconsistencies and blunders.

In reality, there is widespread societal agreement that some individual criminals "deserve" to die. But once our elected officials decide that *some* citizens should die, the difficulty is in drawing the line that tells the executioners when to stop working. Even in a state like Florida, where the death penalty is a central component of the state's criminal justice system, only about 2% of those arrested for murder are sentenced to death.[52] The death penalty is supposedly designed for the worst 2% of the murderers—those with the longest prior records, the most heinous crimes, the most unredeemable features; namely, the most incorrigible. We run into problems when it is realized that reasonable people disagree on the criteria that should be used to define who those "worst" 2% are.

But even if there is consensus, the overwhelming bulk of research that has been done on the death penalty over the past century has demonstrated that the criminal justice system has done, and continues to do, a poor job of selecting that 2% with any consistency or valid claim to accuracy. Some criminals whom most would agree do belong in that "worst 2%" category are offered life imprisonment in exchange for a guilty plea (even notorious serial murderer Ted Bundy was offered such a plea bargain),[53] and if they accept the plea, or have a high-quality defense team, they are not sentenced to death. Others who may not even rank in the top 50th percentile of heinousness and the like—through mediocre defense or racial bias or just plain bad luck—do end up on death row. The races of the defendant and victim, in connection with the heinousness of the crime, may systematically predict who is selected for death row and who is not. With most other cases the outcomes are simply arbitrary.

Once defendants are on death row, who is executed is similarly unpredictable. In some cases, the defense attorney thought to object to something that later, in this or another case, proves to be a winning issue on appeal; in other cases the judge or prosecutor might err in a way that merits a new trial even though the defense attorney did nothing to cause it.

Consider, for example, the words of former Florida Governor LeRoy Collins, who calls the death penalty Florida's "gutter of shame":

> Who gets executed is still a freakish thing, and depends on wealth, power and many unusual circumstances. Most who are killed are poor and friendless. . . . I say the death penalty is Florida's gutter of shame. We have more people on death row than any other state. We also have a higher percentage of our people in jails and prisons than all but a few states. These are signs of failure. They are calling for constructive action, not inhuman violence by state action to satisfy society's revenge. . . . Making tougher laws, executing more people, keeping more and more in jail for longer and longer terms, may make Floridians feel better, but revengeful, violent acts by the state, never have, and never will, influence people to live by a higher moral code of conduct.[54]

Whether one agrees that the death penalty is a "gutter of shame" or causes or reflects a "moral meltdown," Collins's point that it does little to affect crime rates is difficult to fault.

And the death penalty is expensive, draining resources from the state coffers that could be used to deal with violence in more constructive ways. Each execution in American costs millions of dollars more than the cost of life imprisonment.[55] To be sure, a sizable portion of this cost differential is devoted to death penalty appeals, but only cynics unfamiliar with the complexity of death penalty law can argue that these costs can be significantly reduced by further restrictions on federal appeals.

Sentencing the mentally ill and mentally retarded to death is probably even more expensive than other death penalty cases. Before the prisoner is executed there will need to be extensive searches done for materials and information not introduced at trial. More experts will have to be employed. Every court will be inundated with extensive documentation on the case, some of it sophisticated and thus time-consuming for judges to read and digest. Those who see retributive benefit[56] in executing this group fail to balance that "benefit" against the burden of the extra costs.

Meanwhile, if an inmate is indeed found incompetent for execution, as present law stands he will likely be treated, restored to competency, and then put to death. Do the retributive benefits of the death penalty justify the costs of mental health care that will be needed to permit the execution? We know that physicians have physicians' assistants, but should executioners have executioners' assistants—selected from the medical and mental health professions?

The solution to these problems requires more than the necessary first step of banning the execution of the mentally ill or the mentally retarded. Examining their special situations tells us how, in practice, the entire system of capital punishment in the United States is motivated and carried out. Drawing the lines on a continuum of mental status is no more difficult than drawing the lines on issues such as premeditation, criminal intent, and moral responsibility. Indeed, the issues of executing the mentally ill and mentally retarded are excellent binoculars through which the entire system of American death sentencing can be seen and evaluated. Whatever symbolic value the death penalty may have, in the eyes of some, perhaps its worst effect is that it allows politicians to create the false impression that they are actually doing something to make our communities safer.

In the final analysis, we echo the words of Yale Law Professor Charles L. Black, Jr.: "Though the justice of God may indeed ordain that some should die, the justice of man is altogether and always insufficient for saying who these may be."[57]

Notes

1. From solely the state's perspective, the goal of treatment is to speed the prisoner's death. However, some forms of treatment may pursue other goals (e.g., reducing the prisoner's suffering) in a way that does not risk achieving the state's goal. Such treatment would have a low risk of harm. For further discussion, see Heilbrun et al., 1992.

2. The following section relies in part on Radelet and Barnard, 1988.

3. However, see the case of Fred Singleton, discussed below, whose sentence was commuted to life. We make this statement after surveying a dozen of the top capital defense attorneys in the United States in the spring of 1992.

4. *St. Petersburg Times*, November 27, 1984, p. 4B.

5. Radelet and Barnard, 1988.

6. Radelet and Barnard, 1988. Psychiatrist Paul Appelbaum (1986, p. 683) suggested another possibility: totally abolish the exemption from execution because of mental illness. However, in the *Ford* decision, the Supreme Court made this exemption a constitutional right, thus negating the possibility that the exemption could be eliminated.

7. Annotated Code of the Public General Laws of Maryland, 1987 Cumulative Supplement, Article 27, Section 75A.

8. Appelbaum, 1986.

9. Sargent, 1986, p. 5.

10. For a discussion of "next friend" petitions in this context, see Bonnie, 1988, pp. 1366, 1378.

11. Heilbrun et al., 1992. Dr. Heilbrun was employed at the Florida State Hospital in Chattahoochee while Gary Alvord was in residence.

12. See Radelet and Barnard, 1986.

13. The psychiatrists' use of the term *reasonable medical probability* is the first attempt we know of to specify what level of proof is necessary for a finding of competency or incompetency, although we are given no clues about the criterion's meaning.

14. *Singleton v. State,* Newberry County, South Carolina, Order 90-CP-36-66 (May 8, 1991). Singleton's attorney, John Blume, is a co-author of a law review article on executing mentally retarded inmates. See Blume and Bruck, 1988.

15. For an excellent discussion, see Evans, 1991.

16. *State v. Perry,* 502 So.2d 543 (1986).

17. *State v. Perry,* 543 So.2d 487; 545 So.2d 1049 (1988).

18. *Perry v. Louisiana,* 111 S.Ct. 449 (1990).

19. Brief for the American Psychiatric Association and the American Medical Association as *Amici Curiae* in Support of Petitioner, *Perry v. Louisiana,* p. 9-10. See *Perry v. Louisiana,* 111 S.Ct. 449 (1990).

20. Brief for Perry, p. 28.

21. *Washington v. Harper,* 110 S.Ct. 1028 (1990).

22. *The New York Times,* November 14, 1990, p. A30.

23. *Tallahassee Democrat,* April 26, 1991, p. 3A.

24. *Louisiana v. Perry,* 610 So.2d 746 (1992); *The New York Times,* October 21, 1992, p. 21.

25. At least one authority says probably not; see Bonnie, 1990a, p. 85. Bonnie points out that in most courts, defendants who are incompetent to stand trial do not have the right to refuse treatment that will make them competent. Of course, death row inmates have more at stake if rendered competent than do incompetent defendants pretrial.

26. *Bell. v. State,* 547 So.2d 914 (1989).

27. *St. Petersburg Times,* March 24, 1990, p. 3B.

28. *Riggins v. Nevada,* 112 S.Ct. 1810 (1992), p. 1815.

29. Wexler, 1992, p. 32.

30. See Wexler, 1990, 1992; Wexler and Winick, 1991a, 1991b.

31. Winick, 1992, p. 332.

32. Sainsbury, 1991.

33. Sainsbury, 1991.

34. For additional discussion of the special problems faced by mentally retarded defendants, victims, and inmates, see Conley, Luckasson, and Bouthilet, 1992.

35. This estimate comes from the Southern Center on Human Rights in Atlanta. However, because no comprehensive study has ever been done, this is more an

informed guess than a reliable estimate (*San Francisco Examiner,* May 10, 1992, p. A4).

36. *Penry v. Lynaugh,* 107 S.Ct. 2934 (1989). The case was discussed in Chapter 7 as an example of one in which the attorney did a poor job in oral arguments before the Supreme Court.

37. The victim's older brother, Mark, later won the National Football League's Most Valuable Player Award for his kicking abilities with the Washington Redskins.

38. *Washington Post,* January 13, 1989, p. A20; see also *Washington Post,* January 11, 1989, p. A6.

39. Other organizations joining the *amicus* brief were the American Psychological Association, Association for Retarded Citizens of the United States, The Association for Persons with Severe Handicaps, American Association of University Affiliated Programs for the Developmentally Disabled, American Orthopsychiatric Association, New York State Association for Retarded Children, Inc., National Association of Private Residential Resources, National Association of Superintendents of Public Residential Facilities for the Mentally Retarded, Mental Health Law Project, and the National Association of Protection and Advocacy Systems. The American Psychiatric Association was uninvolved in the case. The brief is reprinted in Conley et al., 1992, pp. 245-278.

Not all experts agree with the position that people with mental retardation should be categorically excluded form the death penalty; see Calnen and Blackman, 1992, and the several comments that follow their article.

40. See Ellis and Luckasson, 1985. The American Association on Mental Retardation was previously called the American Association on Mental Deficiency.

41. Resolution on Mental Retardation and the Death Penalty passed by the American Bar Association's House of Delegates, February 7, 1989.

42. *Penry v. Lynaugh,* 107 S.Ct. 2934 (1989).

43. For a suggestion of how state legislatures should react to the *Penry* decision, see Gruttadaurio, 1989.

44. See Blume and Bruck, 1988, pp. 730-734.

45. Perske, 1991, pp. 63-75.

46. A 1991 study on death sentencing in Columbus shows that its use of the death penalty in the years after the *Furman* decision was marked with strong racial bias—as strong as in any other area of the country yet studied. See *The New York Times,* July 10, 1991, p. 1.

47. Perske, 1991, p. 32.

48. *Atlanta Constitution,* June 28, 1986.

49. See, for example, Carver, 1991.

50. Perske, 1991, pp. 28-42.

51. Bruck, 1991, p. 37.

52. In 1989 there were 1,405 murders in Florida, of which 767 were cleared by an arrest. Because of multiple arrests for one murder, this resulted in a total of 1,291 people arrested for murder (Florida Department of Law Enforcement, 1990, p. 38). A rough comparison can be made to the number sentenced to death in 1990 (29), as most inmates sentenced to death for 1989 crimes would not be sentenced until 1990. The ratio of 29/1,291 is 2.2%.

53. Mello, 1990-1991, p. 900.

54. *St. Petersburg Times,* May 19, 1986, p. 9A.

55. See Spangenberg and Walsh, 1989, for review.

56. Carver, 1991.

57. Black, 1981, p. 107.

Appendix

Published Appellate Decisions in the *Ford* Case

Ford v. State, 374 So.2d 496 (7/18/79). Direct appeal of conviction and sentence to Florida Supreme Court.

Ford v. Florida, 445 U.S. 972 (4/14/80). U.S. Supreme Court's refusal to hear appeal of above decision by the Florida Supreme Court.

Ford v. State, 407 So.2d 907 (12/4/81). Decision by Florida Supreme Court, affirming the trial court's denial of postconviction relief.

Ford v. Strickland, 676 F.2d 434 (4/15/82). Decision by a three-judge panel of the Eleventh Circuit U.S. Court of Appeals on petition for habeas corpus relief.

Ford v. Strickland, 696 F.2d 804 (1/7/83). Decision by the full court (Eleventh Circuit U.S. Court of Appeals) on petition for habeas corpus relief; affirms the denial of habeas corpus relief, but vacates the above decision by the three-judge panel and remands the case back to federal district court for further proceedings.

Ford v. Strickland, 464 U.S. 865 (10/3/83). U.S. Supreme Court refuses to hear Ford's appeal of the Eleventh Circuit's decision.

Ford v. Wainwright, 451 So.2d 471 (5/25/84). Florida Supreme Court affirms the trial court's decision to deny Ford's motion for a hearing to determine competency for execution.

Ford v. Strickland, 734 F.2d 538 (5/30/84). Eleventh Circuit U.S. Court of Appeals grants stay of execution on Ford's request that he be granted a procedural due process hearing to determine his sanity.

Wainwright v. Ford, 467 U.S. 1220 (5/31/84). U.S. Supreme Court refuses to overturn the stay of execution issued the preceding day by the Eleventh Circuit.

Ford v. Wainwright, 752 F.2d 526 (1/17/85). A panel of the Eleventh Circuit U.S. Court of Appeals approves Florida's process of determining sanity of condemned prisoners.

Ford v. Wainwright, 474 U.S. 1019 (12/9/85). U.S. Supreme Court agrees to hear Ford's appeal of the above decision.

Ford v. Wainwright, 477 U.S. 699 (6/26/86). U.S. Supreme Court reverses the above decision by the Eleventh Circuit Court of Appeals.

Ford v. Dugger, 522 So.2d 345 (2/18/88). Florida Supreme Court affirms trial court's denial of postconviction relief, holding that there was no harm in telling the jury that their verdict was advisory only and that the error in failing to give proper jury instructions on nonstatutory mitigation was harmless.

References

Adams, R. D., Hoffer, W., & Hoffer, M. M. (1991). *Adams v. Texas*. New York: St. Martin's Press.

American Bar Association. (1989). *ABA criminal justice mental health standards*. Washington, DC: Author.

American Bar Association. (1990). *Toward a more just and effective system of review in state death penalty cases: Report of the ABA task force on death penalty habeas corpus*. Chicago: Author.

American Medical News. (1991, September 23-30).

American Psychiatric Association. (1980). Position statement on medical participation in capital punishment. *American Journal of Psychiatry, 137*, 1487.

American Psychiatric Association. (1987). *Diagnostic and statistical manual of mental disorders*. Washington, DC: Author.

American Psychological Association Symposium. (1986). *The assessment of competency for execution: Ethical and technical issues*. Washington, DC: American Psychological Association.

American Public Health Association. (1986). Policy statement 8521: Participation of health professionals in capital punishment. *American Journal of Public Health, 76*, 339.

American Public Health Association. (1987). Policy statement 8611: Abolition of the death penalty. *American Journal of Public Health, 77*, 105-106.

Andrews, A. B. (1991). Social work expert testimony regarding mitigation in capital sentencing proceedings. *Social Work, 36*, 440-445.

Annas, G. J. (1980, May). Nurses and the death penalty. *Nursing, Law, and Ethics, 1*, 3.

Appelbaum, P. S. (1981). Psychiatrists' role in the death penalty. *Hospital and Community Psychiatry, 32*, 761-762.

Appelbaum, P. S. (1983). Death, the expert witness, and the dangers of going *Barefoot*. *Hospital and Community Psychiatry, 348,* 1003-1004.

Appelbaum, P. S. (1984). Hypotheticals, psychiatric testimony, and the death sentence. *Bulletin of the American Academy of Psychiatry and the Law, 12,* 169-177.

Appelbaum, P. S. (1986). Competence to be executed: Another conundrum for mental health professionals. *Hospital and Community Psychiatry, 37,* 682-684.

Appelbaum, P. S. (1987). In the wake of *Ake*: The ethics of expert testimony in an advocate's world. *Bulletin of the American Academy of Psychiatry and the Law, 15,* 15-25.

Appelbaum, P. S. (1990). The parable of the forensic psychiatrist: Ethics and the problem of doing harm. *International Journal of Law and Psychiatry,13,* 249-259.

Appelbaum, P. S., Bonnie, R. J., Dietz, P. E., & Thorup, O. A., Jr. (1987, Summer). The death penalty: Dilemmas for physicians and society—A panel discussion. *The Pharos, 50,* 23-27.

Arizona Republic. (1992, February 15). Letter to the editor from John C. Keegan.

Atlanta Constitution. (1986, June 28).

Atlanta Constitution. (1991, September 26). P. D3.

Baldus, D. C., Woodworth, G. G., & Pulaski, C. A. (1990). *Equal justice and the death penalty: A legal and empirical analysis.* Boston: Northeastern University Press.

Bayer, R. (1984). Lethal injection and capital punishment: Medicine in the service of the state. *Journal of Prison & Jail Health, 4,* 7-15.

Bedau, H. A. (1982). *The death penalty in America* (3rd ed.). New York: Oxford University Press.

Bedau, H. A. (1987). *Death is different: Studies in the morality, law and politics of capital punishment.* Boston: Northeastern University Press.

Bedau, H. A. (1990-91). The decline of executive clemency in capital cases. *New York University Review of Law & Social Change, 18,* 255-272.

Bedau, H. A. (1991). Imprisonment vs. death: Does avoiding Schwarzschild's paradox lead to Sheleff's dilemma? *Albany Law Review, 54,* 481-495.

Bedau, H. A. (1992). Reflections on psychiatry and the death penalty. In A. Kales, C. M. Pierce, & M. Greenblatt (Eds.), *The mosaic of contemporary psychiatry in perspective* (pp. 44-52). New York: Springer-Verlag.

Bedau, H. A., & Radelet, M. L. (1987). Miscarriages of justice in potentially capital cases. *Stanford Law Review, 40,* 21-179.

Berger, V. (1990-91). The chiropractor as brain surgeon: Defense lawyering in capital cases. *New York University Review of Law & Social Change, 18,* 245-254.

Berns, W. (1979). *For capital punishment: Crime and the morality of the death penalty.* New York: Basic Books.

Black, C. L., Jr. (1981). *Capital punishment: The inevitability of caprice and mistake* (2nd ed.). New York: Norton.

Bluestone, H., & McGahee, C. L. (1962). Reaction to extreme stress: Impending death by execution. *American Journal of Psychiatry, 119,* 393-396.

Blume, J. (1990, August). The elements of a competent and reliable mental health evaluation. *The Advocate, 12,* 42-47.

Blume, J., & Bruck, D. (1988). Sentencing the mentally retarded to death: An eighth amendment analysis. *Arkansas Law Review, 41*, 725-764.

Bohm, R. M. (1991). American death penalty opinion, 1936-1986: A critical examination of the Gallup polls. In R. M. Bohm (Ed.), *The death penalty in America: Current research* (pp. 113-144). Cincinnati: Anderson.

Bonnie, R. J. (1988). The dignity of the condemned. *Virginia Law Review, 74*, 1363-1391.

Bonnie, R. J. (1990a). Dilemmas in administering the death penalty: Conscientious abstention, professional ethics, and the needs of the legal system. *Law and Human Behavior, 14*, 67-90.

Bonnie, R. J. (1990b). Grounds for professional abstention in capital cases: A reply to Brodsky. *Law and Human Behavior, 14*, 99-102.

Bradenton Herald. (1981, November 5). P. 1.

Bright, S. B. (1990). Death by lottery—Procedural bar of constitutional claims in capital cases due to inadequate representation of indigent defendants. *West Virginia Law Review, 92*, 679-695.

British Medical Association. (1992). *Medicine betrayed: The participation of doctors in human rights abuses.* London: Zed Books.

Broderick, D. J. (1979). Insanity of the condemned. *Yale Law Journal, 88*, 533-564.

Brodsky, S. L. (1990). Professional ethics and professional morality in the assessment of competency for execution: A response to Bonnie. *Law and Human Behavior, 14*, 91-97.

Brown, T. A. (1986). Who's qualified to decide who dies? *Nebraska Law Review, 65*, 558-583.

Bruck, D. I. (1991). Does the death penalty matter? Reflections of a death row lawyer. *Reconstruction, 1*, 35-39.

Burt, R. A. (1987). Disorder in the court: The death penalty and the Constitution. *Michigan Law Review, 85*, 1741-1819.

Callans, P. J. (1985). Assembling a jury willing to impose a death penalty: A new disregard for a capital defendant's rights. *Journal of Criminal Law and Criminology, 76*, 1027-1050.

Calnen, T., & Blackman, L. S. (1992). Capital punishment and offenders with mental retardation: Response to the *Penry* brief. *American Journal on Mental Retardation, 6*, 557-564.

Camus, A. (1974). Reflections on the guillotine. In A. Camus, *Resistance, rebellion, and death* (pp. 173-234). New York: Vintage.

Carver, S. A. (1991). Retribution—A justification for the execution of mentally retarded and juvenile murderers. *Oklahoma City University Law Review, 16*, 155-230.

Casscells, W., & Curran, W. J. (1982, December 9). Doctors, the death penalty, and lethal injection: Recent developments. *New England Journal of Medicine, 307*, 1532-1533.

Chicago Tribune. (1982, December 12). P. 1.

Cohen, M. (1983, February 14). Execution by injection. *US Magazine*, pp. 18-21.

Colburn, D. (1990, December 11). Lethal injection. *Washington Post* (Health Section), pp. 12-15.

Conley, R. W., Luckasson, R., & Bouthilet, G. N. (1992). *The criminal justice system and mental retardation: Defendants and victims.* Baltimore: Paul H. Brookes.

Coyle, M., Strasser, F., & Lavelle, M. (1990, June 11). Fatal defense. *National Law Journal*, 30-44.

Curran, W. J. (1982, December 2). Psychiatric evaluations and mitigating circumstances in capital-punishment sentencing. *New England Journal of Medicine, 307*, 1431-1432.

Curran, W. J. (1984, June 21). Uncertainty in prognosis of violent conduct: The Supreme Court lays down the law. *New England Journal of Medicine, 310*, 1651-1652.

Curran, W. J., & Casscells, W. (1980, January 24). The ethics of medical participation in capital punishment by intravenous drug injection. *New England Journal of Medicine, 302*, 226-230.

Dallas Morning News. (1992, February 16). P. 1.

Davis, K. C. (1951). *Handbook on administrative law*. St. Paul, MN: West.

Deitchman, M. A., Kennedy, W. A., & Beckham, J. C. (1991). Self-selection factors in the participation of mental health professionals in competency for execution evaluations. *Law and Human Behavior, 15*, 287-303.

Dershowitz, A. (1989, January 14). Retarded man deserves better legal assistance. *St. Petersburg Times*, p. 18A.

Dick, R. D. (1987). *Ford v. Wainwright*: Warning—Sanity on death row may be hazardous to your health. *Louisiana Law Review, 47*, 1351-1364.

Dix, G. E. (1977a). The death penalty, "dangerousness," psychiatric testimony, and professional ethics. *American Journal of Criminal Law, 5*, 151-224.

Dix, G. E. (1977b). Administration of the Texas death penalty statutes: Constitutional infirmities related to the prediction of dangerousness. *Texas Law Review, 55*, 1343-1414.

Dix, G. E. (1978). Participation by mental health professionals in capital murder sentencing. *International Journal of Law and Psychiatry, 1*, 283-308.

Ehrmann, S. R. (1962, March). For whom the chair waits. *Federal Probation, 26*, 14-25.

Ellis, J. W., & Luckasson, R. A. (1985). Mentally retarded criminal defendants. *George Washington Law Review, 53*, 414-493.

Evans, G. L. (1991). *Perry v. Louisiana*: Can a state treat an incompetent prisoner to ready him for execution? *Bulletin of the American Academy of Psychiatry and the Law, 19*, 249-270.

Ewing, C. P. (1983). "Dr. Death" and the case for an ethical ban on psychiatric and psychological predictions of dangerousness in capital sentencing proceedings. *American Journal of Law and Medicine, 8*, 407-428.

Fitzpatrick, T. (1992, February 28). Two lives, two deaths. *The Texas Observer* pp. 8-10.

The Florida Bar News. (1986, December 1).

The Florida Bar News. (1987, May 1). P. 2.

Florida Department of Law Enforcement. (1990). *Crime in Florida: 1989 annual report*. Tallahassee: Author.

Florida Flambeau. (1984, May 31). P. 1A.

Florida Flambeau. (1987, June 9). P. 1.

Florida Times Union. (1981, December 8). P. B1.

Florida Times Union. (1984, May 31). P. 1B.

Frady, M. (1993, February 22). Death in Arkansas. *The New Yorker*, pp. 105-133.

Ft. Lauderdale News. (1974, July 23). P. 1B.

Ft. Lauderdale News. (1974, July 23). P. 10.

Ft. Lauderdale News. (1974, December 10). P. 1.
Ft. Lauderdale News. (1974, December 18). P. 1.
Ft. Lauderdale News. (1975, January 6). P. 1.
Ft. Lauderdale News. (1976, April 19). P. 1.
Ft. Lauderdale News. (1981, November 26). P. B1.
Ft. Lauderdale News. (1981, December 8). P. B1.
Ft. Lauderdale News. (1981, December 8). P. B3.
Ft. Lauderdale News. (1983, April 30). P. 1A.
Ft. Lauderdale News/Sun-Sentinel. (1983, April 30). P. 1.
Gainesville Sun. (1990, April 29). P. 3B.
Gallemore, J. L., & Panton, J. H. (1972). Inmate responses to lengthy death row confinement. *American Journal of Psychiatry, 129,* 167-171.
Gallup, A., & Newport, F. (1991, June). Death penalty support remains strong. *The Gallup Poll Monthly, 309,* 40-45.
General Accounting Office. (1990). *Death penalty sentencing: Research indicates pattern of racial disparities* (GAO/GGD-90-57). Washington, DC: U.S. General Accounting Agency.
Goldstein, S. M. (1990). Expediting the federal habeas corpus review process in capital cases: An examination of recent proposals. *Capital University Law Review, 19,* 599-647.
Greenberg, J. (1982). Capital punishment as a system. *Yale Law Journal, 91,* 908-936.
Gross, S. R. (1985). Race and death: The judicial evaluation of evidence of discrimination in capital sentencing. *University of California-Davis Law Review, 18,* 1275-1325.
Gross, S. R., & Mauro, R. (1989). *Death and discrimination: Racial disparities in capital sentencing.* Boston: Northeastern University Press.
Gruttadaurio, J. J. (1989). Consistency in the application of the death penalty to juveniles and the mentally impaired: A suggested legislative approach. *Cincinnati Law Review, 58,* 211-241.
Guttmacher, M. S., & Weihofen, H. (1952). *Psychiatry and the law.* New York: Norton.
Haines, H. (1989). *Primum non nocere:* Chemical execution and the limits of medical social control. *Social Problems, 36,* 442-454.
Haines, H. (1992). Flawed executions, the anti-death penalty movement, and the politics of capital punishment. *Social Problems, 39,* 125-138.
Haney, C. (1984a). On the selection of capital juries: The biasing effects of the death-qualification process. *Law and Human Behavior, 8,* 121-132.
Haney, C. (1984b). Examining death qualification: Further analysis of the process effect. *Law and Human Behavior, 8,* 133-151.
Haney, C. (1984c). Epilogue: Evolving standards and the capital jury. *Law and Human Behavior, 8,* 153-158.
Hazard, G. D., Jr., & Louisell, D. W. (1962). Death, the state, and the insane: Stay of execution. *UCLA Law Review, 9,* 381-405.
Heilbrun, K. S. (1987). The assessment of competency for execution: An overview. *Behavioral Sciences and the Law, 5,* 383-396.
Heilbrun, K. S., & McClaren, H. A. (1988). Assessment of competency for execution? A guide for mental health professionals. *Bulletin of the American Academy of Psychiatry and the Law, 16,* 205-216.

Heilbrun, K. S., Radelet, M. L., & Dvoskin, J. 1992. The debate on treating individuals incompetent for execution. *American Journal of Psychiatry, 149*, 596-605.

Heimer, M. (1971). *The cannibal: The case of Albert Fish.* New York: Pinnacle Books.

Hood, R. (1989). *The death penalty: A world-wide perspective.* New York: Oxford University Press.

Jacoby, J. E., & Paternoster, R. (1982). Sentencing disparity and jury packing: Further challenges to the death penalty. *Journal of Criminal Law and Criminology, 73*, 379-387.

Jendrzejczyk, M. (1982, January 10). "Sanitized" execution is still dirty. *Los Angeles Times*, part 4, p. 5.

Johnson, R. (1979). Under sentence of death: The psychology of death row confinement. *Law and Psychology Review, 5*, 141-192.

Johnson, R. (1990). *Death work: A study of the modern execution process.* Pacific Grove, CA: Brooks-Cole.

Jones, G.R.N. (1990, March 24). Judicial electrocution and the prison doctor. *The Lancet, 235*, 713-714.

Kevorkian, J. (1960). *Medical research and the death penalty: A dialogue.* New York: Vantage.

Kevorkian, J. (1985). Medicine, ethics, and execution by lethal injection. *Medicine and Law, 4*, 407-413.

Klein, L. R., Forst, B., & Filatov, V. (1978). The deterrent effect of capital punishment: An assessment of the estimates. In A. Blumstein, J. Cohen, & D. Nagin (Eds.), *Deterrence and incapacitation: Estimating the effects of criminal sanctions on crime rates* (pp. 336-360). Washington, DC: National Academy of Sciences.

Larkin, P. J. (1980). The eighth amendment and the execution of the presently incompetent. *Stanford Law Review, 32*, 765-805.

Lewis, D. O., Pincus, J. H., Feldman, M., Jackson, L., & Bard, B. (1986). Psychiatric, neurological, and psychoeducational characteristics of 15 death row inmates in the United States. *American Journal of Psychiatry, 143*, 838-845.

Lewis, D. O., Pincus, J. H., Bard, B., Richardson, E., Prichep, L., Feldman, M., & Yeager, C. (1988). Neuropsychiatric, psychoeducational, and family characteristics of 14 juveniles condemned to death in the United States. *American Journal of Psychiatry, 145*, 584-589.

Lifton, R. 1986. *The Nazi doctors: Medical killing and the psychology of genocide.* New York: Basic Books.

Los Angeles Times. (1992, August 29). P. 17A.

Mackey, P. E. (1976). *Voices against death: American opposition to capital punishment, 1787-1975.* New York: Burt Franklin.

Mello, M. (1984). Florida's "heinous, atrocious or cruel" aggravating circumstance: Narrowing the class of death-eligible cases without making it smaller. *Stetson Law Review, 13*, 523-554.

Mello, M. (1988). Facing death alone: The post-conviction attorney crisis on death row. *American University Law Review, 37*, 513-607.

Mello, M. (1990-91). On metaphors, mirrors, and murders: Theodore Bundy and the rule of law. *New York University Review of Law & Social Change, 18*, 887-938.

Mello, M., & Robson, R. (1985). Judge over jury: Florida's practice of imposing death over life in capital cases. *Florida State University Law Review, 13*, 31-75.

Meltsner, M. (1973). *Cruel and unusual: The Supreme Court and capital punishment.* New York: Random House.

Menninger, K. (1968). *The crime of punishment.* New York: Viking.

Mezer, R. R., & Rheingold, P. D. (1962). Mental capacity and incompetency: A psycho-legal problem. *American Journal of Psychology, 118*, 827-831.

The Miami Herald. (1988, July 12). P. 1.

The Miami Herald. (1990, December 13). P. 14D.

Miller, K. S. (1980). *The criminal justice and mental health systems: Conflict and collusion.* Cambridge, MA: Oelgeschlager, Gunn & Hain.

Miller, K. S., & Miller, B. D. (1989). *To kill and be killed: Case studies from Florida's death row.* Pasadena, CA: Hope.

Monahan, J. (1981). *Predicting violent behavior: An assessment of clinical techniques.* Rockville, MD: National Institute of Mental Health.

Moore, G. L., III. (1987). *Ford v. Wainwright:* A coda in the executioner's song. *Iowa Law Review, 72*, 1461-1482.

NAACP Legal Defense and Educational Fund. (1992, Winter). Death Row, U.S.A.

National Law Journal. (1991, December 2). P. 6.

Neises, M. L., & Dillehay, R. C. (1987). Death qualification and conviction proneness: *Witt* and *Witherspoon* compared. *Behavioral Sciences and the Law, 5*, 479-494.

Newsday. (1992, January 23). P. 112.

Newsday. (1992, May 4). P. 19.

Newsweek. (1993, March 3). PP. 46-47.

The New York Times. (1988, June 7).

The New York Times. (1990, November 14). P. A30.

The New York Times. (1991, July 10). P. 1.

The New York Times. (1992, January 24). P. 8.

The New York Times. (1992, January 25). P. 8.

The New York Times. (1992, February 12). P. 22.

The New York Times. (1992, September 27). P. 32.

The New York Times. (1992, October 21). P. 21.

Note. (1986). Death penalty. *Harvard Law Review, 100*, 100-107.

Palm Beach Post. (1989, February 14). P. 1A.

Panama City News Herald. (1984, June 12). P. 1.

Paternoster, R. (1991). *Capital punishment in America.* New York: Lexington Books.

Perske, R. (1991). *Unequal justice? What can happen when persons with retardation or other developmental disabilities encounter the criminal justice system.* Nashville: Abingdon Press.

Pierce, G. L., & Radelet, M. L. (1990-91). The role and consequences of the death penalty in American politics. *New York University Review of Law & Social Change, 18*, 713-730.

Podgers, J. (1980). The psychiatrist's role in death sentence debated. *American Bar Association Journal, 66*, 1509.

Rachlin, S., & Weiner, B. A. (1992). Criminal law. In J. A. Talbott, R. E. Hales, & S. L. Keill (Eds.), *Textbook of administrative psychiatry* (pp. 447-470). Washington, DC: American Psychiatric Press.

Radelet, M. L. (1981). Racial characteristics and the imposition of the death penalty. *American Sociological Review, 46*, 918-927.

Radelet, M. L. (1985). Rejecting the jury: The imposition of the death penalty in Florida. *University of California-Davis Law Review, 18*, 1409-1431.

Radelet, M. L. (1989). Executions of whites for crimes against blacks: Exceptions to the rule? *Sociological Quarterly, 30*, 529-544.

Radelet, M. L., & Barnard, G. W. (1986). Ethics and the psychiatric determination of competency to be executed. *Bulletin of the American Academy of Psychiatry and the Law, 14*, 37-53.

Radelet, M. L., & Barnard, G. W. (1988). Treating those found incompetent for execution: Ethical chaos with only one solution. *Bulletin of the American Academy of Psychiatry and the Law, 16*, 297-307.

Radelet, M. L., & Pierce, G. L. (1985). Race and prosecutorial discretion in homicide cases. *Law and Society Review, 19*, 587-621.

Radelet, M. L., & Pierce, G. L. (1991). Choosing those who will die: Race and the death penalty in Florida. *Florida Law Review, 43*, 1-34.

Radelet, M. L., & Vandiver, M. (1988). *Capital punishment in America: An annotated bibliography*. New York: Garland.

Radelet, M. L., & Zsembik, B. A. (1993, Winter). Executive clemency in Post-*Furman* capital cases. *University of Richmond Law Review* (forthcoming).

Radelet, M. L., Bedau, H. A., & Putnam, C. E. (1992). *In spite of innocence*. Boston: Northeastern University Press.

Radelet, M. L., Vandiver, M., & Berardo, F. M. (1983). Families, prisons, and death row inmates: The human impact of structured uncertainty. *Journal of Family Issues, 4*, 593-612.

Resnick, R. (1992, February 10). Fla. jurors hear tales of sex, religion, death. *National Law Journal*.

Rosenbaum, R. (1990, May). Travels with Dr. Death. *Vanity Fair*, pp. 141-147ff.

Roth, L. H. (1987). The council on psychiatry and law. *American Journal of Psychiatry, 144*, 411-412.

Roth, L. H., Meisel, A., & Lidz, C. W. (1977). Tests of competency to consent to treatment. *American Journal of Psychiatry, 134*, 279-284.

Sainsbury, J. (1991, May 31). Moral meltdown. *New Statesman and Society, 4*, 20-21.

Salguero, R. G. (1986). Medical ethics and competency to be executed. *Yale Law Journal, 96*, 167-186.

San Francisco Examiner. (1991, February 17).

San Francisco Examiner. (1992, April 22). P. 14.

San Francisco Examiner. (1992, May 10). P. A4.

Sarasota Herald Tribune. (1991, March 9). P. 10B.

Sargent, D. A. (1986, December). Treating the condemned to death. *Hastings Center Report, 16*, 5-6.

Schopp, R. F. (1991). Wake up and die right: The rationale, standard, and jurisprudential significance of the competency to face execution requirement. *Louisiana Law Review, 51*, 995-1046.

Schwarzschild, H. (1982, December 23). Homicide by injection. *The New York Times*, p. 15.

Scott, G. R. (1950). *The history of capital punishment*. London: Torchstream Books.

Showalter, C. R. (1990, November). Broad-based psychiatric formulation crucial in capital cases. *The Psychiatric Times*, 1, 31-33.

Showalter, C. R., & Bonnie, R. J. (1984). Psychiatrists and capital sentencing: Risks and responsibilities in a unique legal setting. *Bulletin of the American Academy of Psychiatry and the Law, 12,* 159-167.

Showalter, C. R., & Fitch, W. L. (1987). Objectivity and advocacy in forensic psychiatry after *Ake v. Oklahoma. Journal of Psychiatry and Law, 15,* 177-188.

Small, M. A. (1988). Performing "competency to be executed" evaluations: A psycholegal analysis for preventing the execution of the insane. *Nebraska Law Review, 67,* 718-734.

Small, M. A., & Otto, R. K. (1991). Evaluations of competency to be executed: Legal contours and implications for assessment. *Criminal Justice and Behavior, 18,* 146-158.

Soubiran, A. (1964). *The good Dr. Guillotin and his strange device.* London: Souvenir Press.

Spangenberg, R. L., & Walsh, E. R. (1989). Capital punishment or life imprisonment? Some cost considerations. *Loyola of Los Angeles Law Review, 23,* 45-58.

Squire, A. O. (1938). *Sing Sing doctor.* Garden City, NY: Garden City Publishing.

Stewart, D. O., & Nelson, S. (1988, November 1). Hip deep in the death penalty. *American Bar Association Journal, 74,* 40-55.

St. Petersburg Times. (1984, November 27). P. 4B.

St. Petersburg Times. (1985, May 1). P. D1.

St. Petersburg Times. (1986, May 19). P. 9A.

St. Petersburg Times. (1986, April 20). P. 4D.

St. Petersburg Times. (1990, March 24). P. 3B.

St. Petersburg Times, (1993, March 6). P. 1B.

Tabak, R. J., & Lane, J. M. (1989). The execution of injustice: Cost and lack-of-benefit analysis of the death penalty. *Loyola of Los Angeles Law Review, 23,* 59-146.

Tallahassee Democrat. (1981, February 24). P. 1.

Tallahassee Democrat. (1986, April 20).

Tallahassee Democrat. (1986, July 3). P. 6B.

Tallahassee Democrat. (1991, April 26). P. 3A.

Tampa Tribune. (1986, April 20). P. 6A.

Time. (1992, May 19).

Turnbull, C. (1978). Death by decree. *Natural History, 87,* pp. 51-66.

United Press International. (1986, December 1).

van den Haag, E. (1986). The ultimate punishment: A defense. *Harvard Law Review, 99,* 1662-1669.

Walker, N. (1968). *Crime and insanity in England* (Vol. 1). Edinburgh: Edinburgh University Press.

Ward, B. A. (1986). Competency for execution: Problems in law and psychiatry. *Florida State University Law Review, 14,* 35-107.

Washington Post. (1985, November 11). P. A6.

Washington Post. (1989, January 11). P. A6.

Washington Post. (1989, January 13). P. A20.

Weihofen, H. (1951). A question of justice: Trial or execution of the insane. *American Bar Association Journal, 37,* 651-654, 710-711.

Weiner, D. B. (1972, April 3). The real Dr. Guillotin. *Journal of the American Medical Association, 220,* 85-89.

Weisberg, R. (1983). Deregulating death. *Supreme Court Review, 8,* 305-395.

Wertham, F. (1949). *The show of violence.* Garden City, NY: Doubleday.

West, L. J. (1970). Medicine and capital punishment. In hearings before Subcommittee on Criminal Laws and Procedures, Committee of the Judiciary, 90th Congress, 2nd Session, on S1760, *To Abolish the Death Penalty* (pp. 124-129). Washington, DC: Government Printing Office.

West, L. J. (1976). Psychiatric reflections on the death penalty. *American Journal of Orthopsychiatry, 45,* 689-700.

Wexler, D. B. (1990). *Therapeutic jurisprudence: The law as therapeutic agent.* Durham, NC: Carolina Academic Press.

Wexler, D. B. (1992). Putting mental health into mental health law. *Law and Human Behavior, 16,* 27-38.

Wexler, D. B., & Winick, B. J. (1991a). Therapeutic jurisprudence as a new approach to mental health policy analysis and research. *University of Miami Law Review, 45,* 979-1004.

Wexler, D. B., & Winick, B. J. (1991b). *Essays in therapeutic jurisprudence.* Durham, NC: Carolina Academic Press.

White, C. G. (1982). Ethical guidelines for psychologist participation in death penalty proceedings: A survey. *Professional Psychology, 13,* 327-329.

White, L. T. (1987a). Juror decision making in the capital penalty trial: An analysis of crimes and defense strategies. *Law and Human Behavior, 11,* 113-130.

White, L. T. (1987b). The mental illness defense in the capital murder hearing. *Behavioral Sciences and the Law, 5,* 411-421.

White, W. S. (1991). *The death penalty in the nineties.* Ann Arbor: University of Michigan Press.

Wikberg, R., & Rideau, W. (1991, September/October). End of an era. *The Angolite, 16,* 15-24.

Winick, B. J. (1992). Competency to be executed: A therapeutic jurisprudence perspective. *Behavioral Sciences and the Law, 10,* 317-337.

Zeisel, H. (1981). Race bias in the administration of the death penalty: The Florida experience. *Harvard Law Review, 95,* 456-468.

Zimring, F. E., & Hawkins, G. (1986). *Capital punishment and the American agenda.* New York: Cambridge University Press.

Index

195

About the Authors

Kent S. Miller is Professor Emeritus of Psychology at Florida State University. Much of his professional work has focused on mental disability law, and particularly on the relationships between the state and the mentally disabled individual. Previous books he has written have dealt with civil commitment, public guardianship, capital punishment, and the interaction between the criminal justice and mental health systems. He lives in Tallahassee, where he has a private practice in family mediation.

Michael L. Radelet is a Professor of Sociology, University of Florida. He received his Ph.D. in Medical Sociology from Purdue University, and completed 2 years of postdoctoral research in the Department of Psychiatry, University of Wisconsin Medical School, before coming to Florida in 1979. Since then he has published three books and 30 scholarly papers on different aspects of the death penalty. He has testified in several dozen death penalty cases throughout the country, and has worked with far more than 100 death row inmates, primarily in Florida. His most recent work, co-authored with Hugo Adam Bedau and Constance E.

199

Putnam, is *In Spite of Innocence: Erroneous Convictions in Capital Cases*. Among the courses he teaches are Medical Ethics (for second-year medical students), Criminology, and the Sociology of Mental Health.

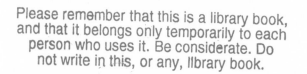
Printed in the United States
24119LVS00004B/322-342

9 780803 951501